Pig Design Patterns

Simplify Hadoop programming to create complex
end-to-end Enterprise Big Data solutions with Pig

Pradeep Pasupuleti

PUBLISHING

BIRMINGHAM - MUMBAI

Pig Design Patterns

First published: April 2014

Production Reference: 1100414

Published by Packt Publishing Ltd.
Livery Place
35 Livery Street
Birmingham B3 2PB, UK.

ISBN 978-1-78328-555-6

www.packtpub.com

Cover Image by Pradeep Pasupuleti (pasupuleti.pradeepkumar@gmail.com)

Credits

Author
Pradeep Pasupuleti

Reviewers
Aaron Binns

Shingo Furuyama

Shashwat Shriparv

Fábio Uechi

Acquisition Editor
Owen Roberts

Content Development Editor
Priya Singh

Technical Editors
Aparna Kumar

Pooja Nair

Nikhil Potdukhe

Copy Editors
Alisha Aranha

Brandt D'Mello

Gladson Monteiro

Adithi Shetty

Project Coordinator
Wendell Palmer

Proofreaders
Ting Baker

Elinor Perry-Smith

Indexer
Hemangini Bari

Graphics
Sheetal Aute

Ronak Dhruv

Yuvraj Mannari

Abhinash Sahu

Production Coordinator
Aditi Gajjar Patel

Cover Work
Aditi Gajjar Patel

Foreword

Nearly 30 years ago, when I started my career, a 10 MB upgrade on a hard-disk drive was a big purchase and had to go through many approvals in the enterprise. The drawing office of a medium-sized engineering enterprise stored their drawings in this extra large storage! Over the years, storage became cheaper and bigger. The supply side proved the Moore's law and its variations accurately.

Much more has happened on the demand side though. User organizations have realized the potential of data and analytics. So, the amount of data generated at each level in the enterprise has gone up much more steeply. Some of this data comes through well-defined processes; on the other hand though, a large majority of it comes through numerous unstructured forms, and as a result, ends up as unstructured data. Analytics tried to keep pace and mostly succeeded. However, the diversity of both the data and the desired analytics demands newer and smarter methods for working with the data. The Pig platform surely is one of these methods. Nevertheless, the power of such a platform is best tapped by extending it efficiently. Extending requires great familiarity of the platform. More importantly, extending is fun when the process of building such extensions is easy.

The Pig Latin platform offers great simplicity. However, a practitioner's advice is immensely valuable in leveraging this simplicity to an enterprise's own requirement. This is where I find this book to be very apt. It makes you productive with the platform pretty quickly through very well-researched design patterns. This helps simplify programming in Hadoop and create complex end-to-end enterprise-grade Big Data solutions through a building block and best-pattern approach.

This book covers the journey of Big Data from the time it enters the enterprise to its eventual use in analytics, either in the form of a dashboard or a predictive model.

I particularly liked the presentation of the content. You need not go sequentially through the book; you can go straight to the pattern of your interest, skipping some of the preceding content. The fact that every pattern you see in this book will be relevant to you at some point in your journey with Big Data should be a good reason to spend time with those patterns as well. The simplicity of the quoted examples puts the subject in the right perspective, in case you already browsed through some pages and felt that the examples were not exactly from your domain.

Most likely, you will find a few patterns that exactly fit your requirement. So go ahead, adopt them, and gain productivity right away.

As of writing this foreword, the world is still struggling with analyzing incomprehensibly large data, which is like trying to locate a passenger plane that went missing in the sky! This is the way things seem to work. Just when we think we have all the tools and technologies, we realize that we need much more power beyond what we have available today. Extending this, one would realize that data (creation, collection, and so on) and analytics will both play an extremely important role in our future. A knowledge tool that helps us move toward this future should always be welcomed, and what could be a better tool than a good book like this!

I had a very enriching experience while working with Pradeep earlier in my career. I spotted talent in him that was beyond the ordinary. However, in an environment that is driven primarily by a customer project and where technologies and platforms are defined by the customer, I must admit that we did not give sufficient room for him to show his creativity in designing new technologies. Even here, I fondly recollect a very creative work of distributed processing of a huge vector map data by Pradeep and his colleagues. This monster of a job would run overnight on many desktop systems that were otherwise lying unused in our organization. A consolidation engine would later stitch up the results from individual systems to make one seamless large dataset. This might look very trivial today, but more than a decade ago, it was a big innovation that helped greatly compress our release cycles.

Throughout the years, he continued this passion of using machine learning on Big Data to solve complex problems and find answers that touch human lives. Possessing a streak of hard-to-hide innovativeness, Pradeep is bold enough to think beyond what is possible. His works on computational linguistics (NLP) and deep-learning techniques to build expert systems are all examples of this.

That he made a transition from being the lead of a development-focused team to an established technology author makes me immensely pleased. His constant and unlimited appetite for knowledge is something to emulate for people like me, who are in the technology space! Although not directly related to this book, it is appropriate that I mention even his strong value system as an individual. This quality is what makes him a successful professional, a great leader, and a guru to learn from!

He was kind enough to ask me to review this book. However, the boss in me jumped out and tried to grill him as I often did when he worked in my team. He responded very positively to my critique, which at times was harsh when I look back at it! For you see, both of us share a common belief that it is better to realize the existing errors and potential improvements in processes ourselves, and not simply leave them to reach our customers or you, the audience of this book.

I always felt that a good book can be authored only with a specific end user profile in mind. A book written for beginners may not appeal to a professional at all. The opposite of this is even truer. However, this work by Pradeep benefits both beginners and professionals equally well. This is the biggest difference that I found in this book.

An initiation, a book, or a training program are all meant to give you the essentials and point you to the right direction. There is no replacement to practicing what you learn. I encourage you to practice what you learn from this book and push up your efficiencies of Big Data development!

Srinivas Uppuluri

Founder Director, Valueware Technologies
www.valueware.co.in
srinivas.uppuluri@valueware.co.in

About the Author

Pradeep Pasupuleti has over 16 years of experience in architecting and developing distributed and real-time data-driven systems. Currently, his focus is on developing robust data platforms and data products that are fuelled by scalable machine-learning algorithms, and delivering value to customers by addressing business problems by juxtaposing his deep technical insights into Big Data technologies with future data management and analytical needs. He is extremely passionate about Big Data and believes that it will be the cradle of many innovations that will save humans their time, money, and lives.

He has built solid data product teams with experience spanning through every aspect of data science, thus successfully helping clients to build an end-to-end strategy around how their current data architecture can evolve into a hybrid pattern that is capable of supporting analytics in both batch and real time—all of this is done using the lambda architecture. He has created COE's (Center of Excellence) to provide quick wins with data products that analyze high-dimensional multistructured data using scalable natural language processing and deep learning techniques.

He has performed roles in technology consulting advising Fortune 500 companies on their Big Data strategy, product management, systems architecture, social network analysis, negotiations, conflict resolution, chaos and nonlinear dynamics, international policy, high-performance computing, advanced statistical techniques, risk management, marketing, visualization of high dimensional data, human-computer interaction, machine learning, information retrieval, and data mining. He has a strong experience of working in ambiguity to solve complex problems using innovation by bringing smart people together.

His other interests include writing and reading poetry, enjoying the expressive delights of ghazals, spending time with kids discussing impossible inventions, and searching for archeological sites.

You can reach him at http://www.linkedin.com/in/pradeeppasupuleti and pasupuleti.pradeepkumar@gmail.com.

Acknowledgments

Writing a technical book takes an unpredictable amount of sacrifice every single day. I sincerely believe that nobody could ever complete writing a book alone without the willing sacrifices of family, friends, and coworkers. It is an honor to give credit where credit is due. I am truly blessed to have been in the company of some of the consistently bright people in the world while working on this book.

I owe a deep sense of gratitude to my parents, Prabhakar and Sumathy, who have constantly guided, encouraged, and blessed me; I am sure mere words can never express the magnitude of my gratitude to them. On the home front, I gave up more time with my wife, Sushma, and sons, Sresht and Samvruth, than I'm proud to admit. Thanks most of all to you for your support, love, and patience while I researched, wrote, reviewed, and rewrote the book by stealing your valuable time.

More than anything else, this book has been a team effort right from the beginning. Every member of my team has contributed in one way or another, whether they realize it or not. I am grateful to Salome, Vasundhara Boga, and Pratap for their extraordinary efforts and endless fortitude to help put together the environment, develop the code, and test the output. Without their stellar performances, this book would be incomplete. Their effort reinforces my faith in teamwork—the key ingredient for the success of any endeavor.

Srinivas Uppuluri has been an inspiration right from the beginning of my career, and I am extremely proud to be associated with him. I would like to profusely thank him for reviewing this book at every step and allowing me to be exposed to many great ideas, points of view, and zealous inspiration.

I would also like to thank Dr. Dakshina Murthy who eased me into the world of Big Data analytics and is my mentor and role model in the field of data sciences.

I would like to express my appreciation to all the staff of Packt Publishing for assisting me while editing this book. It was a marvelous effort on their part to shape its outcome for the best. They also made writing my first book an enjoyable experience. I thank everyone involved with Apache Pig. This includes committers, contributors, as well as end users for documenting so much in so little time.

I also want to show appreciation to an e-mail by my previous manager, Sandeep Athavale, which was sent to me a few years ago. In that e-mail, he reposed faith in my writing abilities and encouraged me to write a book one day, thus sowing the seed that culminated in the writing of this book—thank you Sandeep for that action-provoking mail. Through this, I want to let you know that little words of encouragement definitely leave an indelible impression to make improvements to both your personal and professional life.

Thanks to the readers for giving this book a chance. I hope you will definitely find something that can enrich your ideas and trigger new thoughts in you.

Above all, I want to thank all the folks who have helped me in some way or the other to write this book. These are a few of them who happen to be on the top of my mind: Pallavi P, Praveen P, Srini Mannava, Sunil Sana, Ravi Jordan, Haribabu T, Syam A, Robin H, Roopa, Satish B and his family, and so on.

This book is dedicated to the beloved memory of my teammate:
Subramanyam Pagadala

About the Reviewers

Aaron Binns spent over five years at the Internet Archive where he designed and built a petabyte-scale Hadoop cluster supporting full-text search and Big Data analytics, the majority of which was implemented in Pig. He was responsible for the construction and deployment of full-text search of domain-scale web archives of hundreds of millions of archived web pages, as well as the over two billion web pages indexed for full-text search in the Archive-It service. He also developed custom software, built on Lucene, to provide special functionality required for full-text search of archival web documents.

He currently works at TaskRabbit as a data scientist. He holds a Bachelor of Science degree in Computer Science from Case Western Reserve University.

Shingo Furuyama is a software engineer, who has specialized in domain logic implementation to realize the value of software in the financial industry. At weekends, he enjoys cycling, scuba diving, wind surfing, and coding. Currently, he is studying English in the Philippines to expand his career opportunities.

He started his career as a software engineer at Simplex Technology, taking major responsibility in developing interest rate derivatives and a Forex option management system for a Japanese mega bank. Before going to the Philippines, he was working for Nautilus Technologies, a Japanese start-up that specializes in Big Data technologies and cloud-related enterprise solutions.

You can get more information from his blog (`http://marblejenka.blogspot.jp/`) or LinkedIn (`http://jp.linkedin.com/in/shingofuruyama`). You can also follow him on Twitter (`@marblejenka`).

Shashwat Shriparv holds a master's degree in Computer Application from Cochin University of Science and Technology and currently working as Senior. System Engineer HPC with Cognilytics. With a total IT experience of six years, he spent three and a half years working on core Big Data technologies, such as Hadoop, Hive, HBase, Pig, Sqoop, Flume, and Mongo in the field of development and management, and the rest of his time in handling projects in technologies, such as .Net, Java, web programming languages, and mobile development.

He has worked with companies, such as HCL, C-DAC, PointCross, and Genilok. He actively participates and contributes to online Big Data forums and groups. He has also contributed to Big Data technologies by creating and uploading several videos for Big Data enthusiasts and practitioners on YouTube free of cost.

He likes writing articles, poems, and technology blogs, and also enjoys photography. More information about him can be found at `https://github.com/shriparv` and `http://helpmetocode.blogspot.com`. You can connect to him on LinkedIn at `http://www.linkedin.com/pub/shashwat-shriparv/19/214/2a9` and can mail him at `dwivedishashwat@gmail.com`.

Fábio Franco Uechi has a bachelor's degree in Computer Science and is a Senior Software Engineer at CI&T Inc. He has been the architect of enterprise-grade solutions in the software industry for around 11 years and has been using Big Data and cloud technologies over the past four to five years to solve complex business problems.

He is highly interested in machine learning and Big Data technologies, such as R, Hadoop, Mahout, Pig, Hive, and related distributed processing platforms to analyze datasets to achieve informative insights.

Other than programming, he enjoys playing pinball, slacklining, and wakeboarding. You can learn more from his blog (`http://fabiouechi.blogspot.com`) and GitHub (`https://github.com/fabito`).

www.PacktPub.com

Support files, eBooks, discount offers and more

You might want to visit www.PacktPub.com for support files and downloads related to your book.

Did you know that Packt offers eBook versions of every book published, with PDF and ePub files available? You can upgrade to the eBook version at www.PacktPub.com and as a print book customer, you are entitled to a discount on the eBook copy. Get in touch with us at service@packtpub.com for more details.

At www.PacktPub.com, you can also read a collection of free technical articles, sign up for a range of free newsletters and receive exclusive discounts and offers on Packt books and eBooks.

http://PacktLib.PacktPub.com

Do you need instant solutions to your IT questions? PacktLib is Packt's online digital book library. Here, you can access, read and search across Packt's entire library of books.

Why Subscribe?
- Fully searchable across every book published by Packt
- Copy and paste, print and bookmark content
- On demand and accessible via web browser

Free Access for Packt account holders

If you have an account with Packt at www.PacktPub.com, you can use this to access PacktLib today and view nine entirely free books. Simply use your login credentials for immediate access.

Table of Contents

Preface

This book is a practical guide to realizing the power of analytics in Big Data.
It walks the Big Data technologist in you through the process of getting the data
ready, applying analytics, and creating a value out of the data. All of this is done
using appropriate design patterns in Pig. We have chosen Pig to demonstrate how
useful it is, which is evident from the following:

- The inherent amenability of Pig through its simple language constructs, which
  can be learned very easily, and its extensibility and applicability to structured
  and unstructured Big Data makes it the preferred choice over others.

- The ease and speed with which patterns can be implemented by Pig to derive
  meaning out of the apparent randomness in any Big Data is commendable.

- This book guides system architects and developers so they become
  more proficient at creating complex analytics solutions using Pig. It
  does so by exposing them to a variety of Pig design patterns, UDFs,
  tools, and best practices.

By reading this book, you will achieve the following goals:

- Simplify the process of creating complex data pipelines by performing
  data movement across platforms, data ingestion, profiling, validation,
  transformations, data reduction, and egress; you'll also be able to use Pig in
  these design patterns

- Create solutions that use patterns for exploratory analysis of multistructured
  unmodeled data to derive structure from it and move the data to
  downstream systems for further analysis

- Decipher how Pig can coexist with other tools in the Hadoop ecosystem
  to create Big Data solutions using design patterns

What this book covers

Chapter 1, Setting the Context for Design Patterns in Pig, lays a basic foundation for design patterns, Hadoop, MapReduce and its ecosystem components gradually exposing Pig, its dataflow paradigm, and the language constructs and concepts with a few basic examples that are required to make Pig work. It sets the context to understand the various workloads Pig is most suitable for and how Pig scores better. This chapter is more of a quick practical reference and points to additional references if you are motivated enough to know more about Pig.

Chapter 2, Data Ingest and Egress Patterns, explains the data ingest and egress design patterns that deal with a variety of data sources. The chapter includes specific examples that illustrate the techniques to integrate with external systems that emit multistructured and structured data and use Hadoop as a sink to ingest. This chapter also explores patterns that output the data from Hadoop to external systems. To explain these ingest and egress patterns, we have considered multiple filesystems, which include, but are not limited to, logfiles, JSON, XML, MongoDB, Cassandra, HBase, and other common structured data sources. After reading this chapter, you will be better equipped to program patterns related to ingest and egress in your enterprise context, and will be capable of applying this knowledge to use the right Pig programming constructs or write your own UDFs to accomplish these patterns.

Chapter 3, Data Profiling Patterns, focuses on the data profiling patterns applied to a multitude of data formats and realizing these patterns in Pig. These patterns include different approaches to using Pig and applying basic and innovative statistical techniques to profile data and find data quality issues. You will learn about ways to program similar patterns in your enterprise context using Pig and write your own UDFs to extend these patterns.

Chapter 4, Data Validation and Cleansing Patterns, is about the data validation and cleansing patterns that are applied to various data formats. The data validation patterns deal with constraints, regex, and other statistical techniques. The data cleansing patterns deal with simple filters, bloom filters, and other statistical techniques to make the data ready for transformations to be applied.

Chapter 5, Data Transformation Patterns, deals with data transformation patterns applied to a wide variety of data types ingested into Hadoop. After reading this chapter, you will be able to choose the right pattern for basic transformations and also learn about widely used concepts such as creating joins, summarization, aggregates, cubes, rolling up data, generalization, and attribute construction using Pig's programming constructs and also UDFs where necessary.

Chapter 6, Understanding Data Reduction Patterns, explains the data reduction patterns applied to the already ingested, scrubbed, and transformed data. After reading this chapter, you will be able to understand and use patterns for dimensionality reduction, sampling techniques, binning, clustering, and irrelevant attribute reduction, thus making the data ready for analytics. This chapter explores various techniques using the Pig language and extends Pig's capability to provide sophisticated usages of data reduction.

Chapter 7, Advanced Patterns and Future Work, deals with the advanced data analytics patterns. These patterns cover the extensibility of the Pig language and explain with use cases the methods of integrating with executable code, map reduce code written in Java, UDFs from PiggyBank, and other sources. Advanced analytics cover the patterns related to natural language processing, clustering, classification, and text indexing.

Motivation for this book

The inspiration for writing this book has its roots in the job I do for a living, that is, heading the enterprise practice for Big Data where I am involved in the innovation and delivery of solutions built on the Big Data technology stack.

As part of this role, I am involved in the piloting of many use cases, solution architecture, and development of multiple Big Data solutions. In my experience, Pig has been a revelation of sorts, and it has a tremendous appeal for users who want to quickly pilot a use case and demonstrate value to business. I have used Pig to prove rapid gains and solve problems that required a not-so-steep learning curve. At the same time, I have found out that the documented knowledge of using Pig in enterprises was nonexistent in some cases and spread out wide in cases where it was available. I personally felt the need to have a use case pattern based reference book of knowledge. Through this book, I wanted to share my experiences and lessons, and communicate to you the usability and advantages of Pig for solving your common problems from a pattern's viewpoint.

One of the other reasons I chose to write about Pig's design patterns is that I am fascinated with the Pig language, its simplicity, versatility, and its extensibility. My constant search for repeatable patterns for implementing Pig recipes in an enterprise context has inspired me to document it for wider usage. I wanted to spread the best practices that I learned while using Pig through contributing to a pattern repository of Pig. I'm intrigued by the unseen possibilities of using Pig in various use cases, and through this book, I plan to stretch the limit of its applicability even further and make Pig more pleasurable to work with.

This book portrays a practical and implementational side of learning Pig. It provides specific reusable solutions to commonly occurring challenges in Big Data enterprises. Its goal is to guide you to quickly map the usage of Pig to your problem context and to design end-to-end Big Data systems from a design pattern outlook.

In this book, a design pattern is a group of enterprise use cases logically tied together so that they can be broken down into discrete solutions that are easy to follow and addressable through Pig. These design patterns address common enterprise problems involved in the creation of complex data pipelines, ingress, egress, transformation, iterative processing, merging, and analysis of large quantities of data.

This book enhances your capability to make better decisions on the applicability of a particular design pattern and use Pig to implement the solution.

Pig Latin has been the language of choice for implementing complex data pipelines, iterative processing of data, and conducting research. All of these use cases involve sequential steps in which data is ingested, cleansed, transformed, and made available to upstream systems. The successful creation of an intricate pipeline, which integrates skewed data from multiple data platforms with varying structure, forms the cornerstone of any enterprise, which leverages Big Data and creates value out of it through analytics.

This book enables you to use these design patterns to simplify the creation of complex data pipelines using Pig, ingesting data from multiple data sources, cleansing, profiling, validating, transformation and final presentation of large volumes of data.

This book provides in-depth explanations and code examples using Pig and the integration of UDFs written in Java. Each chapter contains a set of design patterns that pose and then solve technical challenges that are relevant to the enterprise's use cases. The chapters are relatively independent of each other and can be completed in any order since they address design patterns specific to a set of common steps in the enterprise. As an illustration, a reader who is looking forward to solving a data transformation problem, can directly access *Chapter 5, Data Transformation Patterns*, and quickly start using the code and explanations mentioned in this chapter. The book recommends that you use these patterns for solving the same or similar problems you encounter and create your own patterns if the design pattern is not suitable in a particular case.

This book's intent is not to be a complete guide to Pig programming but to be more of a reference book that brings in the design patterns' perspective of applying Pig. It also intends to empower you to make creative use of the design patterns and build interesting mashups with them.

What you need for this book

You will need access to a single machine (VM) or multinode Hadoop cluster to execute the Pig scripts given in this book. It is expected that the tools needed to run Pig are configured. We have used Pig 0.11.0 to test the examples of this book, and it is highly recommended that you have this version installed.

The code for the UDFs in this book is written in different languages such as Java; therefore, it is advisable for you to have access to a machine with development tools (such as Eclipse) that you are comfortable with.

It is recommended to use Pig Pen (Eclipse plugin) on the developer's machine for developing and debugging Pig scripts.

Pig Pen can be downloaded from `https://issues.apache.org/jira/secure/attachment/12456988/org.apache.pig.pigpen_0.7.5.jar`.

Who this book is for

This book is for experienced developers who are already familiar with Pig and are looking forward to referring to a use case standpoint that they can relate to the problems of ingestion, profiling, cleansing, transformation, and egress of data encountered in the enterprises. These power users of Pig will use the book as a reference for understanding the significance of Pig design patterns to solve their problems.

Knowledge of Hadoop and Pig is mandatory for you to grasp the intricacies of Pig design patterns better. To address this, *Chapter 1, Setting the Context for Design Patterns in Pig*, contains introductory concepts with simple examples. It is recommended that readers be familiar with Java and Python in order to better comprehend the UDFs that are used as examples in many chapters.

Conventions

In this book, you will find a number of styles of text that distinguish between different kinds of information. Here are a few examples of these styles and an explanation of their meaning.

Code words in text are shown as follows: "From this point onward, we shall call the unpacked Hadoop directory `HADOOP_HOME`."

A block of code for UDFs written in Java is set as follows:

```
package com.pigdesignpatterns.myudfs;

public class DeIdentifyUDF extends EvalFunc<String> {

    @Override
    public String exec(Tuple input){

            try {
                String plainText = (String)input.get(0);
                String encryptKey = (String)input.get(1);
                String str="";
                str = encrypt(plainText,encryptKey.getBytes());
                return str;
            }
            catch (NullPointerException npe) {
                warn(npe.toString(), PigWarning.UDF_WARNING_2);
                return null;
            } catch (StringIndexOutOfBoundsException npe) {
                warn(npe.toString(), PigWarning.UDF_WARNING_3);
                return null;
            } catch (ClassCastException e) {
                warn(e.toString(), PigWarning.UDF_WARNING_4);
                return null;
            }
```

Pig Script is displayed as follows:

```
Users = load 'users' as (name, age);
Fltrd = filter Users by
 age >= 18 and age <= 25;
Pages = load 'pages' as (user, url);
Jnd = join Fltrd by name, Pages by user;
Grpd = group Jnd by url;
Smmd = foreach Grpd generate group,
COUNT(Jnd) as clicks;
Srtd = order Smmd by clicks desc;
Top5 = limit Srtd 5;
store Top5 into 'top5sites'
```

Any command-line input or output is written as follows:

```
>tar -zxvf hadoop-1.x.x.tar.gz
```

New terms and **important words** are shown in bold. Words that you see on the screen, in menus or dialog boxes for example, appear in the text like this: "Clicking the **Next** button moves you to the next screen."

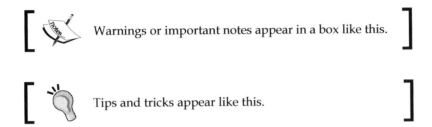

Warnings or important notes appear in a box like this.

Tips and tricks appear like this.

Reader feedback

Feedback from our readers is always welcome. Let us know what you think about this book—what you liked or may have disliked. Reader feedback is important for us to develop titles that you really get the most out of.

To send us general feedback, simply send an e-mail to feedback@packtpub.com, and mention the book title via the subject of your message.

If there is a topic that you have expertise in and you are interested in either writing or contributing to a book, see our author guide on www.packtpub.com/authors.

Customer support

Now that you are the proud owner of a Packt book, we have a number of things to help you to get the most from your purchase

Downloading the example code

You can download the example code files for all Packt books you have purchased from your account at http://www.packtpub.com. If you purchased this book elsewhere, you can visit http://www.packtpub.com/support and register to have the files e-mailed directly to you. The examples in this book are tested by compiling against Pig Version 0.11.0. Many of the Pig scripts, UDFs, and data are available from the publisher's website or GitHub.

You can also use https://github.com/pradeep-pasupuleti/pig-design-patterns.

The Pig Latin script examples are organized by chapter in their respective directories. UDFs of Java and Python are also part of the chapter directory organized in a separate subdirectory by the name src. All datasets are in the datasets directory. Readme files are included to help you get the UDFs built and to understand the contents of the data files.

Each script is written with the assumption that the input and output are in the HDFS path.

Third-party libraries

A number of third-party libraries are used for the sake of convenience. They are included in the Maven dependencies so there is no extra work required to work with these libraries. The following table contains a list of the libraries that are in prevalent use throughout the code examples:

Library name	Description	Link
dataFu	DataFu is a collection of user-defined functions for working with large-scale data in Hadoop and Pig especially for data mining and statistics	http://search.maven.org/remotecontent?filepath=com/linkedin/datafu/datafu/0.0.10/datafu-0.0.10.jar
mongo-hadoop-core	This is the plugin for Hadoop that provides the ability to use MongoDB as an input source and/or an output source	http://repo1.maven.org/maven2/org/mongodb/mongo-hadoop-core_1.0.0/1.0.0-rc0/mongo-hadoop-core_1.0.0-1.0.0-rc0.jar
mongo-hadoop-pig	This is to load records from the MongoDB database to use them in a Pig script and to write to a MongoDB instance	http://repo1.maven.org/maven2/org/mongodb/mongo-hadoop-pig/1.0.0/mongo-hadoop-pig-1.0.0.jar
mongo-java-driver	This is a Java driver for MongoDB	http://repo1.maven.org/maven2/org/mongodb/mongo-java-driver/2.9.0/mongo-java-driver-2.9.0.jar
elephant-bird-pig	This is Twitter's open source library of Pig LoadFuncs	http://repo1.maven.org/maven2/com/twitter/elephantbird/elephant-bird-pig/3.0.5/elephant-bird-pig-3.0.5.jar

Library name	Description	Link
elephant-bird-core	This is Twitter's collection of core utilities	`http://repo1.maven.org/maven2/com/twitter/elephantbird/elephant-bird-pig/3.0.5/elephant-bird-pig-3.0.5.jar`
hcatalog-pig-adapter	This contains utilities to access data from Hcatalog-managed tables	`http://search.maven.org/remotecontent?filepath=org/apache/hcatalog/hcatalog-pig-adapter/0.11.0/hcatalog-pig-adapter-0.11.0.jar`
cb2java	This JAR has libraries to dynamically parse the COBOL copybook	`http://sourceforge.net/projects/cb2java/files/latest/download`
Avro	This is the Avro core components' library	`http://repo1.maven.org/maven2/org/apache/avro/avro/1.7.4/avro-1.7.4.jar`
json-simple	This library is a Java toolkit for JSON to encode or decode JSON text	`http://www.java2s.com/Code/JarDownload/json-simple/json-simple-1.1.1.jar.zip`
commons-math	This library contains few mathematical and statistical components	`http://repo1.maven.org/maven2/org/apache/commons/commons-math3/3.2/commons-math3-3.2.jar`

Datasets

Throughout this book, you'll work with these datasets to provide some variety for the examples. Copies of the exact data used are available in the GitHub repository in the directory `https://github.com/pradeep-pasupuleti/pig-design-patterns`. Wherever relevant, data that is specific to a chapter exists within chapter-specific subdirectories under the same GitHub location.

The following are the major classifications of datasets, which are used in this book as relevant to the use case discussed:

- The logs dataset contains a month's worth of HTTP requests to the NASA Kennedy Space Center WWW server in Florida. These logs are in the format of Apache access logs.

> The dataset is downloaded from the links `ftp://ita.ee.lbl.gov/traces/NASA_access_log_Jul95.gz` and `ftp://ita.ee.lbl.gov/traces/NASA_access_log_Aug95.gz`.
>
> Acknowledgement: The logs were collected by Jim Dumoulin of the Kennedy Space Center, and contributed by Martin Arlitt (`mfa126@cs.usask.ca`) and Carey Williamson (`carey@cs.usask.ca`) of the University of Saskatchewan.

- The custom logs dataset contains logs generated by a web application in the custom log format. Web service request and response information is embedded along with the event logs. This is a synthetic dataset created specifically to illustrate the examples in this book.

- The historical NASDAQ stock data from 1970 to 2010, including daily open, close, low, high, and trading volume figures. Data is organized alphabetically by ticker symbol.

> This dataset is downloaded from the link `http://www.infochimps.com/datasets/nasdaq-exchange-daily-1970-2010-open-close-high-low-and-volume/downloads/166853`.

- The customer retail transactions dataset has details on category of the product being purchased and customer demographic information. This is a synthetic dataset created specifically to illustrate the examples in this book.

- The automobile insurance claims dataset consists of two files. The `automobile_policy_master.csv` file contains the vehicle price and the premium paid for it. The file `automobile_insurance_claims.csv` contains automobile insurance claims data, specifically vehicle repair charges claims. This is a synthetic dataset created specifically to illustrate the examples in this book.

- The MedlinePlus health topic XML files contain records of health topics. Each health topic record includes data elements associated with that topic.

  This dataset is downloaded from the link `http://www.healthdata.gov/data/dataset/medlineplus-health-topic-xml-files-0`.

- This dataset contains a large set of e-mail messages from the Enron corpus which has about 150 users with an average of 757 messages per user; the dataset is in AVRO format and we have converted it to JSON format for the purpose of this book.

  This dataset is downloaded from the link `https://s3.amazonaws.com/rjurney_public_web/hadoop/enron.avro`.

- Manufacturing dataset for electrical appliances is a synthetic dataset created for the purpose of this book. This dataset contains the following files:

  - `manufacturing_units.csv`: This contains information about each manufacturing unit
  - `products.csv`: This contains details of the products that are manufactured
  - `manufacturing_units_products.csv`: This holds detailed information of products that are manufactured in different manufacturing units
  - `production.csv`: This holds the production details

- The unstructured text dataset contains parts of articles from Wikipedia on Computer science and Information Technology, Big Data, Medicine, invention of telephone, stop words list, and dictionary words list.

- The Outlook contacts dataset is a synthetic dataset created by exporting the Outlook contacts for the purpose of this book; it is a CSV file with attributes contact names and job titles.

- The German credit dataset in CSV format classifies people as good or bad credit risks based on a set of attributes. There are 20 attributes (7 numerical and 13 categorical) with 1,000 instances.

> This dataset is downloaded from the link `http://archive.ics.uci.edu/ml/machine-learning-databases/statlog/german/german.data`.
>
> Acknowledgement: Data collected from UCI Machine Learning Repository (`http://archive.ics.uci.edu/ml/datasets/Statlog+(German+Credit+Data)`), source: Professor Dr. Hans Hofmann, Institut fuer Statistik und Oekonometrie, Universitaet Hamburg.

Errata

Although we have taken every care to ensure the accuracy of our content, mistakes do happen. If you find a mistake in one of our books—maybe a mistake in the text or the code—we would be grateful if you would report this to us. By doing so, you can save other readers from frustration and help us improve subsequent versions of this book. If you find any errata, please report them by visiting `http://www.packtpub.com/support`, selecting your book, clicking on the **errata submission form** link, and entering the details of your errata. Once your errata are verified, your submission will be accepted and the errata will be uploaded to our website, or added to any list of existing errata, under the Errata section of that title.

Piracy

Piracy of copyright material on the Internet is an ongoing problem across all media. At Packt, we take the protection of our copyright and licenses very seriously. If you come across any illegal copies of our works, in any form, on the Internet, please provide us with the location address or website name immediately so that we can pursue a remedy.

Please contact us at `copyright@packtpub.com` with a link to the suspected pirated material.

We appreciate your help in protecting our authors, and our ability to bring you valuable content.

Questions

You can contact us at `questions@packtpub.com` if you are having a problem with any aspect of the book, and we will do our best to address it.

1
Setting the Context for Design Patterns in Pig

This chapter is aimed at providing a broad introduction to multiple technologies and concepts addressed in this book. We start with exploring the concepts related to design patterns by defining them and understanding how they are discovered and applied in real life, and through this, we seek to understand how these design patterns are applied and implemented in Pig.

Before we start looking into the intricacies of the Pig programming language, we explore the background of why Pig came into existence, where Pig is used in an enterprise, and understand how Hadoop fits in the distributed computing landscape in the age of Big Data. We then perform a quick dive into the Hadoop ecosystem, introducing you to its important features. The Pig programming language has been covered from the language features perspective, giving you a ready-made example that is elaborated to explain the language features, such as common operators, extensibility, input and output operators, relational operators, schemas, nulls, and ways to understand the intermediate MapReduce code.

Understanding design patterns

Design patterns provide a consistent and common solutions approach to similar problems or requirements. A designer working with diverse systems often comes across a similarity in the way a problem manifests itself or a requirement that needs to be met. Eventually, he/she gains enough knowledge of the subtle variations, and starts seeing a common thread connecting these otherwise different and recurring problems. Such common behavior or characteristics are then abstracted into a pattern. This pattern or solution approach is thus a generalized design that can also be applied to a broader set of requirements and newer manifestations of the problem. For example, the widely acclaimed software design patterns book, *Design Patterns: Elements of Reusable Object-Oriented Software* by *Erich Gamma*, *Richard Helm*, *Ralph Johnson*, and *John Vlissides*, *Addison-Wesley Professional*, mentions five creational patterns. These patterns can also be understood by analyzing real-life situations that trace their origin to a non-software field. The factory method pattern mentioned in this book defines an interface for the creation of class objects, but it lets the subclasses perform the decision making on which class to instantiate. This software pattern seems to have a parallel in the non-software industry where toys are manufactured by the injection molding process. The machine processes the plastic powder and injects the powder into molds of the required shapes. The class of the toy (car, action figure, and so on) is determined by its mold.

The intent of the design pattern is not to act like a perfect tailor-made solution for a specific problem that can be converted into code. Rather, it is like a template to solve specific and well-defined problems. Usually, design patterns are uncovered in real life; they are not created. The following are general ways in which patterns are discovered:

- The evolution of a new group of technologies that solve the latest problems together; these technologies have a perceived need for a pattern catalog
- Encountering a solution that has recurring problems

Adapt the existing patterns to new situations and modify the existing pattern itself. Discovering a pattern implies defining it, giving it a name, and documenting it in a very clear way so that users can read, understand, and apply them when faced with similar problems. A pattern is worth publishing after it is used by real users and they have worked on real-world problems rather than hypothetical issues. These patterns are not rules or laws; they are guidelines that may be modified to fit the needs of the solution.

This book takes inspiration from other books written on design patterns on various subject areas. It also follows the pattern documentation format as outlined by the GoF pattern catalog *Design Patterns: Elements of Reusable Object-Oriented Software*, by *Gamma, Helm, Johnson & Vlissides (Addison-Wesley Professional)*.

Every design pattern in this book follows a template and is identified by a name, followed by a few sections that tell the user more about the patterns.

- The pattern name gives the pattern a unique identifier and can be a good means of communication.

- The pattern details section succinctly describes the what and why of the pattern.

- The *Background* section describes the motivation and in-detail applicability of the pattern.

- The *Motivation* section describes a concrete scenario that describes the problem and how the pattern fits as a solution. Applicability describes different situations where the pattern is used.

- The *Use cases* section deals with various use cases in real systems where we can see evidence of the pattern.

- The *Code snippets* section consists of the code through which the pattern is implemented.

- The *Results* section has the consequences of the pattern that deal with the intended and unintended effect of the output of the pattern.

- The *Additional information* section deals with how the patterns relate to each other, and any other relevant information related to the pattern.

You apply a pattern when you identify a problem, which a pattern can solve, and recognize the similarity to other problems that might be solved using known patterns. This can happen during the initial design, coding, or maintenance phase. In order to do this, you need to get familiar with the existing patterns and their interrelationships first, and then look at the *Background* section that delves deeper into the motivation and applicability of the pattern for the design problem.

The scope of design patterns in Pig

This book deals with patterns that were encountered while solving real-world, recurrent Big Data problems in an enterprise setting. The need for these patterns takes root in the evolution of Pig to solve the emerging problems of large volumes and a variety of data, and the perceived need for a pattern catalog to document their solutions.

The emerging problems of handling large volumes of data, typically deal with getting a firm grip on understanding whether the data can be used or not to generate analytical insights and, if possible, how to efficiently generate these insights. Imagine yourself to be in the shoes of a data scientist who has been given a massive volume of data that does not have a proper schema, is messy, and has not been documented for ages. You have been asked to integrate this with other enterprise data sources and generate spectacular analytical insights. How do you start? Would you start integrating data and fire up your favorite analytics sandbox and begin generating results? Would it be handy if you knew beforehand the existence of design patterns that can be applied systematically and sequentially in this kind of scenario to reduce the error and increase the efficiency of Big Data analytics? The design patterns discussed in this book will definitely appeal to you in this case.

Design patterns in Pig are geared to enhance your ability to take a problem of Big Data and quickly apply the patterns to solve it. Successful development of Big Data solutions using Pig requires considering issues early in the lifecycle of development, and these patterns help to uncover those issues. Reusing Pig design patterns helps identify and address such subtleties and prevents them from growing into major problems. The by-product of the application of the patterns is readability and maintainability of the resultant code. These patterns provide developers a valuable communication tool by allowing them to use a common vocabulary to discuss problems in terms of what a pattern could solve, rather than explaining the internals of a problem in a verbose way. Design patterns for Pig are not a cookbook for success; they are a rule of thumb. Reading specific cases in this book about Pig design patterns may help you recognize problems early, saving you from the exponential cost of reworks later on.

The popularity of design patterns is very much dependent on the domain. For example, the state patterns, proxies, and facades of the *Gang of Four* book are very common with applications that communicate a lot with other systems. In the same way, the enterprises, which consume Big Data to understand analytical insights, use patterns related to solving problems of data pipelines since this is a very common use case. These patterns specifically elaborate the usage of Pig in data ingest, profiling, cleansing, transformation, reduction, analytics, and egress.

A few patterns discussed in *Chapter 5, Data Transformation Patterns* and *Chapter 6, Understanding Data Reduction Patterns,* adapt the existing patterns to new situations, and in the process modify the existing pattern itself. These patterns deal with the usage of Pig in incremental data integration and creation of quick prototypes.

These design patterns also go deeper and enable you to decide the applicability of specific language constructs of Pig for a given problem. The following questions illustrate this point better:

- What is the recommended usage of projections to solve specific patterns?
- In which pattern is the usage of scalar projections ideal to access aggregates?
- For which patterns is it not recommended to use COUNT, SUM, and COUNT_STAR?
- How to effectively use sorting in patterns where key distributions are skewed?
- Which patterns are related to the correct usage of spill-able data types?
- When not to use multiple FLATTENS operators, which can result in CROSS on bags?
- What patterns depict the ideal usage of the nested FOREACH method?
- Which patterns to choose for a JOIN operation when one dataset can fit into memory?
- Which patterns to choose for a JOIN operation when one of the relations joined has a key that dominates?
- Which patterns to choose for a JOIN operation when two datasets are already ordered?

Hadoop demystified – a quick reckoner

We will now discuss the need to process huge multistructured data and the challenges involved in processing such huge data using traditional distributed applications. We will also discuss the advent of Hadoop and how it efficiently addresses these challenges.

The enterprise context

The last decade has been a defining moment in the history of data, resulting in enterprises adopting new business models and opportunities piggybacking on the large-scale growth of data.

The proliferation of Internet searches, personalization of music, tablet computing, smartphones, 3G networks, and social media contributed to the change in rules of data management, from organizing, acquiring, storing, and retrieving data to managing perspectives. The need for decision making for these new sources of data and getting valuable insights has become a valuable weapon in the enterprise arsenal, aimed to make the enterprise successful.

Traditional systems, such as RDBMS-based data warehouses, took the lead to support the decision-making process by being able to collect, store, and manage data by applying traditional and statistical methods of measurement to create a reporting and analysis platform. The data collected within these traditional systems were highly structured in nature with minimal flexibility to change with the needs of the emerging data types, which were more unstructured.

These data warehouses are capable of supporting distributed processing applications, but with many limitations. Such distributed processing applications are generally oriented towards taking in structured data, transforming it, and making it usable for analytics or reporting, and these applications were predominantly batch jobs. In some cases, these applications are run on a cluster of machines so that the computation and data are distributed to the nodes of the cluster. These applications take a chunk of data, perform a computationally intense operation on it, and send it to downstream systems for another application or system to consume.

With the competitive need to analyze both structured and unstructured data and gain insights, the current enterprises need the processing to be done on an unprecedentedly massive scale of data. The processing mostly involves performing operations needed to clean, profile, and transform unstructured data in combination with the enterprise data sources so that the results can be used to gain useful analytical insights. Processing these large datasets requires many CPUs, sufficient I/O bandwidth, Memory, and so on. In addition, whenever there is large-scale processing, it implies that we have to deal with failures of all kinds. Traditional systems such as RDBMS do not scale linearly or cost effectively under this kind of tremendous data load or when the variety of data is unpredictable.

In order to process the exceptional influx of data, there is a palpable need for data management technology solutions; this allows us to consume large volumes of data in a short amount of time across many formats, with varying degrees of complexity to create a powerful analytical platform that supports decisions.

Common challenges of distributed systems

Before the genesis of Hadoop, distributed applications were trying to cope with the challenges of data growth and parallel processing in which processors, network, and storage failure was common. The distributed systems often had to manage the problems of failure of individual components in the ecosystem, arising out of low disk space, corrupt data, performance degradations, routing issues, and network congestion. Achieving linear scalability in traditional architectures was next to impossible and in cases where it was possible to a limited extent, it was not without incurring huge costs.

High availability was achieved, but at a cost of scalability or compromised integrity. The lack of good support for concurrency, fault tolerance, and data availability were unfavorable for traditional systems to handle the complexities of Big Data. Apart from this, if we ever want to deploy a custom application, which houses the latest predictive algorithm, distributed code has its own problems of synchronization, locking, resource contentions, concurrency control, and transactional recovery.

Few of the previously discussed problems of distributed computing have been handled in multiple ways within the traditional RDBMS data warehousing systems, but the solutions cannot be directly extrapolated to the Big Data situation where the problem is amplified exponentially due to huge volumes of data, and its variety and velocity. The problems of data volume are solvable to an extent. However, the problems of data variety and data velocity are prohibitively expensive to be solved by these attempts to rein in traditional systems to solve Big Data problems.

As the problems grew with time, the solution to handle the processing of Big Data was embraced by the intelligent combination of various technologies, such as distributed processing, distributed storage, artificial intelligence, multiprocessor systems, and object-oriented concepts along with Internet data processing techniques

The advent of Hadoop

Hadoop, a framework that can tolerate machine failure, is built to outlast challenges concerning the distributed systems discussed in the previous section. Hadoop provides a way of using a cluster of machines to store and process, in parallel, extremely huge amounts of data. It is a File System-based scalable and distributed data processing architecture, designed and deployed on a high-throughput and scalable infrastructure.

Hadoop has its roots in Google, which created a new computing model built on a File System, **Google File System (GFS)**, and a programming framework, MapReduce, that scaled up the search engine and was able to process multiple queries simultaneously. *Doug Cutting* and *Mike Cafarella* adapted this computing model of Google to redesign their search engine called Nutch. This eventually led to the development of Nutch as a top-level Apache project under open source, which was adopted by Yahoo in 2006 and finally metamorphosed into Hadoop.

The following are the key features of Hadoop:

- Hadoop brings the power of embarrassingly massive parallel processing to the masses.

- Through the usage of File System storage, Hadoop minimizes database dependency.

- Hadoop uses a custom-built distributed file-based storage, which is cheaper compared to storing on a database with expensive storages such as **Storage Area Network (SAN)** or other proprietary storage solutions. As data is distributed in files across the machines in the cluster, it provides built-in redundancy using multinode replication.

- Hadoop's core principle is to use commodity infrastructure, which is linearly scalable to accommodate infinite data without degradation of performance. This implies that every piece of infrastructure, be it CPU, memory, or storage, added will create 100 percent scalability. This makes data storage with Hadoop less costly than traditional methods of data storage and processing. From a different perspective, you get processing done for every TB of storage space added to the cluster, free of cost.

- Hadoop is accessed through programmable **Application Programming Interfaces (APIs)** to enable parallel processing without the limitations imposed by concurrency. The same data can be processed across systems for different purposes, or the same code can be processed across different systems.

- The use of high-speed synchronization to replicate data on multiple nodes of the cluster enables a fault-tolerant operation of Hadoop.

- Hadoop is designed to incorporate critical aspects of high availability so that the data and the infrastructure are always available and accessible by users.

- Hadoop takes the code to the data rather than the other way round; this is called data locality optimization. This local processing of data and storage of results on the same cluster node minimizes the network load gaining overall efficiencies.

- To design fault tolerant applications, the effort involved to add the fault tolerance part is sometimes more than the effort involved in solving the actual data problem at hand. This is where Hadoop scores heavily. It enables the application developer to worry about writing applications by decoupling the distributed system's fault tolerance from application logic. By using Hadoop, the developers no longer deal with the low-level challenges of failure handling, resource management, concurrency, loading data, allocating, and managing the jobs on the various nodes in the cluster; they can concentrate only on creating applications that work on the cluster, leaving the framework to deal with the challenges.

Hadoop under the covers

Hadoop consists of the Hadoop core and Hadoop subprojects. The Hadoop core is essentially the MapReduce processing framework and the HDFS storage system.

The integral parts of Hadoop are depicted in the following diagram:

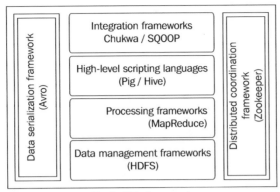

Typical Hadoop stack

The following is an explanation of the integral parts of Hadoop:

- **Hadoop Common**: This includes all the library components and utilities that support the ecosystem

- **Hadoop Distributed File System (HDFS)**: This is a filesystem that provides highly available redundant distributed data access for processing using MapReduce

- **Hadoop MapReduce**: This is a Java-based software framework to operate on large datasets on a cluster of nodes, which store data (HDFS)

Few Hadoop-related top level Apache projects include the following systems:

- **Avro**: This a data serialization and deserialization system

- **Chukwa**: This is a system for log data collection

- **SQOOP**: This is a structured data collection framework that integrates with RDBMS

- **HBase**: This is a column-oriented scalable, distributed database that supports millions of rows and columns to store and query in real-time structured data using HDFS

- **Hive**: This is a structured data storage and query infrastructure built on top of HDFS, which is used mainly for data aggregation, summarization, and querying

- **Mahout**: This is a library of machine-learning algorithms written specifically for execution on the distributed clusters

- **Pig**: This is a data-flow language and is specially designed to simplify the writing of MapReduce applications

- **ZooKeeper**: This is a coordination service designed for distributed applications

Understanding the Hadoop Distributed File System

The **Hadoop Distributed File System (HDFS)** is a File System that provides highly available redundant data access to process using MapReduce. The HDFS addresses two major issues in large-scale data storage and processing. The first problem is that of data locality in which code is actually *sent* to the location of the data in the cluster, where the data has already been divided into manageable blocks so that each block can be independently processed and the results combined. The second problem deals with the capability to tolerate faults at any subsystem level (it can be at the CPU, network, storage, memory, or application level) owing to the reliance on commodity hardware, which is assumed to be less reliant, unless proven otherwise. In order to address these problems, the architecture of HDFS was inspired by the early lead taken by the GFS.

HDFS design goals

The three primary goals of HDFS architecture are as follows:

- Process extremely large files ranging from multiple gigabytes to petabytes.

- Streaming data processing to read data at high-throughput rates and process data while reading.

- Capability to execute on commodity hardware with no special hardware requirements.

Working of HDFS

HDFS has two important subsystems. One is NameNode, which is the master of the system that maintains and manages the blocks that are present in the other nodes. The second one is DataNodes, which are slave nodes working under the supervision of the NameNode and deployed on each machine to provide the actual storage. These nodes collectively serve read and write requests for the clients, which store and retrieve data from them. This is depicted in the following diagram:

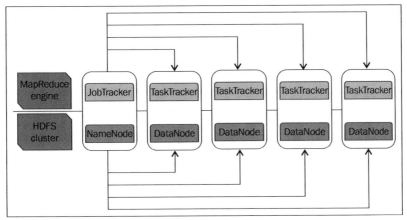

JobTracker and NameNode

The master node is the place where the metadata of the data splits is stored in the memory. This metadata is used at a later point in time to reconstruct the complete data stored in the slave nodes, enabling the job to run on various nodes. The data splits are replicated on a minimum of three machines (the default replication factor). This helps in situations when the hardware of the slave nodes fails and the data can be readily recoverable from the machines where the redundant copy was stored, and the job was executed on one of those machines. Together, these two account for the storage, replication, and management of the data in the entire cluster.

On a Hadoop cluster, the data within the filesystem nodes (data nodes) are replicated on multiple nodes in the cluster. This replication adds redundancy to the system in case of machine or subsystem failure; the data stored in the other machines will be used for the continuation of the processing step. As the data and processing coexist on the same node, linear scalability can be achieved by simply adding a new machine and gaining the benefit of an additional hard drive and the computation capability of the new CPU (scale out).

It is important to note that HDFS is not suitable for low-latency data access, or storage of many small files, multiple writes, and arbitrary file modifications.

Understanding MapReduce

MapReduce is a programming model that manipulates and processes huge datasets; its origin can be traced back to Google, which created it to solve the scalability of search computation. Its foundations are based on principles of parallel and distributed processing without any database dependency. The flexibility of MapReduce lies in its ability to process distributed computations on large amounts of data in clusters of commodity servers, with a facility provided by Hadoop and MapReduce called data locality, and a simple task-based model for management of the processes.

Understanding how MapReduce works

MapReduce primarily makes use of two components; a JobTracker, which is a Master node daemon, and the TaskTrackers, which run in all the slave nodes. It is a slave node daemon. This is depicted in the following diagram:

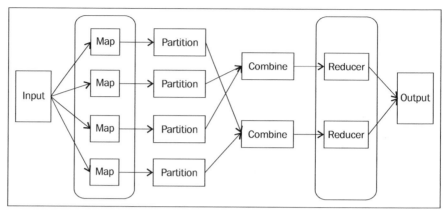

MapReduce internals

The developer writes a job in Java using the MapReduce framework, and submits it to the master node of the cluster, which is responsible for processing all the underlying data with the job.

The master node consists of a daemon called `JobTracker`, which assigns the job to the slave nodes. The `JobTracker` class, among other things, is responsible for copying the JAR file containing the task on to the node containing the task tracker so that each of the slave node spawns a new JVM to run the task. The copying of the JAR to the slave nodes will help in situations that deal with slave node failure. A node failure will result in the master node assigning the task to another slave node containing the same JAR file. This enables resilience in case of node failure.

The MapReduce internals

A MapReduce job is implemented as two functions:

- **The Map function**: A user writes a Map function, which receives key-value pairs as input, processes it, and emits a list of key-value pairs.

- **The Reduce function**: The Reduce function, written by the user, will accept the output of the Map function, that is, the list of intermediate key-value pairs. These values would be typically merged to form a smaller set of values and hence the name Reduce. The output could be just zero or one output value per each reducer invocation.

The following are the other components of the MapReduce framework as depicted in the previous diagram:

- **Combiner**: This is an optimization step and is invoked optionally. It is a function specified to execute a Reduce-like processing on the Mapper side and perform map-side aggregation of the intermediate data. This will reduce the amount of data transferred over the network from the Mapper to the Reducer.

- **Partitioner**: This is used to partition keys of the map output. The key is used to develop a partition by grouping all values of a key together in a single partition. Sometimes default partitions can be created by a hash function.

- **Output**: This collects the output of Mappers and Reducers.

- **Job configuration**: This is the primary user interface to manage MapReduce jobs to specify the Map, Reduce functions, and the input files.

- **Job input**: This specifies the input for a MapReduce job.

Pig – a quick intro

Pig is MapReduce simplified. It is a combination of the Pig compiler and the Pig Latin script, which is a programming language designed to ease the development of distributed applications for analyzing large volumes of data. We will refer to the whole entity as Pig.

The high-level language code written in the Pig Latin script gets compiled into sequences of the MapReduce Java code and it is amenable to parallelization. Pig Latin promotes the data to become the main concept behind any program written in it. It is based on the dataflow paradigm, which works on a stream of data to be processed; this data is passed through instructions, which processes the data. This programming style is analogous to how electrical signals flow through circuits or water flows through pipes.

This dataflow paradigm is in stark contrast to the control flow language, which works on a stream of instructions, and operates on external data. In a traditional program, the conditional executions, jumps, and procedure calls change the instruction stream to be executed.

Processing statements in Pig Latin consist of operators, which take inputs and emit outputs. The inputs and outputs are structured data expressed in bags, maps, tuples, and scalar data. Pig resembles a dataflow graph, where the directed vertices are the paths of data and the nodes are operators (such as FILTER, GROUP, and JOIN) that process the data. In Pig Latin, each statement executes as soon as all data reaches them in contrast to a traditional program that executes as soon as it encounters the statement.

A programmer writes code using a set of standard data-processing Pig operators, such as JOIN, FILTER, GROUP BY, ORDER BY, and UNION. These are then translated into MapReduce jobs. Pig itself does not have the capability to run these jobs and it delegates this work to Hadoop. Hadoop acts as an execution engine for these MapReduce jobs.

It is imperative to understand that Pig is not a general purpose programming language with all the bells and whistles that come with it. For example, it does not have the concept of control flow or scope resolution, and has minimal variable support, which many developers are accustomed to in traditional languages. This limitation can be overcome by using **User Defined Functions (UDFs)**, which is an extensibility feature of Pig.

For a deeper understanding, you may have to refer the Apache web site at http://pig.apache.org/docs/r0.11.0/ to understand the intricacies of the syntax, usage, and other language features.

Understanding the rationale of Pig

Pig Latin is designed as a dataflow language to address the following limitations of MapReduce:

- The MapReduce programming model has tightly coupled computations that can be decomposed into map phase, shuffle phase, and a reducer phase. This limitation is not appropriate for real-world applications that do not fit into this pattern and tasks having a different flow like joins or n-phases. Few other real-world data pipelines require additional coordination code to combine separate MapReduce phases for management of the intermediate results between pipeline phases. This takes its toll in terms of the learning curve for new developers to understand the computation.

- Complex workarounds have to be implemented in MapReduce even for the simplest of operations like projection, filtering, and joins.

- The MapReduce code is difficult to develop, maintain, and reuse, sometimes taking the order of the magnitude than the corresponding code written in Pig.

- It is difficult to perform optimizations in MapReduce because of its implementation complexity.

Pig Latin brings the double advantage of being a SQL-like language with its declarative style and the power of a procedural programming language such as MapReduce using various extensibility features.

Pig supports nested data and enables complex data types to be embedded as fields of a table. The support for nested data models makes data modeling more intuitive since this is closer to the reality of how data exists than the way a database models it in the first normal form. The nested data model also reflects how the data is stored on the disk and enables users to write custom UDFs more intuitively.

Pig supports creation of user-defined functions, which carry out specialized data processing tasks; almost all aspects of programming in Pig are extensible using UDFs. What it implies is that a programmer can customize Pig Latin functions like grouping, filtering, and joining using the `EvalFunc` method. You can also customize load/store capabilities by extending `LoadFunc` or `StoreFunc`. *Chapter 2, Data Ingest and Egress Patterns*, has examples showing Pig's extensibility.

Pig has a special feature, called the `ILLUSTRATE` function to aid the Big Data developer to develop code using sample data quickly. The sample data closely resembles the real data as much as possible and fully illustrates the semantics of the program. This example data evolves automatically as the program grows in complexity. This systematic example data can help in detecting errors and its sources early.

One other advantage of using Pig is that there is no need to perform an elaborate data import process prior to parsing the data into tuples as in conventional database management systems. What it implies is, if you have a data file, the Pig Latin queries can be run on it directly without importing it. Without importing means that the data can be accessed and queried in any format as long as it can be read by Pig as tuples. We don't need to import data as we do it while working with a database, for example, importing a CSV file into a database before querying it. Still, you need to provide a function to parse the content of the file into tuples.

Understanding the relevance of Pig in the enterprise

In the current enterprises, the Big Data processing cycle is remarkable for its complexity and it widely differs from a traditional data processing cycle. The data collected from a variety of data sources is loaded to a target platform; then a base level analysis is performed so that a discovery happens through a metadata layer being applied to the data. This will result in the creation of a data structure or schema for the content in order to discover the context and relevance of the data. Once the data structure is applied, the data is then integrated, transformed, aggregated, and prepared to be analyzed. This reduced and structured dataset is used for reporting and ad hoc analytics. The result from the process is what provides insights into the data and any associated context (based on the business rules processed). Hadoop can be used as a processing and storage framework at each of the stages.

The following diagram shows a typical Big Data processing flow:

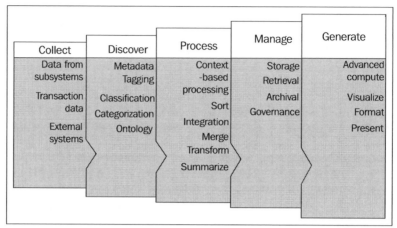

Big Data in the enterprise

The role of Pig as per the preceding diagram is as follows:

- In the *collect phase*, Pig is used to interface with the acquired data from multiple sources including real-time systems, near-real-time systems, and batch-oriented applications. Another way to use Pig is to process the data through a knowledge discovery platform, which could be upstream and store the subset of the output rather than the whole dataset.

- Pig is used in the data *discovery stage* where Big Data is first analyzed and then processed. It is in this stage that Big Data is prepared for integration with the structured analytical platforms or the data warehouse. The discovery and analysis stage consists of tagging, classification, and categorization of data, which closely resembles the subject area and results in the creation of data model definition or metadata. This metadata is the key to decipher the eventual value of Big Data through analytical insights.

- Pig is used in the data *processing phase*, where the context of the data is processed to explore the relevance of the data within the unstructured environment; this relevance would facilitate the application of appropriate metadata and master data in Big Data. The biggest advantage of this kind of processing is the ability to process the same data for multiple contexts, and then looking for patterns within each result set for further data mining and data exploration. For example, consider the word "cold", the context of the word has to be ascertained correctly based on the usage, semantics, and other relevant information. This word can be related to the weather or to a common disease. After getting the correct context for this word, further master data related to either weather or common diseases can be applied on the data.

- In the processing phase, Pig can also be used to perform data integration right after the contextualization of data, by cleansing and standardizing Big Data with metadata, master data, and semantic libraries. This is where the data is linked with the enterprise dataset. There are many techniques to link the data between structured and unstructured datasets with metadata and master data. This process is the first important step in converting and integrating the unstructured and raw data into a structured format. This is the stage where the power of Pig is used extensively for data transformation, and to augment the existing enterprise data warehouse by offloading high volume, low value data, and workloads from the expensive enterprise data warehouse.

- As the processing phase in an enterprise is bound by tight SLAs, Pig, being more predictable and having the capability to integrate with other systems, makes it more suitable to regularly schedule data cleansing, transformation, and reporting workloads.

Pig scores in situations where incoming data is not cleansed and normalized. It gracefully handles situations where data schemas are unknown until runtime or are inconsistent. Pig's procedural language model and schema-less approach offers much more flexibility and efficiency in data access so that data scientists can build research models on the raw data to quickly test a theory.

Pig is typically used in situations where the solution can be expressed as a **Directed Acyclic Graph (DAG)**, involving the combination of standard relational operations of Pig (join, aggregation, and so on) and utilizing custom processing code via UDFs written in Java or a scripting language. This implies that if you have a very complex chain of tasks where the outputs of each job feeds as an input to the next job, Pig makes this process of chaining the jobs easy to accomplish.

Pig is useful in Big Data workloads where there is one very large dataset, and processing on that dataset includes constantly adding in new small pieces of data that will change the state of the large dataset. Pig excels in combining the newly arrived data so that the whole of the data is not processed, but only the delta of the data along with the results of the large data is processed efficiently. Pig provides operators that perform this incremental processing of data in a reasonable amount of time.

Other than the previously mentioned traditional use cases where Pig is generally useful, Pig has the inherent advantage in the form of much less development time needed to write and optimize code than to write in Java MapReduce. Pig is a better choice when performing optimization-by-hand is tedious. Pig's extensibility capabilities, through which you can integrate your existing executable and UDFs with Pig Latin scripts, enables even faster development cycles.

Working of Pig – an overview

This subsection is where an example Pig script gets dissected threadbare and is explained to illustrate the language features of Pig.

Firing up Pig

This subsection helps you to get a very quick understanding of booting Pig into the action mode by installing and configuring it.

The primary prerequisite for Pig to work in a Hadoop cluster is to maintain the Hadoop version compatibility, which in essence means Pig 0.11.0 works with Hadoop versions 0.20.X, 1.X, 0.23.X, and 2.X. This is done by changing the directory for HADOOP_HOME. The following table shows version compatibility between Apache Pig and Hadoop.

The following table summarizes the Pig versus Hadoop compatibility:

Apache Pig Version	Compatible Hadoop Versions
0.12.0	0.20.x, 1.x, 0.23.x, 2.x
0.11.0	0.20.x, 1.x, 0.23.x, 2.x
0.10.1	0.20.x, 1.x, 0.23.x, 2.x
0.10.0	0.20.x, 1.0.x, 0.23.x
0.9.2	0.20, 1.0.0
0.9.1	0.2
0.9.0	0.2
0.8.1	0.2
0.8.0	0.2
0.7.0	0.2
0.6.0	0.2
0.5.0	0.2
0.4.0	0.18
0.3.0	0.18
0.2.0	0.18
0.1.1	0.18
0.1.0	0.17

Pig core is written in Java and it works across operating systems. Pig's shell, which executes the commands from the user, is a bash script and requires a UNIX system. Pig can also be run on Windows using Cygwin and Perl packages.

Java 1.6 is also mandatory for Pig to run. Optionally, the following can be installed on the same machine: Python 2.5, JavaScript 1.7, Ant 1.7, and JUnit 4.5. Python and JavaScript are for writing custom UDFs. Ant and JUnit are for builds and unit testing, respectively. Pig can be executed with different versions of Hadoop by setting HADOOP_HOME to point to the directory where we have installed Hadoop. If HADOOP_HOME is not set, Pig will run with the embedded version by default, which is currently Hadoop 1.0.0.

The following table summarizes the prerequisites for installing Pig (we have considered major versions of Pig until 0.9.1):

Apache Pig Version	Prerequisites
0.12.0	Hadoop 0.20.2, 020.203, 020.204, 0.20.205, 1.0.0, 1.0.1, or 0.23.0, 0.23.1
	Java 1.6
	Cygwin(for windows)
	Perl(for windows)
0.11.0,0.11.1	Hadoop 0.20.2, 020.203, 020.204, 0.20.205, 1.0.0, 1.0.1, or 0.23.0, 0.23.1
	Java 1.6
	Cygwin(for windows)
	Perl(for windows)
0.10.0,0.10.1	Hadoop 0.20.2, 020.203, 020.204, 0.20.205, 1.0.0, 1.0.1, or 0.23.0, 0.23.1
	Java 1.6
	Cygwin(for windows)
	Perl(for windows)
0.9.2	Hadoop 0.20.2, 0.20.203, 0.20.204, 0.20.205, or 1.0.0
	Java 1.6
	Cygwin(for windows)
	Perl(for windows)

Apache Pig Version	Prerequisites
0.9.1	Hadoop 0.20.2, 0.20.203, 0.20.204 or 0.20.205
	Java 1.6
	Cygwin(for windows)
	Perl(for windows)

Pig is typically installed in a machine, which is not a part of the Hadoop cluster. This can be a developer's machine, which has connectivity to the Hadoop cluster. This machine is called a gateway or edge machine.

The installation of Pig is a straightforward process. Download Pig from your favorite distribution site, be it Apache, Cloudera, or Hortonworks and follow the instructions specified in the installation guide specific to the distribution. These instructions generally involve steps to untar the tarball in a directory of your choice and setting the only configuration required, which is the JAVA_HOME property to the location that contains the Java distribution.

To verify if Pig was indeed installed correctly, try the command $ `pig -help`.

Pig can be run in two modes: local and MapReduce.

- **The local mode**: To run Pig in the local mode, install this mode on a machine where Pig is run using your local File System. The `-x` local flag is used to denote the local mode (`$ pig -x local ...`). The result of this command is the Pig shell called *Grunt* where you can execute command lines and scripts. The local mode is useful when a developer wants to prototype, debug, or use small data to quickly perform a proof of concept locally and then apply the same code on a Hadoop cluster (the MapReduce mode).

```
$ pig -x local
... - Connecting to ...
grunt>
```

Downloading the example code

You can download the example code files for all Packt books you have purchased from your account at http://www.packtpub.com. If you purchased this book elsewhere, you can visit http://www.packtpub.com/support and register to have the files e-mailed directly to you.

- **The MapReduce mode**: This mode is used when you need to access a Hadoop cluster and run the application on it. This is the default mode and you can specify this mode using the -x flag ($ pig or $ pig -x mapreduce). The result of this command is the Pig shell called *Grunt* where you can execute commands and scripts.

```
$ pig -x mapreduce
... - Connecting to ...
grunt>
```

You can also perform the following code snippet instead of the previous one:

```
$ pig
... - Connecting to ...
grunt>
```

It is important to understand that in both the local and MapReduce modes, Pig does the parsing, checking, compiling, and planning locally. Only the job execution is done on the Hadoop cluster in the MapReduce mode and on the local machine in the local mode. This implies that parallelism cannot be evidenced in the local mode.

In the local and MapReduce mode, Pig can be run interactively and also in the batch mode. Running Pig interactively implies executing each command on the Grunt shell, and running it in the batch mode implies executing the combination of commands in a script file (called Pig script) on the Grunt shell.

Here is a quick example of the interactive mode:

```
grunt> raw_logs_Jul = LOAD 'NASA_access_logs/Jul/access_log_Jul95'
   USING ApacheCommonLogLoader AS (jaddr, jlogname, juser, jdt,
   jmethod, juri, jproto, jstatus, jbytes);

grunt> jgrpd = GROUP raw_logs_Jul BY DayExtractor(jdt);

grunt> DESCRIBE jgrpd;
```

Please note that in the previous example, each of the Pig expressions are specified on the Grunt shell. Here is the example for the batch mode execution:

```
grunt> pigexample.pig
```

In the previous example, a Pig script (pigexample.pig) is created initially and it is executed on the Grunt shell. Pig scripts can also be executed outside the grunt shell at the command prompt. The following is the method to do it:

```
$>pig <filename>.pig (mapreduce mode)
```

You can also use the following code line instead of the previous one:

```
$>pig -x local <filename>.pig (local mode)
```

The use case

This section covers a quick introduction of the use case. Log data is generated by nearly every web-based software application. The applications log all the events into logfiles along with the timestamps at which the events occurred. These events may include changes to system configurations, access device information, information on user activity and access locations, alerts, transactional information, error logs, and failure messages. The value of the data in logfiles is realized through the usage of Big Data processing technologies and is consistently used across industry verticals to understand and track applications or service behavior. This can be done by finding patterns, errors, or suboptimal user experience, thereby converting *invisible* log data into useful performance insights. These insights can be leveraged across the enterprise with use cases providing both operational and business intelligence.

The Pig Latin script in the following *Code listing* section loads two month's logfiles, analyses the logs, and finds out the number of unique hits for each day of the month. The analysis results in two relations: one for July and the other for August. These two relations are joined on the day of month that produces an output where we can compare number of visits by day for each month (for example, the number of visits on the first of July versus the number of visits on the first of August).

Code listing

The following is the complete code listing:

```
-- Register the jar file to be able to use the UDFs in it
REGISTER 'your_path_to_piggybank/piggybank.jar';

/* Assign aliases ApacheCommonLogLoader, DayMonExtractor,
   DayExtractor to the CommonLogLoader and DateExtractor UDFs
*/
DEFINE ApacheCommonLogLoader org.apache.pig.piggybank.storage.
   apachelog.CommonLogLoader();
DEFINE DayMonExtractor org.apache.pig.piggybank.evaluation.
   util.apachelogparser.DateExtractor
   ('dd/MMM/yyyy:HH:mm:ss Z','dd-MMM');
DEFINE DayExtractor org.apache.pig.piggybank.evaluation.
   util.apachelogparser.DateExtractor('dd-MMM','dd');

/* Load July and August logs using the alias ApacheCommonLogLoader
   into the relations raw_logs_Jul and raw_logs_Aug
*/
```

```
raw_logs_Jul = LOAD '/user/cloudera/pdp/datasets/logs/
  NASA_access_logs/Jul/access_log_Jul95' USING
  ApacheCommonLogLoader AS (jaddr, jlogname, juser, jdt, jmethod,
  juri, jproto, jstatus, jbytes);
raw_logs_Aug = LOAD '/user/cloudera/pdp/datasets/logs/
  NASA_access_logs/Aug/access_log_Aug95' USING
  ApacheCommonLogLoader AS (aaddr, alogname, auser, adt, amethod,
  auri, aproto, astatus, abytes);


-- Group the two relations by date
jgrpd = GROUP raw_logs_Jul BY DayMonExtractor(jdt);
DESCRIBE jgrpd;
agrpd = GROUP raw_logs_Aug BY DayMonExtractor(adt);
DESCRIBE agrpd;

-- Count the number of unique visits for each day in July
jcountd = FOREACH jgrpd
{
  juserIP =  raw_logs_Jul.jaddr;
  juniqIPs = DISTINCT juserIP;
  GENERATE FLATTEN(group) AS jdate,COUNT(juniqIPs) AS jcount;
}

-- Count the number of unique visits for each day in August
acountd = FOREACH agrpd
{
  auserIP =  raw_logs_Aug.aaddr;
  auniqIPs = DISTINCT auserIP;
  GENERATE FLATTEN(group) AS adate,COUNT(auniqIPs) AS acount;
}

-- Display the schema of the relations jcountd and acountd
DESCRIBE jcountd;
DESCRIBE acountd;

/* Join the relations containing count of unique visits in July
   and August where a match is found for the day of the month
*/
joind = JOIN jcountd BY DayExtractor(jdate), acountd BY
  DayExtractor(adate);

/* Filter by removing the records where the count is less than
   2600
*/
filterd = FILTER joind BY jcount > 2600 and acount > 2600;
```

```
/* Debugging operator to understand how the data passes through
   FILTER and gets transformed
*/
ILLUSTRATE filterd;

/* Sort the relation by date, PARALLEL specifies the number of
   reducers to be 5
*/
srtd = ORDER filterd BY jdate,adate PARALLEL 5;

-- Limit the number of output records to be 5
limitd = LIMIT srtd 5;

/* Store the contents of the relation into a file in the directory
   unique_hits_by_month on HDFS
*/
STORE limitd into '/user/cloudera/pdp/output/unique_hits_by_month';
```

The dataset

As an illustration, we would be using logs for two month's web requests in a web server at NASA. These logs were collected from July 1 to 31, 1995 and from August 1 to 31, 1995. The following is the description of the fields in the files:

- Hostname (or the Internet address), which initiates the request, for example, 109.172.181.143 in the next code snippet.

- Logname is empty in this dataset and is represented by – in the next code snippet.

- The user is empty in this dataset and is represented by – in the next code snippet.

- The timestamp is in the DD/MMM/YYYY HH:MM:SS format. In the next code snippet, the time zone is -0400, for example, [02/Jul/1995:00:12:01 -0400].

- HTTP request is given in quotes, for example, GET /history/xxx/ HTTP/1.0 in the next code snippet.

- HTTP response reply code, which is 200 in the next code snippet.

The snippet of the logfile is as follows:

```
109.172.181.143 - - [02/Jul/1995:00:12:01 -0400] "GET
/history/xxx/ HTTP/1.0" 200 6545
```

Understanding Pig through the code

The following subsections have a brief description of the operators and their usage:

Pig's extensibility

In the use case example, the REGISTER function is one of the three ways to incorporate external custom code in Pig scripts. Let's quickly examine the other two Pig extensibility features in this section to get a better understanding.

- REGISTER: The UDFs provide one avenue to include the user code. To use the UDF written in Java, Python, JRuby, or Groovy, we use the REGISTER function in the Pig script to register the container (JAR and Python script). To register a Python UDF, you also need to explicitly provide which compiler the Python script will be using. This can be done using Jython.

  In our example, the following line registers the Piggybank JAR:

  ```
  REGISTER '/opt/cloudera/parcels/CDH-4.3.0-
      1.cdh4.3.0.p0.22/lib/pig/piggybank.jar';
  ```

- MAPREDUCE: This operator is used to embed MapReduce jobs in Pig scripts. We need to specify the MapReduce container JAR along with the inputs and outputs for the MapReduce program.

  An example is given as follows:

  ```
  input = LOAD 'input.txt';
  result = MAPREDUCE 'mapreduceprg.jar' [('other.jar', ...)]
      STORE input INTO 'inputPath' USING storeFunc LOAD
      'outputPath' USING loadFunc AS schema ['params, ... '];
  ```

  The previous statement stores the relation named input into inputPath using storeFunc; native mapreduce uses storeFunc to read the data. The data received as a result of executing mapreduceprg.jar is loaded from outputPath into the relation named result using loadFunc as schema.

- STREAM: This allows data to be sent to an external executable for processing as part of a Pig data processing pipeline. You can intermix relational operations, such as grouping and filtering with custom or legacy executables. This is especially useful in cases where the executable has all the custom code, and you may not want to change the code and rewrite it in Pig. The external executable receives its input from a standard input or file, and writes its output either to a standard output or file.

The syntax for the operator is given as follows:

```
alias = STREAM alias [, alias ...] THROUGH {'command' |
  cmd_alias } [AS schema] ;
```

Where `alias` is the name of the relation, `THROUGH` is the keyword, `command` is the executable along with arguments, `cmd_alias` is the alias defined for the command using the `DEFINE` operator, `AS` is a keyword, and `schema` specifies the schema.

Operators used in code

The following is an explanation of the operators used in the code:

- `DEFINE`: The `DEFINE` statement is used to assign an alias to an external executable or a UDF function. Use this statement if you want to have a crisp name for a function that has a lengthy package name.

  For a `STREAM` command, `DEFINE` plays an important role to transfer the executable to the task nodes of the Hadoop cluster. This is accomplished using the `SHIP` clause of the `DEFINE` operator. This is not a part of our example and will be illustrated in later chapters.

  In our example, we define aliases by names `ApacheCommonLogLoader`, `DayMonExtractor`, and `DayExtractor` for the corresponding fully qualified class names.

  ```
  DEFINE ApacheCommonLogLoader
    org.apache.pig.piggybank.storage.
    apachelog.CommonLogLoader();

  DEFINE DayMonExtractor org.apache.pig.piggybank.
    evaluation.util.apachelogparser.
    DateExtractor('dd/MMM/yyyy:HH:mm:ss Z','dd-MMM');

  DEFINE DayExtractor org.apache.pig.piggybank.
    evaluation.util.apachelogparser.DateExtractor('dd-
    MMM','dd');
  ```

- `LOAD`: This operator loads data from the file or directory. If a directory name is specified, it loads all the files in the directory into the relation. If Pig is run in the local mode, it searches for the directories on the local File System; while in the MapReduce mode, it searches for the files on HDFS. In our example, the usage is as follows:

```
raw_logs_Jul = LOAD 'NASA_access_logs/Jul/access_log_Jul95'
  USING ApacheCommonLogLoader AS (jaddr, jlogname, juser,
  jdt, jmethod, juri, jproto, jstatus, jbytes);

raw_logs_Aug = LOAD 'NASA_access_logs/Aug/access_log_Aug95'
  USING ApacheCommonLogLoader AS (aaddr, alogname, auser,
  adt, amethod, auri, aproto, astatus, abytes);
```

The content of `tuple raw_logs_Jul` is as follows:

```
(163.205.85.3,-,-,13/Jul/1995:08:51:12 -
  0400,GET,/htbin/cdt_main.pl,HTTP/1.0,200,3585)
(163.205.85.3,-,-,13/Jul/1995:08:51:12 -0400,GET,/cgi-
  bin/imagemap/countdown70?287,288,HTTP/1.0,302,85)
(109.172.181.143,-,-,02/Jul/1995:00:12:01 -
  0400,GET,/history/xxx/,HTTP/1.0,200,6245)
```

By using globs (such as `*.txt`, `*.csv`, and so on), you can read multiple files (all the files or selective files) that are in the same directory. In the following example, the files under the folders `Jul` and `Aug` will be loaded as a union.

```
raw_logs = LOAD 'NASA_access_logs/{Jul,Aug}' USING
ApacheCommonLogLoader AS (addr, logname, user, dt, method, uri,
proto, status, bytes);
```

- `STORE`: The `STORE` operator has dual purposes, one is to write the results into the File System after completion of the data pipeline processing, and another is to actually commence the execution of the preceding Pig Latin statements. This happens to be an important feature of this language, where logical, physical, and MapReduce plans are created after the script encounters the `STORE` operator.

  In our example, the following code demonstrates their usage:

  ```
  DUMP limitd;
  STORE limitd INTO 'unique_hits_by_month';
  ```

- `DUMP`: The `DUMP` operator is almost similar to the `STORE` operator, but it is used specially to display results on the command prompt rather than storing it in a File System like the `STORE` operator. `DUMP` behaves in exactly the same way as `STORE`, where the Pig Latin statements actually begin execution after encountering the `DUMP` operator. This operator is specifically targeted for the interactive execution of statements and viewing the output in real time.

In our example, the following code demonstrates the usage of the DUMP operator:

```
DUMP limitd;
```

- UNION: The UNION operator merges the contents of more than one relation without preserving the order of tuples as the relations involved are treated as unordered bags.

  In our example, we will use UNION to merge the two relations raw_logs_Jul and raw_logs_Aug into a relation called combined_raw_logs.

  ```
  combined_raw_logs = UNION raw_logs_Jul, raw_logs_Aug;
  ```

  The content of tuple combined_raw_logs is as follows:

  ```
  (163.205.85.3,-,-,13/Jul/1995:08:51:12 -
    0400,GET,/htbin/cdt_main.pl,HTTP/1.0,200,3585)
  (163.205.85.3,-,-,13/Jul/1995:08:51:12 -0400,GET,/cgi-
    bin/imagemap/countdown70?287,288,HTTP/1.0,302,85)
  (198.4.83.138,-,-,08/Aug/1995:22:25:28 -
    0400,GET,/shuttle/missions/sts-69/mission-sts-
    69.html,HTTP/1.0,200,11264)
  ```

- SAMPLE: The SAMPLE operator is useful when you want to work on a very small subset of data to quickly test if the data flow processing is giving you correct results. This statement provides a random data sample picked from the entire population using an arbitrary sample size. The sample size is passed as a parameter. As the SAMPLE operator internally uses a probability-based algorithm, it is not guaranteed to return the same number of rows or tuples every time SAMPLE is used.

  In our example, the SAMPLE operator returns, at most, 1 percent of the data as an illustration.

  ```
  sample_combined_raw_logs = SAMPLE combined_raw_logs 0.01;
  ```

  The content of tuple sample_combined_raw_logs is as follows:

  ```
  (163.205.2.43,-,-,17/Jul/1995:13:30:34 -
    0400,GET,/ksc.html,HTTP/1.0,200,7071)
  (204.97.74.34,-,-,27/Aug/1995:12:07:37 -
    0400,GET,/shuttle/missions/sts-
    69/liftoff.html,HTTP/1.0,304,0)
  (128.217.61.98,-,-,21/Aug/1995:08:59:26 -
    0400,GET,/images/ksclogo-medium.gif,HTTP/1.0,200,5866)
  ```

- GROUP: The GROUP operator is used to group all records with the same value into a bag. This operator creates a nested structure of output tuples.

  The following snippet of code from our example illustrates grouping logs by day of the month.

```
jgrpd = GROUP raw_logs_Jul BY DayMonExtractor(jdt);
DESCRIBE jgrpd;
```

  Schema content of jgrpd: The following output shows the schema of the relation jgrpd where we can see that it has created a nested structure with two fields, the key and the bag of collected records. The key is named group, and value is the name of the alias that was grouped with raw_logs_Jul and raw_logs_Aug, in this case.

```
jgrpd: {group: chararray,raw_logs_Jul: {(jaddr:
  bytearray,jlogname: bytearray,juser: bytearray,jdt:
  bytearray,jmethod: bytearray,juri: bytearray,jproto:
  bytearray,jstatus: bytearray,jbytes: bytearray)}}

agrpd = GROUP raw_logs_Aug BY DayExtractor(adt);
DESCRIBE agrpd;

agrpd: {group: chararray,raw_logs_Aug: {(aaddr:
  bytearray,alogname: bytearray,auser: bytearray,adt:
  bytearray,amethod: bytearray,auri: bytearray,aproto:
  bytearray,astatus: bytearray,abytes: bytearray)}}
```

- FOREACH: The FOREACH operator is also known as a projection. It applies a set of expressions to each record in the bag, similar to applying an expression on every row of a table. The result of this operator is another relation.

  In our example, FOREACH is used for iterating through each grouped record in the group to get the count of distinct IP addresses.

```
jcountd = FOREACH jgrpd
{
  juserIP =  raw_logs_Jul.jaddr;
  juniqIPs = DISTINCT juserIP;
  GENERATE FLATTEN(group) AS jdate,COUNT(juniqIPs) AS }

acountd = FOREACH agrpd
{
  auserIP =  raw_logs_Aug.aaddr;
  auniqIPs = DISTINCT auserIP;
  GENERATE FLATTEN(group) AS adate,COUNT(auniqIPs) AS
    acount;
}
```

Contents of the tuples: The following output shows the tuples in the relations jcountd and acountd. The first field is the date in the format of DD-MMM and the second field is the count of distinct hits.

```
 jcountd
(01-Jul,4230)
(02-Jul,4774)
(03-Jul,7264)

 acountd
(01-Aug,2577)
(03-Aug,2588)
(04-Aug,4254)
```

* DISTINCT: The DISTINCT operator removes duplicate records in a relation. DISTINCT should not be used where you need to preserve the order of the contents.

   The following example code demonstrates the usage of DISTINCT to remove duplicate IP addresses and FLATTEN to remove the nest of jgrpd and agrpd.

```
jcountd = FOREACH jgrpd
{
  juserIP =  raw_logs_Jul.jaddr;
  juniqIPs = DISTINCT juserIP;
  GENERATE FLATTEN(group) AS jdate,COUNT(juniqIPs) AS
    jcount;
}
acountd = FOREACH agrpd
{
  auserIP =  raw_logs_Aug.aaddr;
  auniqIPs = DISTINCT auserIP;
  GENERATE FLATTEN(group) AS adate,COUNT(auniqIPs) AS
    acount;
}
DESCRIBE jcountd;
DESCRIBE acountd;
```

   Content of the tuples: The following output shows the schema of the relation of jcountd and acountd. We can see that the nesting created by GROUP is now removed.

```
jcountd: {jdate: chararray,jcount: long}
acountd: {adate: chararray,acount: long}
```

- JOIN: The JOIN operator joins more than one relation based on shared keys.

  In our example, we join two relations by day of the month; it returns all the records where the day of the month matches. Records for which no match is found are dropped.

  ```
  joind = JOIN jcountd BY jdate, acountd BY adate;
  ```

  Content of tuples: The following output shows the resulting values after JOIN is performed. This relation returns all the records where the day of the month matches; records for which no match is found are dropped. For example, we have seen in sample output of FOREACH, the section jcountd shows 4774 hits on 2-Jul and acountd does not have any record for 2-Aug. Hence after JOIN, the tuple having 2-Jul hits is omitted as there is no match found for 2-Aug.

  ```
  (01-Jul,4230,01-Aug,2577)
  (03-Jul,7264,03-Aug,2588)
  (04-Jul,5806,04-Aug,4254)
  (05-Jul,7144,05-Aug,2566))
  ```

- DESCRIBE: The DESCRIBE operator is a diagnostic operator in Pig and is used to view and understand the schema of an alias or a relation. This is a kind of command line log, which enables us to understand how preceding operators in the data pipeline are changing the data. The output of the DESCRIBE operator is the description of the schema.

  In our example, we use DESCRIBE to understand the schema.

  ```
  DESCRIBE joind;
  ```

  The output is as follows:

  ```
  joind: {jcountd::jdate: chararray,jcountd::jcount:
    long,acountd::adate: chararray,acountd::acount: long}
  ```

- FILTER: The FILTER operator allows you to select or filter out the records from a relation based on a condition. This operator works on tuples or rows of data.

  The following example filters records whose count is greater than 2,600:

  ```
  filterd = FILTER joind BY jcount > 2600 and acount > 2600;
  ```

  Content of filtered tuple: All the records which are less than 2600 are filtered out.

  ```
  (04-Jul,5806,04-Aug,4254)
  (07-Jul,6951,07-Aug,4062)
  (08-Jul,3064,08-Aug,4252)
  ```

- ILLUSTRATE: The ILLUSTRATE operator is the debugger's best friend, and it is used to understand how data passes through the Pig Latin statements and gets transformed. This operator enables us to create good test data in order to test our programs on datasets, which are a sample representing the flow of statements.

  ILLUSTRATE internally uses an algorithm, which uses a small sample of the entire input data and propagates this data through all the statements in the Pig Latin scripts. This algorithm intelligently generates sample data when it encounters operators such as FILTER, which have the ability to remove the rows from the data, resulting in no data following through the Pig statements.

  In our example, the ILLUSTRATE operator is used as shown in the following code snippet:

  ```
  filterd = FILTER joind BY jcount > 2600 and acount > 2600;
  ILLUSTRATE filterd;
  ```

  The dataset used by us does not have records where the count is less than 2,600. ILLUSTRATE has manufactured a record with two counts to ensure that values below 2,600 get filtered out. This record passes through the FILTER condition and gets filtered out and hence, no values are shown in the relation filtered.

  The following screenshot shows the output:

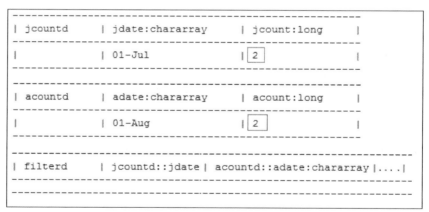

Output of illustrate

- ORDER BY: The ORDERBY operator is used to sort a relation using the sort key specified. As of today, Pig supports sorting on fields with simple types rather than complex types or expressions. In the following example, we are sorting based on two fields (July date and August date).

  ```
  srtd = ORDER filterd BY jdate,adate PARALLEL 5;
  ```

- PARALLEL: The PARALLEL operator controls reduce-side parallelism by specifying the number of reducers. It is defaulted to one while running in a local mode. This clause can be used with operators, such as ORDER, DISTINCT, LIMIT, JOIN, GROUP, COGROUP, and CROSS that force a reduce phase.

- LIMIT: The LIMIT operator is used to set an upper limit on the number of output records generated. The output is determined randomly and there is no guarantee if the output will be the same if the LIMIT operator is executed consequently. To request a particular group of rows, you may consider using the ORDER operator, immediately followed by the LIMIT operator.

  In our example, this operator returns five records as an illustration:

  ```
  limitd = LIMIT srtd 5;
  ```

  The content of the limitd tuple is given as follows:

  ```
  (04-Jul,5806,04-Aug,4254)
  (07-Jul,6951,07-Aug,4062)
  (08-Jul,3064,08-Aug,4252)
  (10-Jul,4383,10-Aug,4423)
  (11-Jul,4819,11-Aug,4500)
  ```

- FLATTEN: The FLATTEN operator is used to make relations such as bags and tuple flat by removing the nesting in them. Please refer to the example code in *DISTINCT* for the sample output and usage of FLATTEN.

The EXPLAIN operator

A Pig program goes through multiple stages as shown in the next diagram, before being executed in the Hadoop cluster, and the EXPLAIN operator provides the best way to understand what transpires underneath the Pig Latin code. The EXPLAIN operator generates the sequence of plans that go into converting the Pig Latin scripts to a MapReduce JAR.

The output of this operator can be converted into a graphical format by the use of the -dot option to generate graphs of the program. This writes the output to a DOT file containing diagrams explaining the execution of our script.

The syntax for the same is as follows:

```
pig -x mapreduce -e 'pigexample.pig' -dot -out <filename> or
  <directoryname>
```

Next is an example of usage. If we specify a filename directory after `-out`, all the three output files (logical, physical, and MapReduce plan files) will get created in that directory. In the next case, all files will get created in the `pigexample_output` directory.

```
pig -x mapreduce -e ' pigexample.pig' -dot -out pigexample_output
```

Follow the given steps to convert the DOT files into an image format:

1. Install graphviz on your machine.

2. Plot a graph written in Dot language by executing the following command:

```
dot -Tpng filename.dot  >  filename.png
```

The following diagram shows each step in Pig processing:

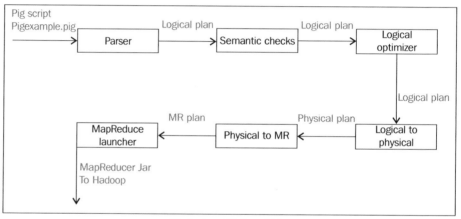

Pig Latin to Hadoop JAR

- **The query parser**: The parser uses **ANother Tool for Language Recognition (ANTLR)**, a language parser, to verify whether the program is correct syntactically and if all the variables are properly defined. The parser also checks the schemas for type correctness and generates intermediate representation, **Abstract Syntax Tree (AST)**.

- **The logical plan**: The intermediate representation, AST, is transformed into a logical plan. This plan is implemented internally as a directed graph with all the operators in the Pig Latin script mapped to the logical operators. The following diagram illustrates this plan:

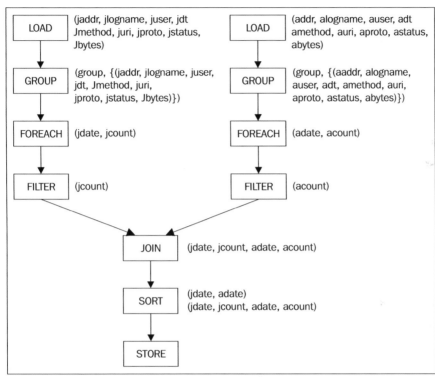

Logical plan

- **The logical optimization**: The logical plan generated is examined for opportunities of optimization such as filter-projection pushdown and column pruning. These are considered depending on the script. Optimization is performed and then the plan is compiled into a series of physical plans.

- **The physical plan**: The physical plan is a physical description of the computation that creates a usable pipeline, which is independent of MapReduce. We could use this pipeline and target other processing frameworks such as Dryad. The opportunities for optimizations in this stage are in memory aggregations instead of using combiners. The physical planning stage is also the right place where the plan is examined for the purpose of reducing the number of reducers.

For clarity, each logical operator is shown with an ID. Physical operators that are produced by the translation of a logical operator are shown with the same ID. For the most part, each logical operator becomes a corresponding physical operator. The logical GROUP operator maps into a series of physical operators: local and global rearrange plus package. Rearrange is just like the Partitioner class and Reducer step of the MapReduce where sorting by a key happens.

The following diagram shows the logical plan translated to a physical plan example:

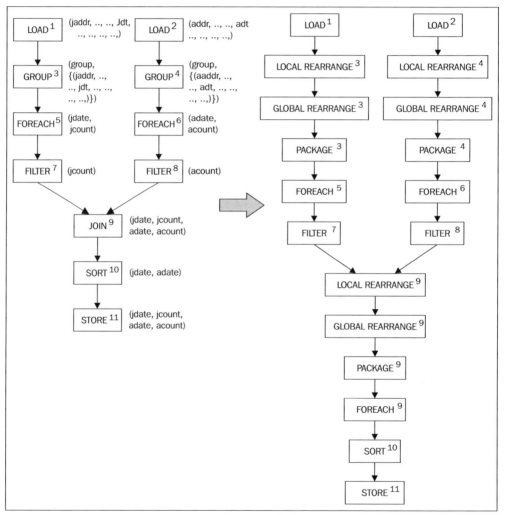

Logical to physical plan

- **MapReduce plan**: This is the phase where the physical plan is converted into a graph of actual MapReduce jobs with all the inputs and outputs specified. Opportunities for optimization in the MapReduce phase are examined to see if it is possible to combine multiple MapReduce jobs into one job for reducing the data flow between Mappers and Reducers. The idea of decoupling the Logical and Physical plans from the MapReduce plan is to divorce them from the details of running on Hadoop. This level of abstraction is necessary to port the application to a different processing framework like Dryad.

The following Physical to MapReduce Plan shows the assignment of the physical operators to Hadoop stages for our running example (only the map and reduce stages are shown). In the MapReduce plan, the local rearrange operator interprets tuples with keys and input stream's identifiers.

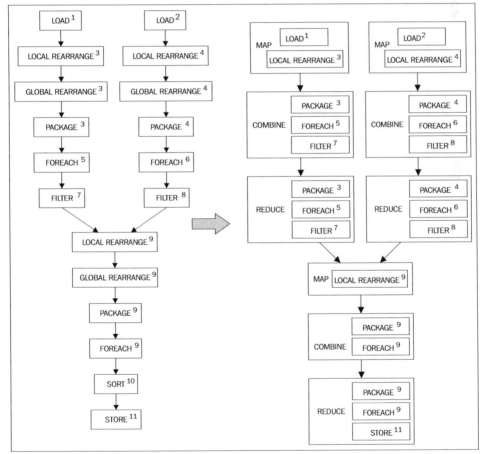

Physical to the MapReduce plan

Understanding Pig's data model

The Pig's data model consists of both primitive and complex types. The following sections give a brief overview of these data types:

Primitive types

Pig supports primitive data types such as `Int`, `Float`, `Long`, `Double`, and `Chararray`.

Complex types

The following are the complex data types, formed by combining the primitive data types:

- **Atom**: An atom contains a single value and can be composed of any one of the primitive data types.

- **Tuple**: A tuple is like a row of a table in an RDBMS, or a sequence of fields, each of which can be any of the data types including primitive and complex types. Tuples are enclosed in parentheses, `()`. An example is shown as follows:

  ```
  (163.205.85.3,-,-,13/Jul/1995:08:51:12 -
   0400,GET,/htbin/cdt_main.pl,HTTP/1.0,200,3585)
  ```

- **Bag**: A bag is analogous to a table and a collection of tuples, which may have duplicates too. Bag is Pig's only spillable data structure, which implies that when the full structure does not fit in memory, it is spilled on to the disk and paged in when necessary. In a Bag, the schema of the constituent tuples is flexible and doesn't need to have a consistent number and type of fields. Bags are represented by data or tuple in curly braces, `{}`. An example is shown as follows:

  ```
  {(163.205.85.3,-,-,13/Jul/1995:08:51:12 -
    0400,GET,/htbin/cdt_main.pl,HTTP/1.0,200,3585)
  (100.305.185.30,-,-,13/AUG/1995:09:51:12 -
    0400,GET,/htbin/cdt_main.pl,HTTP/1.0,200,3585)}
  ```

- **Map**: This is a key value data structure. The schema of the data items in a Map is not strictly enforced, giving the option to take the form of any type. Map is useful to prototype datasets where schemas may change over time. Maps are enclosed in square braces, `[]`.

The relevance of schemas

Pig has a special way to handle known and unknown schemas. *Schemas exist to give fields their identity by naming them and categorizing them into a data type.* Pig has the ability to discover schemas at runtime by making appropriate assumptions about the data types. In case the data type is not assigned, Pig defaults the type to bytearray and performs conversions later, based on the context in which that data is used. This feature gives Pig an edge when you want to use it for research purposes to create quick prototypes on data with the unknown schema. Notwithstanding these advantages of working with unspecified schemas, it is recommended to specify the schema wherever or whenever it is possible for more efficient parse-time checking and execution. However, there are a few idiosyncrasies of how Pig handles unknown schemas when using various operators.

For the relational operators that perform JOIN, GROUP, UNION, or CROSS, if any one of the operators in the relation doesn't have a schema specified, then the resultant relation would be null. Similarly, a null would be the result when you try to flatten a bag with unknown schema.

Extending the discussion of how nulls can be resulted in Pig as in the preceding section, there are a few other ways nulls could result through the interaction of specific operators. As a quick illustration, if any of the subexpression operand in the comparison operators, such as ==, <, >, and MATCHES are null, then the result would be null. The same is applicable to arithmetic operators (such as +, -, *, /) and the CONCAT operators too. It is important to remember subtle differences between how various functions respect a null. While the AVG, MAX, MIN, SUM, and COUNT functions disregard nulls, the COUNT_STAR function does not ignore it and counts a null as if there is a value to it.

Summary

In this chapter, we have covered a wide array of ideas, with the central theme of keeping your focus latched on to Pig and then exploring its periphery. We understood what design patterns are and the way they are discovered and applied, from the perspective of Pig. We explored what Hadoop is, but we did it from a viewpoint of the historical enterprise context and figured out how Hadoop rewrote the history of distributed computing by addressing the challenges of the traditional architectures.

We understood how Pig brought in a fresh approach to programming Hadoop in an intuitive style, and we could comprehend the advantages it offers over other approaches of programming, plus it has given us the facility to write code in scripting-like language, which is easy to understand for those who already know scripting or don't want to code in Java MapReduce; with a small set of functions and operators, it provides us with the power to process an enormous amount of data quickly. We used a code example through which we understood the internals of Pig. The emphasis of this section was to cover as much ground as possible without venturing too deep into Pig and give you a ready reckoner to understand Pig.

In the next chapter, we will extend our understanding of the general concepts of using Pig in enterprises to specific use cases where Pig can be used for the input and output of data from a variety of sources. We shall begin by getting a ring-side view of all the data that gets into the enterprise and how it is consumed, and then we will branch out to look at a specific type of data more closely, and apply our patterns to it. These branches deal with unstructured, structured, and semi-structured data. Within each branch, we will learn how to apply patterns for each of the subbranches that deal with multiple aspects and attributes.

2
Data Ingest and Egress Patterns

In the previous chapter, you were introduced to the high-level concepts of design patterns and saw how they were implemented using Pig. We explored the evolution of Hadoop and Pig, the limitations with traditional systems, and how Hadoop and Pig relate to the enterprise to solve specific issues related to Big Data. The Pig programming language was explained using a ready-made example that elaborated the language features.

We are about to see the power of using Pig design patterns to ingest and egress various data to and from Hadoop. This chapter's overarching goal is to act as a launch pad for a Hadoop practitioner to rapidly load data, start processing and analyzing it as quickly as possible, and then egress it to other systems, without being bogged down in the maze of writing complex MapReduce code.

This chapter begins with an overview of various types of data typically encountered in the Big Data environment and the source of this data. We then discuss several data ingest design patterns to import multistructured data stored in various source systems into Hadoop. We will also discuss the data egress design patterns that export the data stored in Hadoop to target systems in their native format. To illustrate the ingest and egress patterns, we consider various data formats, such as log files, images, CSV, JSON, and XML. The data sources considered to illustrate these patterns are filesystems, mainframes, and NoSQL databases.

The context of data ingest and egress

Data ingest is the process of getting the data into a system for later processing or storage. This process involves connecting to the data source, accessing the data, and then importing the data into Hadoop. Importing implies the copying of data from external sources into Hadoop and storing it in HDFS.

Data egress is the process of sending data out of the Hadoop environment after the data is processed. The output data will be in a format that matches that of the target systems. Data egress is performed in cases where downstream systems consume the data to create visualizations, serve web applications or web services, or perform custom processing.

With the advent of Hadoop, we are witnessing the capability to ingest and egress data at an unprecedented scale, quickly and efficiently. Enterprises are adopting newer paradigms to ingest and egress data according to the needs of their analytical value. There is a potential value in every data feed that enters an enterprise. These feeds primarily consist of the legacy enterprise data, unstructured data, and external data. The data ingest process deals with a variety of these feeds that are synchronized at regular intervals with the existing enterprise assets. Data egress deals with restricting the outbound data so that it meets the data requirements of the integrated downstream systems.

Once the data is within the enterprise perimeter, there is an increase in its ability to perform meaningful analysis on the raw data itself, even before it is converted into something more structured in the traditional sense (that is, information). We no longer require the data to be extremely organized and structured so that insights are gathered from it. However, with the proliferation of new aged algorithms, any type or form of data can be analyzed. This recently led to exciting business models in which enterprises suddenly found themselves unspooling data from tapes, stored for compliance purposes all these years, to uncover the hidden treasure and value from them. Enterprises are beginning to realize that no data is dispensable or useless, regardless of how unstructured or unrelated it may seem. They have started to scramble for every scrap of data that might hold the potential to give them a competitive edge in the industry.

The unstructured data is examined with renewed interest: if it can be integrated with the existing structured data sources in the enterprise and if this integration can result in better business outcomes through predictive analytics. Today's data scientists revel in heterogeneity. To explore unstructured data is their new challenge, and to find patterns from random distributions is the new normal. Spinning up a few Hadoop nodes on a cloud provider of choice, importing data, and running sophisticated algorithms have become regular chores for many of data scientists; this makes it relatively simple to process tons of various types of data from many disparate sources. All this underscores the importance of data ingest and egress to and from various sources, which forms the bedrock for the eventual value. In this chapter, we will discuss the *how* of ingest and egress through design patterns in Pig as well as give special impetus to the *why*.

Types of data in the enterprise

The following section details the enterprise-centric view of data and its relevance to the Big Data processing stack as depicted in the following diagram:

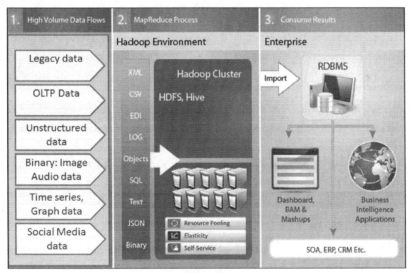

Data Variety in the enterprise

The following is an explanation of various categories of high-volume data:

- **Legacy data**: This data type includes data from all legacy systems and applications, encompassing the structured and semi-structured formats of data stored online or offline. There are lots of use cases for data types—seismic data, hurricane data, census data, urban planning data, and socioeconomic data. These types can be ingested into Hadoop and combined with the master data to create interesting, predictive mash-ups.

- **Transactional (OLTP) data**: Data from the transactional systems is traditionally loaded to the data warehouse. The advent of Hadoop has addressed the lack of extreme scalability in traditional systems; thus, transactional data is often modeled so that not all the data from the source systems is used in the analysis. Hadoop can be used to load and analyze the OLTP data in its entirety as a pre-processing or second-pass processing step. It can also be used to ingest, egress, and integrate transactional data from ERP, mainframe, SCM, and CRM systems to create powerful data products.

- **Unstructured data**: This data type includes documents, notes, memos, and contracts residing in enterprise content management platforms. These enterprise systems are geared toward producing and storing content without much analysis being performed on the data. Hadoop provides interfaces to ingest the content and process it by discovering context-based, user-defined rules. The output of content processing is used to define and design analytics to explore the mining of unstructured data using semantic technologies.

- **Video**: Many enterprises have started to harness into video-based data to gain key insights into use cases related to security surveillance, weather, media, and so on. Hadoop enables the ingest of the components in a video, such as the content, audio, and associated metadata. Hadoop integrates the contextualized video data and associated metadata with structured data in the **Enterprise Data Warehouses (EDW)** to further process the data using advanced algorithms.

- **Audio**: Data from call centers contains a lot of intelligence about customers, competition, and other categories. While the current data warehouse has limitations on the processing and integration of this type of data, Hadoop ingests this data seamlessly by integrating it with the existing data in the warehouse. Audio data extracts can be processed and stored as contextual data with the associated metadata in Hadoop.

- **Images**: Static images carry a lot of information that can be very useful for government agencies (geospatial integration), healthcare (X-ray and CAT scans), and other areas. Ingesting this data in Hadoop and integrating it with the data warehouse will provide large enterprises with benefits through analytical insights, which generate business opportunities where initially none existed, due to lack of data availability or processing capability.

- **Numerical/patterns/graphs**: This data type belongs to the semi-structured category. It includes seismic data, sensor data, weather data, stock market data, scientific data, RFID, cellular tower data, automotive on-board computer chips, GPS data, and streaming video. Other such data are patterns that occur, or numeric data or graphs that repeat their manifests in periodic time intervals. Hadoop helps to ingest this type of data and process it by integrating the results with the data warehouse. This processing will provide analytical opportunities to perform correlation analysis, cluster analysis, or Bayesian types of analysis, which will help identify opportunities in revenue leakage, customer segment behavior, and business risk modeling.

- **Social media data**: Typically classified as Facebook, LinkedIn, or Twitter data, the social media data transcends those channels. This data can be purchased from third-party aggregators, such as DataSift, Gnip, and Nielsen. Ingesting these types of data and combining them in Hadoop with structured data enables a wide variety of social network analysis applications, such as sentiment detection.

In the upcoming sections, we will examine the numerous ingest and egress patterns dealing with the aforementioned data types.

Ingest and egress patterns for multistructured data

The next sections describe the specific design patterns for ingesting unstructured data (images) and semi-structured text data (Apache log and custom log).The following is a brief overview of the formats:

- **Apache Log formats**: Extracting intelligence from this format is a widely used enterprise use case and is relevant across the board.

- **Custom log format**: This format represents an arbitrary log that can be parsed through a regex. Understanding this pattern will help you to extend it for many other similar use cases where a custom loader has to be written.

- **Image format**: This is the only pattern dealing with nontext data, and the pattern described to ingest images can be tweaked and applied to any type of binary data. We will also discuss the image egress pattern to illustrate the ease of egressing the binary data using Pig's extensibility features.

Considerations for log ingestion

The storage of logs depends on the characteristics of the use case. Typically, in the enterprise, logs are stored, indexed, processed, and used for analytics. The role of MapReduce starts from the point of ingestion to index and process the log data. Once the processing is done, it has to be stored on a system that provides read performance for real-time querying on the log indexes. In this section, we will examine the various options to store the log data for real-time read performance:

- One of the options is a wide variety of SQL-based relational databases. They are not a good fit to store large volumes of log data for the use cases that need querying in real time to gain insights.

- NoSQL databases seem to be a good option to store unstructured data due to the following characteristics:

  - Document databases, such as CouchDB and MongoDB, store the data in documents, where each document can contain a variable number of fields or schemas. In the case of log processing, generally, the schemas are predetermined and will not change so frequently. Hence, document databases can be used in the use cases where schema flexibility (logs with different schemas) is the primary criterion.

  - Column-oriented databases, such as HBase and Cassandra, store closely related data in columns, which are extendable. These databases are good for distributed storage and are performance centric. These are very efficient in reading operations and calculating on a set of columns. However, at the same time, these databases are not schema flexible like the other NoSQL counterparts. The database structure has to be predetermined before storing the data. Most of the common use cases of log file processing can be implemented in column-oriented databases.

  - Graph databases, such as GraphLab and Neo4j, are not suitable for log file processing because the logs cannot be represented as the nodes or vertices of a graph.

  - Key-value databases such as SimpleDB store values that are accessible by a certain key. A key-value database works well when the database scheme is flexible and for data that needs to be accessed frequently. Ideally, these databases are not suitable for log file processing where there is no explicit change in the schema over a period.

Considering the previously mentioned characteristics, the best practice is to choose the performance and distribution capabilities of columnar databases over the schema flexibility of a key value and document databases for logfile storage and processing. Another important criterion to help make a better decision is to choose a columnar database that has a good read performance instead of a good write performance, as millions of logs have to be read and aggregated for analysis.

In light of all the criteria, enterprises have successfully implemented log analytics platforms using HBase as their database of choice.

The Apache log ingestion pattern

The logfile ingestion pattern describes how you can use Pig Latin to ingest Apache logs into the Hadoop File System to further process them on your data pipeline.

We will discuss the relevance of Apache logs to the enterprise, and get an understanding of the various logs formats, how each format differs, and the use cases where logs are used in conjunction with Pig. You will also understand how Pig makes the ingestion of these logs a lot easier than programming them in MapReduce.

The subsequent discussion of the implementation-level detail of this pattern is meant to familiarize you with the important concepts and alternatives as applicable. An example code snippet is used to enable better understanding of the pattern from the Pig language perspective, followed by the results of using the pattern.

Background

The Apache Server logs are used for general purpose tracking and monitoring of server health. The Apache web servers create the Apache logs and store them in the local storage. These logs are moved periodically to the Hadoop cluster for storage on the Hadoop File System through the Apache Flume framework, which is distributed in major Hadoop distributions such as Cloudera.

The following is a quick high-level introduction to Flume:

- Flume is a distributed and reliable producer-consumer system to move large volumes of logs (automatically after they are configured) into Hadoop for processing
- The Flume agents run on the web servers (producer)
- The producer agent collects the log data periodically using collectors (consumer)
- The producer agent pushes the log data to the destination filesystem, HDFS

A snapshot of this architecture is depicted in following diagram:

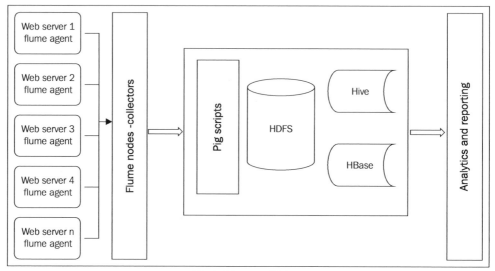

Typical log acquisition

Motivation

The log data is analyzed to understand and track the behavior of any application or web service. It contains a wealth of information about the application and its users, which is aggregated to find patterns, errors, or suboptimal user experience, thereby converting *invisible* log data into useful performance insights. These insights are leveraged across the enterprise in the form of specific use cases that range from product support to engineering and marketing, providing both operational and business intelligence.

A computer cluster contains many individual servers, each with its own logging facility. This makes it difficult for server administrators to analyze the overall performance of an entire cluster. Combining log files of the individual servers into one log file can be very useful to get information about the performance of the cluster. The combined log files make it possible to visualize the cluster's performance and detect problems in the cluster in a short period of time. However, storing server logs of a cluster for a few days results in datasets of several gigabytes. Analyzing such a large quantity of data requires a lot of processing power and memory. A distributed system such as Hadoop is best suited for this kind of processing power and memory.

The size of web logs can grow to hundreds of GB, and Hadoop ingests these files for further analysis and considers various dimensions, such as time, geography of origin, and type of browser, to extract patterns and vital information.

Use cases

This design pattern can be used in the following use cases:

- To find the users who are linked to the website.
- To find the number of website visitors and unique users. This can be done across spatial and temporal dimensions.
- To find peak load hours in temporal and spatial directions.
- To analyze the visits of bots and worms.
- To find stats relevant to site performance.
- To analyze the server's responses and requests and gain insights into the root causes of web server issues.
- To analyze which page or part of the website is more interesting to the user.

Pattern implementation

The Apache access log ingestion pattern is implemented in Pig through the usage of the `ApacheCommonLogLoader` and `ApacheCombinedLogLoader` classes of piggybank. These functions extend the `LoadFunc` class of Pig.

Code snippets

The two different types of logs that are used in the following example are the **Common Log Format** named `access_log_Jul95` and the **Combined Log Format** named `access.log`. In the enterprise setting, these logs are extracted using the Flume agent residing on the web server where the log is generated.

The following table illustrates the constituent attributes of each type:

Attribute	Common log format	Combined log format
IP address	Yes	Yes
User ID	Yes	Yes
Time of request	Yes	Yes
Text of request	Yes	Yes
Status code	Yes	Yes
Size in bytes	Yes	Yes
Referer		Yes
HTTP agent		Yes

Code for the CommonLogLoader class

The following Pig script illustrates the usage of the CommonLogLoader class to ingest the access_log_Jul95 log file into the Pig relation logs:

```
/*
Register the piggybank jar file to be able to use the UDFs in it
*/
REGISTER '/usr/share/pig/contrib/piggybank/java/piggybank.jar';

/*
Assign the aliases ApacheCommonLogLoader and DayExtractor to
  piggybank's CommonLogLoader and DateExtractor UDFs
*/
DEFINE ApacheCommonLogLoader org.apache.pig.piggybank.storage.
  apachelog.CommonLogLoader();
DEFINE DayExtractor org.apache.pig.piggybank.evaluation.
  util.apachelogparser.DateExtractor('yyyy-MM-dd');

/*
Load the logs dataset using the alias ApacheCommonLogLoader into
  the relation logs
*/
logs = LOAD '/user/cloudera/pdp/datasets/logs/access_log_Jul95'
  USING ApacheCommonLogLoader
    AS (addr: chararray, logname: chararray, user: chararray,
      time: chararray,
    method: chararray, uri: chararray, proto: chararray,
    status: int, bytes: int);
/*
* Some processing logic goes here which is deliberately left out
  to improve readability
*/

/*
Display the contents of the relation logs on the console
*/
DUMP logs;
```

Code for the CombinedLogLoader class

The following Pig script illustrates the usage of the CombinedLogLoader class to ingest the access.log file into the Pig relation logs:

```
/*
Register the piggybank jar file to be able to use the UDFs in it
*/
REGISTER '/usr/share/pig/contrib/piggybank/java/piggybank.jar';
```

```
/*
Load the logs dataset using piggybank's CombinedLogLoader into the
  relation logs
*/
logs = LOAD '/user/cloudera/pdp/datasets/logs/access.log'
  USING org.apache.pig.piggybank.storage.apachelog.
    CombinedLogLoader()
  AS (addr: chararray, logname: chararray, user: chararray,
    time: chararray,
    method: chararray, uri: chararray, proto: chararray,
    status: int, bytes: int,
    referer: chararray, useragent: chararray);
/*
* Some processing logic goes here which is deliberately left out
  to improve readability
*/

-- Display the contents of the relation logs on the console
DUMP logs;
```

Results

As a consequence of using this pattern, data from the Apache log file is stored in a bag. The following are a few ways in which a Pig relation can be stored with invalid values:

* If the log file has invalid data, then nulls are stored in the bag.

* If the data types are not defined in the schema after the AS clause, then all the columns are defaulted to bytearray in the bag. Pig performs conversions later, based on the context in which that data is used. It is sometimes required to typecast the columns explicitly to reduce parse time errors.

Additional information
* http://pig.apache.org/docs/r0.11.0/api/org/apache/pig/
  piggybank/storage/apachelog/CombinedLogLoader.html

* http://pig.apache.org/docs/r0.11.0/api/org/apache/pig/
  piggybank/storage/apachelog/CommonLogLoader.html

* http://pig.apache.org/docs/r0.11.0/api/org/apache/pig/
  piggybank/evaluation/util/apachelogparser/package-summary.html

The complete code and datasets for this section are in the following GitHub directories:

- `chapter2/code/`
- `chapter2/datasets/`

The Custom log ingestion pattern

The custom log ingestion pattern describes how you can use Pig Latin to ingest any kind of logs into the Hadoop File System to further process logs on your data pipeline.

We will discuss the relevance of custom logs in the enterprise, and get an understanding of how these logs are generated and transferred to the Hadoop cluster and of the use cases where logs are used in conjunction with Pig. You will also understand how Pig makes ingestion of these logs a lot easier than programming them in MapReduce.

The subsequent discussion of the implementation-level detail of this pattern is meant to familiarize you with the important concepts and alternatives as applicable. An example code snippet is used to enable the better understanding of the pattern from the Pig language perspective, followed by the results of using the pattern.

Background

Most of the logs use certain conventions to delimit the constituent fields, similar to a CSV file, but there are situations where we encounter text files, which are not properly separated (by a tab or a comma).These logs are required to be cleaned before they can be analyzed. Data can be cleaned before it arrives in HDFS via Flume, Chukwa, or Scribe and stored in a format where Pig or Hive can easily process it for analytics. If data is already stored in an uncleaned format in HDFS, you can write a Pig script to clean up the data and analyze it by loading it in Hive or HBase for it to be used later.

Motivation

Pig's reputation for handling unstructured data stems from its native support for data with partial or unknown schemas. While loading data, it is optional to specify the schema, and it is possible that the schema can be specified after the loading has been completed. This is in stark contrast with other systems such as Hive, where you have to enforce a schema before loading.

Use this pattern when the text data is not standardized and formatted yet.

Use cases

The following are the generic use cases where this pattern can be applied:

- To ingest any text or log file that doesn't have a well-defined schema
- To ingest text or log files and experimentally figure out what schema can be imposed on it, based on the suitability for analytics

Pattern implementation

The unstructured text ingestion pattern is implemented in Pig through the usage of the TextLoader function of piggybank. These functions inherit the LoadFunc class.

Pig has a nice feature that deciphers the type of data if the schema is not explicitly specified. In such cases, fields are set to the default bytearray type and then the correct type is inferred based on the usage and context of the data in the next statements.

The TextLoader function of piggybank enables you to load the text file, splitting on new lines and loading each line into a Pig tuple. If a schema is specified using the AS clause, each of the tuple is considered chararray. If no schema is specified by omitting the clause, then the resultant tuples will not have the schema.

Similarly, you can use the MyRegexLoader class to load the contents of the file after filtering the rows using the regex pattern specified. A regular expression format can be specified using MyRegExLoader. This function returns a matched regex as chararray if a pattern is passed to it as a parameter.

Code snippets

In this use case, we illustrate the ingestion of application log files to help identify potential performance issues in a web server by analyzing the request/response patterns. We will use the sample_log.1 dataset to calculate the average response time taken by each service. This log file contains event logs embedded along with the web service request and response information generated by a web application in the format shown in the following code. Here, we are interested in extracting only the request response pairs, ignoring the event information related to INFO, DEBUG, and ERRORS:

```
/* other unstructured event logs related to INFO, DEBUG, and ERROR
   logs are depicted here */
Request <serviceName> <requestID> <Timestamp>
Response <serviceName> <requestID> <Timestamp>
/* other unstructured event logs related to INFO, DEBUG, and ERROR
   logs are depicted here */
```

The following code snippet shows the usage of `MyRegexLoader` to load the lines that match the specified regular expression:

```
/*
Register the piggybank jar file to be able to use the UDFs in it
*/
REGISTER '/usr/share/pig/contrib/piggybank/java/piggybank.jar';

/*
Load the logs dataset using piggybank's MyRegExLoader into the
  relation logs.
MyRegexLoader loads only the lines that match the specified regex
  format
*/
logs = LOAD '/user/cloudera/pdp/datasets/logs/sample_log.1'
  USING org.apache.pig.piggybank.storage.MyRegExLoader(
    '(Request|Response)(\\s+\\w+)(\\s+\\d+)(\\s+\\d\\d/\\d\\d/\\d
    \\d\\s+\\d\\d:\\d\\d:\\d\\d:\\d\\d\\d\\s+CST)')
    AS (type:chararray, service_name:chararray, req_id:chararray,
      datetime:chararray);

/*
* Some processing logic goes here which is deliberately left out
  to improve readability
*/

-- Display the contents of the relation logs on the console
DUMP logs;
```

Further processing would be done on the extracted logs to calculate the average response time taken by each service and identifying potential performance issues.

The following code snippet shows the usage of `TextLoader` to load the custom log:

```
/*
Load the logs dataset using TextLoader into the relation logs
*/
logs = LOAD '/user/cloudera/pdp/datasets/logs/sample_log.1' USING
  TextLoader  AS (line:chararray);

/*
The lines matching the regular expression are stored in
  parsed_logs.
FILTER function filters the records that do not match the pattern
*/
```

```
parsed_logs = FILTER logs BY $0 MATCHES '(Request|Response)(\\s+\\w+)
(\\s+\\d+)(\\s+\\d\\d/\\d\\d/\\d\\d\\
  s+\\d\\d:\\d\\d:\\d\\d:\\d\\d\\d\\s+CST)';

/*
* Some processing logic goes here which is deliberately left out
  to improve readability
*/

-- Display the contents of the relation parsed_logs on the console

DUMP parsed_logs;
```

Results

As a consequence of using this pattern, data from the log file is stored in a bag. This bag is used in the subsequent steps for analysis.

The following are a few ways in which a Pig relation could be stored with invalid values:

- If the log file has invalid data, then nulls are stored in the Bag.
- If the data types are not defined in the schema after the AS clause, then all the columns are defaulted to bytearray in the bag. Pig performs conversions later based on the context in which that data is used. It is sometimes required to typecast the columns explicitly to reduce parse time errors.
    - You can define data types after the AS clause, but care has to be taken when defining appropriate data types for each of the columns. A null will be stored in the Bag when the data type casting cannot happen such as in cases where a chararray type is forcibly typecasted to an int result in a null. However, int can be casted to chararray. (For example, int 27 can be typecast into chararray "27".)
- You have to pay special attention to data in a relation that could result in a null. Relational operators such as COUNT disregard nulls, but the COUNT_STAR function does not ignore it and counts a null as if there is a value to it.

Additional information

- http://pig.apache.org/docs/r0.11.0/api/org/apache/pig/
  piggybank/storage/MyRegExLoader.html
- http://pig.apache.org/docs/r0.11.1/func.html#textloader

The complete code and datasets for this section can be found in the following GitHub directories:

- `chapter2/code/`
- `chapter2/datasets/`

The image ingress and egress pattern

The design patterns in this section describe how you can use Pig Latin to ingest and egress a set of images into and from the Hadoop File System to further process images in your data pipeline.

We will discuss the relevance of images in the enterprise and get an understanding of the various ways images can be created and stored, the optimal way of gathering images to be processed on Hadoop, and the use cases where images are used in conjunction with Pig. You will also understand how Pig makes it easy to ingest these images with a custom UDF written in Java.

The subsequent discussion of the implementation-level detail of this pattern is meant to familiarize you with the important concepts and alternatives as applicable. An example code snippet is used to enable better understanding of the pattern from the Pig language perspective, followed by the results of using the pattern.

Background

There are many documented use cases of Hadoop that deal with structured data and unstructured text data. However, we have evidence of many cases that exploit the real power of Hadoop to process the other forms of unstructured data, such as images, videos, and sound files.

In terms of processing images, Hadoop plays a key role in analyzing images taken by weather/military/civil satellites, that is, when the image size is large and the resolution is high and they need to be processed by a farm of servers.

Hadoop offers an effective storage mechanism for large images or a set of small images. Unlike the process of storing images in a RDBMS as a BLOB without the ability to perform a massive-scaled, meaningful analysis on them using SQL, specific image processing algorithms can be written on Hadoop, which can work on individual images and on a bundle of images for performing high-end image analysis in a parallel way.

Motivation

This pattern is applicable in cases where you want to load and process a large number of image files in Hadoop. The loading of the images into the data pipeline is accomplished by a UDF written in Java.

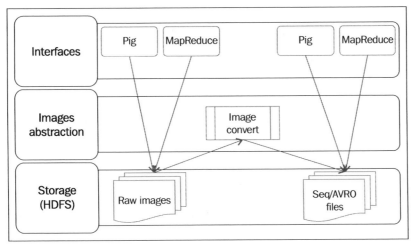

Image ingress and egress

Ingesting the unstructured image data and combining it with the structured image metadata, such as tags, EXIF information, and object tags, which provide the contextual information, has led to newer developments in social media analytics and other areas—such as security, intelligence gathering, weather predictions, and facial recognition. This idea could be extended to a wider range of image features that allow us to examine and analyze images in a revolutionary way.

After ingesting the images into Hadoop, the actual processing of raw images is a complex task involving multiple calculations on the raw pixels level. These calculations are accomplished by the low-level C and C++ algorithms. Hadoop is integrated with these algorithms using Hadoop streaming to wrap these and work as a standard Hadoop job.

The image egress pattern attempts to show a simple mechanism in which the binary images existing as a sequence file in the HDFS are output as image files. The motivation for this pattern lies in the ability of Hadoop-based image processing algorithms to perform complex computations on images to join its constituent tiles to create a bigger image.

Hadoop works effectively by grouping image files into a small number of large files as opposed to an enormous number of tiny image files. Using a large number of small image files, whose size is less than the HDFS block size of 64 MB, could cause many reads from the disk and heavy lookup in the NameNode, resulting in a huge amount of network traffic to transfer these files from one node to another. This causes unproductive data access. This design pattern explores a way to overcome this limitation in Hadoop by grouping these image files into sequence files. You can extend this pattern to ingest and process other types of binary files such as sound and video.

The ingestion design pattern is applicable to images that are part of a large corpus of image files, where each image is distinct and combining them is not natural. The pattern is not applicable to a very large image that is split among the nodes of the Hadoop cluster. An illustration of the architecture is shown in the previous diagram.

Use cases

You may consider applying the image ingestion pattern as a pre-processing step in the following use cases:

- Ingest multiple images to apply the various types of image filters on each of the images
- Perform batch enhancements to the image quality
- Understand the content of the images, for example, apply AI-based unsupervised computer vision algorithms to extract features such as roads, canals, or buildings from within the image
- Use images for pattern matching as in the case of medical and GIS imagery

You may consider applying the image egress pattern in use cases where noise has to be removed from the images. The original images are loaded in Hadoop and processed to remove noise; the noise-filtered images are egressed back by combining multiple tiles of the images to create a new image.

Pattern implementation

The following sections describe the pattern implementation of the image ingest pattern followed by image egress.

The image Ingress Implementation

The image ingestion pattern is implemented in Pig through the usage of a custom loader function that is implemented as a UDF in Java. This `ImageToSequenceFileUDF` converts the image(s) into a sequence file. The input is the HDFS path of the images directory and the output is the sequence file path.

The sequence file stores the contents of the image file as a value, mapped to the filename key. As the sequence file can be split, it can be processed by streaming or using MapReduce. MapReduce internally uses a marker to split the files into block-sized chunks and operates on them independently. The sequence file supports compression with many codecs, and block compression is used for the maximum efficiency of storage and retrieval. There will not be any reducer in this case to prevent the shuffling of data and consumption of bandwidth. This will enable using Hadoop for its scalable advantages in case you have a large amount of image data stored in the sequence files.

The image egress implementation

The image egress pattern is implemented in Pig through the usage of a custom storage function that is implemented as a UDF in Java. This `SequenceToImageStorage` class converts the sequence file into images and stores it in the specified location on the disk. The input to this function is the path of the sequence files.

Code snippets

The following sections describes the code of the image ingest pattern followed by the image egress.

The image ingress

To illustrate the working of this pattern, we considered a set of image files stored in a folder accessible to the Hadoop File System, HDFS. There is no pre-processing done on the images; they are stored in the raw format (JPEG). The following code primarily has two major parts. Firstly, the Pig Latin script, which loads the file containing the path to images folder, and secondly, the custom UDF written in Java that does the actual work behind the scenes to decompose an image or a set of images to a sequence file.

Pig script

The following is the Pig script to read image files and convert them into a sequence file:

```
/*
Register the custom loader imagelibrary.jar, it has UDFs to
  convert images to sequence file and sequence file to images
*/
REGISTER '/home/cloudera/pdp/jars/imagelibrary.jar';

/*
```

```
Load images_input file, it contains the path to images directory
*/
images_file_path = LOAD
  '/user/cloudera/pdp/datasets/images/images_input' AS
  (link:chararray);


/*
ImageToSequenceFileUDF converts multiple image files to a sequence
  file.
This ensures that there are no large number of small files on
  HDFS, instead multiple small images are converted into a single
  sequence file.
Another advantage of sequence file is that it is splittable.
The sequence file contains key value pairs, key is the image
  file name and value is the image binary data.
It returns the path of the sequence file.
*/
convert_to_seq = FOREACH images_file_path GENERATE
  com.mycustomudf.ImageToSequenceFileUDF();


/*
* Some processing logic goes here which is deliberately left out
  to improve readability
*/


-- Display the contents of the convert_to_seq on the console
DUMP convert_to_seq;
```

Image to a sequence UDF snippet

The following is the Java code snippet of ImagetoSequenceFileUDF that shows the conversion of image file(s) to a sequence file:

```
public static String createSequenceFile(Path inPutPath)
{
.
.

for(int i=0;i<status.length;i++)
  {
    //FSDataInputStream is opened at the given path
    dataInputStream = fileSystem.open(status[i].getPath());
    // extracting image name from the absolute path
    fileName = status[i].getPath().toString().
    substring(status[i].getPath().toString().
    lastIndexOf("/")+1);
```

```
        byte buffer[] = new byte[dataInputStream.available()];
        //buffer.remaining() bytes will be read into buffer.
        dataInputStream.read(buffer);
        /*Add a key/value pair. Key is the image filename and
          value is the BytesWritable object*/
        seqFileWriter.append(new Text(fileName),
        new BytesWritable(buffer));
        .
        .
    }
}
```

The image egress

The following section describes the code for the image egress.

Pig script

The following is the Pig script to egress contents of the sequence file into images:

```
/*
Register the custom jar, it has UDFs to convert images to sequence
  file and sequence file to images
*/
REGISTER '/home/cloudera/pdp/jars/imagelibrary.jar';

/*
Load images_input file, it contains the path to images directory
*/
images_file_path = LOAD '/user/cloudera/pdp/datasets/images/images_
input' AS
  (link:chararray);

/*
ImageToSequenceFileUDF function converts multiple image files to a
  sequence file.
This ensures that there are no large number of small files on
  HDFS, instead multiple small images are converted into a single
  sequence file.
Another advantage of sequence file is that it is splittable.
The sequence file contains key value pairs, key is the image
  file name and value is the image binary data.
It returns the path of the sequence file.
*/
convert_to_seq = FOREACH images_file_path GENERATE
  com.mycustomudf.ImageToSequenceFileUDF();
```

```
/*
* Some processing logic goes here which is deliberately left out
  to improve readability.
* It is assumed that in-between the load and store steps, a user
  performs some image processing step such as stitching multiple
  image tiles together.
*/

/*
The custom UDF SequenceToImageStorage reads the sequence file and
  writes out images.
It reads each key/value pair and writes out the contents as images
  with keyname as the filename in the folder seq_to_img_output
*/
STORE convert_to_seq INTO
  '/user/cloudera/pdp/output/images/seq_to_img_output' USING
  com.mycustomudf.SequenceToImageStorage();
```

Sequence to an image UDF

The following is a snippet of the custom store function, SequenceToImageStorage, to read a sequence file and write out the contents to image file(s):

```
@Override
public void putNext(Tuple tuples) throws IOException {
  .
  .
  // Do this for each key/value pair
  while (seqFilereader.next(key, value))
  {
    bufferString = value.toString().split(" ");
    buffer =new byte[bufferString.length];
    for(int i=0;i<bufferString.length;i++)
    {
    /*
      String parameter parsed as signed integer in the radix given
        by the second parameter
      */
      buffer[i] = (byte)
      Integer.parseInt(bufferString[i], 16);
    }
    /*
    output path of the image which is the path specified, key is
      the image name
    */
    outPutPath=new Path(location+"/"+key);
    // FSDataOutputStream will be created at the given Path.
```

```
      seqFileWriter = fileSystem.create(outPutPath);
      // All bytes in array are written to the output stream
      seqFileWriter.write(buffer);
   }
   .
   .
   .
}
```

The `SequenceFile.Reader` class of Hadoop API is used to read the sequence file to get the key-value pairs. The key-value pairs are iterated and then for each pair, a new file is created with a key name, and the value is written as bytes into the file, thus generating multiple image files.

Results

As a consequence of applying the image ingestion pattern, the corpus of images is parsed by the Java UDF into sequence files. Each of the sequence files is decomposed later into the RGB values and stored in a Pig Latin map relation. The next stages of data pipeline use the map relation to further process the sequence files.

As a result of the image egress pattern, the sequence file stored in HDFS is converted into image files so that the upstream image display systems can use these images.

Additional information

- http://pig.apache.org/docs/r0.11.0/api/org/apache/pig/ piggybank/storage/SequenceFileLoader.html
- http://pig.apache.org/docs/r0.11.1/udf.html#load-store- functions

The complete code and datasets for this section is in the following GitHub directories:

- chapter2/code/
- chapter2/datasets/

The ingress and egress patterns for the NoSQL data

This section describes the patterns that deal with ingesting data from two classes of NoSQL data. To illustrate the power of Pig to readily support NoSQL databases and the use cases associated with it, we have chosen document databases such as MongoDB and columnar databases such as HBase.

MongoDB ingress and egress patterns

The MongoDB ingress and egress patterns describe how you can use Pig Latin to store the contents of MongoDB document collections in the Hadoop File System (Pig relations) to process data and then write the processed data back into the MongoDB.

We will discuss the relevance of the data stored in MongoDB to the enterprise and understand the various ways in which the MongoDB data can be accessed, the motivation to perform ingest and egress, and the use cases where MongoDB data is used in conjunction with Pig. You will also understand how Pig makes the ingestion and egression of this data a lot more intuitive than doing it using MapReduce code written in Java.

The subsequent discussion of the implementation-level detail of this pattern is meant to familiarize you with the important concepts and alternatives as applicable. The example code snippets enable better understanding of the patterns from the Pig language perspective, followed by the results of using the pattern.

Background

MongoDB is a NoSQL database designed from the ground up to store data in the form of document collections, unlike the rows and columns of RDBMS. It is highly scalable and makes the retrieval of documents easy, owing to the extensive indexing capability and the use of JSON for integration with external applications. MongoDB is extremely flexible and handles variable schemas. (It is not mandatory to have the same schema for each of the documents in the collection.) As MongoDB stores data as documents and almost all attributes of these document collections are indexed, it is a highly effective solution as an operational store to process real-time queries, unlike Hadoop which excels in offline batch processing and aggregating of data from various sources.

Motivation

In a typical enterprise, MongoDB and Hadoop are integrated in scenarios where Hadoop is required to handle more extreme data loads compared to what MongoDB is capable of to aggregate data and facilitate complex analytics.

The data from MongoDB is ingested into Hadoop and processed with MapReduce jobs. Hadoop combines the data with additional data from other enterprise sources using the Pig data pipelines to develop a multidata aggregation solution. After processing the data in the Pig data pipelines, it is written back into MongoDB for ad-hoc analysis and querying. This ensures that existing applications can use the egressed data from Hadoop to create visualizations or drive other systems.

In many enterprise use cases, Hadoop functions as a central data repository that integrates the data with different data stores. In this case, MongoDB can function as one of the data sources that feeds Hadoop periodically using MapReduce jobs. Once the MongoDB data is ingested into Hadoop, the combined bigger datasets are processed and made available to further query them.

MongoDB also acts as one of the **Operational Data Store (ODS)**, which connects to other data stores and data warehouses. Obtaining analytical insights involves the movement of data from these connected data sources and the performing of ETL, for which Pig can be effectively used. Hadoop acts as an ETL hub to pull data from one store, perform various transformations using the MapReduce jobs, and load the data onto another store.

 It is important to note that ingesting data directly from an external source (MongoDB) has very different operational performance characteristics than data already loaded/transferred into HDFS.

Use cases

You might want to consider using the patterns of data ingress and egress in the following scenarios where integrating MongoDB with Hadoop reaps rich dividends:

- MongoDB and Hadoop handle different workloads, near real time and batch, respectively. Consider using the ingress design pattern in use cases where you want to offload loads to Hadoop to be batch processed and thus, free up resources in MongoDB. Consider using the egress design pattern to make the MongoDB a sink to export data from Hadoop and enable real-time query operations.

- MongoDB itself has a MapReduce implementation, which runs on the MongoDB database. However, it is slower than the Hadoop MapReduce as it is implemented in JavaScript, and it has fewer data types and libraries to perform complex analytics. Consider using the ingress design pattern in use cases that has data to be offloaded to Hadoop to take advantage of Hadoop's library support, machine learning, ETL capabilities, and the scale of processing. Consider using the egress design pattern to move data from Hadoop into MongoDB and to take advantage of Mongo DB's MapReduce implementation.

- MongoDB has support for few basic data aggregation capabilities to generate aggregates in the SQL style that requires a higher learning curve to understand the aggregation framework. Consider using the ingress design pattern in cases where you want to take advantage of Hadoop to perform complex aggregation tasks.

- This design pattern can be used in cases where there is a huge amount of unstructured data and you need to use MongoDB for real-time analysis. In this case, you can use the ingress design pattern to create a structure out of the ingested raw data in Hadoop and export the data into MongoDB using the egress design pattern to facilitate optimized storage in MongoDB for real-time querying and analytics.

Pattern implementation

The following diagram shows the MongoDB connector integration:

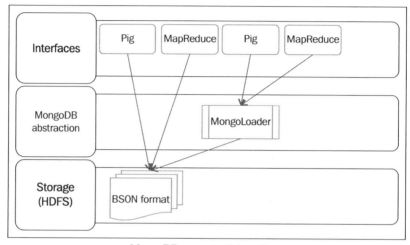

MongoDB connector integration

Hadoop and MongoDB can be integrated using the MongoDB connector for Hadoop. This connector helps to move data to and from MongoDB into the Hadoop ecosystem and allows access through other programming languages (Hadoop streaming). The connector's integration with Pig is depicted in the previous diagram.

The ingress implementation

Pig uses the `MongoLoader` function to load MongoDB data into a Pig Latin relation. Using this function, the data is loaded directly from the database. Pig can also read from the MongoDB native format (BSON) using the `BSONLoader` function.

The `MongoLoader` function can work in the schema-less mode in which the field names are not specified. In this mode, the records are interpreted as tuples containing a single map (document). This case is useful when you do not know the schema of the MongoDB collection. The `MongoLoader` function can also work in the schema mode where you specify field names that maps the fields in the Pig script with those in the document.

The egress implementation

The data in a Pig relation can be written into MongoDB in two ways. The first way is to use the BSONStorage function to perform the storage of a relation into a .BSON file that can be imported later into MongoDB. This method has the advantage of writing at high throughput in the native storage format of MongoDB. The second way uses MongoDB's wrapper to connect to the database and write directly into it through the usage of the MongoStorage function. This function will operate on a tuple level by storing each tuple it receives into the corresponding document in MongoDB. The schema of the Pig relation and the MongoDB document is mapped before the writing commences. Using the second method will give you a lot of flexibility to write data at record or tuple level, but it compromises on the speed of I/O.

The MongoStorage function can also be used to update the existing document collection in MongoDB by specifying the update key in the constructor. If the update key is specified, the first document (value) corresponding to the key will be updated by the contents of the Pig tuple.

Code snippets

In the following example code, we have considered the contents of the nasdaqDB. store_stock data already residing in MongoDB. This dataset consists of NASDAQ data spanning from the 1970s to 2010; this includes the stock tracking data of various companies and how they performed on a specific day with its trading volume figures. This dataset is alphabetically organized by the ticker symbol and stored as JSON objects in MongoDB.

The ingress code

The following code performs the task of connecting to MongoDB, setting up the connection, loading the MongoDB native file, parsing it, and retrieving only the specified schema in the MongoLoader constructor by mapping the fields of the MongoDB document with the fields specified in the schema. This abstraction is performed by just one call to the MongoLoader function.

```
/*
Register the mongo jar files to be able to use MongoLoader UDF
*/
REGISTER '/home/cloudera/pdp/jars/mongo.jar';
REGISTER '/home/cloudera/pdp/jars/mongo-hadoop-pig.jar';

/*
Load the data using MongoLoader UDF, it connects to MongoDB, loads
   the native file and parses it to retrieve only the specified
   schema.
```

```
*/
stock_data = LOAD 'mongodb://slave1/nasdaqDB.store_stock' USING
    com.mongodb.hadoop.pig.MongoLoader('exchange:chararray,
    stock_symbol:chararray, date:chararray, stock_price_open:float,
    stock_price_high:float, stock_price_low:float,
    stock_price_close:float, stock_volume:long,
    stock_price_adj_close:chararray') AS
    (exchange,stock_symbol,date,stock_price_open,stock_price_high,
    stock_price_low,stock_price_close,stock_volume,
    stock_price_adj_close);

/*
* Some processing logic goes here which is deliberately left out
  to improve readability
*/

/*
Display the contents of the relation stock_data on the console
*/
DUMP stock_data;
```

The egress code

The following code depicts the writing of data existing in a `stock_data` Pig relation to a MongoDB document collection:

```
/*
Register the mongo jar files and piggybank jar to be able to use
  the UDFs
*/
REGISTER '/home/cloudera/pdp/jars/mongo.jar';
REGISTER '/home/cloudera/pdp/jars/mongo_hadoop_pig.jar';
REGISTER '/usr/share/pig/contrib/piggybank/java/piggybank.jar';

/*
Assign the alias MongoStorage to MongoStorage class
*/
DEFINE MongoStorage com.mongodb.hadoop.pig.MongoStorage();

/*
Load the contents of files starting with NASDAQ_daily_prices_ into
  a Pig relation stock_data
*/
```

```
stock_data= LOAD '/user/cloudera/pdp/datasets/mongo/
  NASDAQ_daily_prices/NASDAQ_daily_prices_*' USING
  org.apache.pig.piggybank.storage.CSVLoader() as
  (exchange:chararray, stock_symbol:chararray, date:chararray,
  stock_price_open:chararray, stock_price_high:chararray,
  stock_price_low:chararray, stock_price_close:chararray,
  stock_volume:chararray, stock_price_adj_close:chararray);

/*
 * Some processing logic goes here which is deliberately left out
   to improve readability
 */

/*
Store data to MongoDB by specifying the MongoStorage serializer.
  The MongoDB URI nasdaqDB.store_stock is the document collection
  created to hold this data.
*/
STORE stock_data INTO 'mongodb://slave1/nasdaqDB.store_stock'
  using MongoStorage();
```

Results

As a consequence of applying the ingest design pattern on a MongoDB document collection, the contents of the collection specified by the MongoDB URI are loaded into a stock_data Pig relation. Similarly, the egress design pattern stores the contents of a stock_data Pig relation into the nasdaqDB.store.stock MongoDB document collection.

The following are a few ways specific to MongoLoader implementation in which a Pig relation can be stored with invalid values:

- If the input MongoDB document contains a field that is not mapped in the schema of the constructor, the MongoLoader function will store nulls for that field in a Pig relation.

- If the MongoDB document does not contain a field that is specified in the schema of the constructor, the entire row or tuple of a relation is set to null.

- If there is a type mismatch between MongoDB documents fields and the schema specified, MongoLoader will set the field as a null in a Pig relation.

Additional information

- https://github.com/mongodb/mongo-hadoop/blob/master/pig/README.md

The complete code and datasets for this section is in the following GitHub directories:

- chapter2/code/
- chapter2/datasets/

The HBase ingress and egress pattern

The HBase ingress and egress pattern describes how you can use Pig Latin to ingest the contents of the HBase tables into the Pig relations to further process data and then egress the processed data into HBase.

We will discuss the relevance of HBase to the enterprise and understand the various ways in which the HBase data is stored internally and accessed externally as well as of the use cases where HBase data is used in conjunction with Pig. You will also understand how Pig makes the ingestion and egression of the HBase data a lot easier with the ready-made functions provided.

The subsequent discussion of the implementation-level detail of this pattern is meant to familiarize you with the important concepts and alternatives as applicable. The example code snippets enable the better understanding of the pattern from the Pig language perspective, followed by the results of using the pattern.

Background

HBase is a column-oriented NoSQL database created by taking inspiration from Google's Big Table implementation and is specifically designed to store schema-flexible data and access it in real time. It is linearly scalable for data containing billions of columns and features compression of data and in memory operations for lightning fast access.

The HBase data is internally stored in a custom optimized format called the **Indexed Storefiles** in the HDFS. HBase uses HDFS to take advantage of its storage and high availability features. As HDFS cannot store data to perform random reads and writes, HBase uses a binary format optimized for random read-write access to overcome the limitation of HDFS. The storage of HBase-indexed store files on HDFS makes it perfectly suitable for MapReduce to work on it without the need to import the data from elsewhere.

Logically, HBase stores data in a nested multidimensional map abstraction that has sorted key value pairs and a time stamp associated with the key value. The time stamp enables the latest version of the data to be stored in a sorted order so that the lookup can be easier. HBase implements the concept of fast and slow changing data to store them accordingly using the versions. The data in the multidimensional nested map is retrieved using a primary key, called a rowkey in HBase, through which all the nested data can be dereferenced.

The multidimensional map has two important nested structures (implemented as a map), called the column family and the columns belonging to the column family. The schema of the column family cannot change over the storage lifetime, whereas the schema of the columns inside a column family can have flexible schema, which may change per row. This data organization is inherently suitable to store unrelated and unstructured data suitable for real-time access (as everything is in a map).

Motivation

The need to ingest HBase tables into Pig facilitates its batch processing using the MapReduce framework to achieve the use case goals. After the HBase data has been processed in the Pig data pipeline, it is sometimes required to store it back into HBase to provide real-time access to queries that run natively on HBase. It is in this context that the ingress and egress patterns of HBase data have a special appeal.

The data in HBase is natively accessed through the HBase Java client API calls to put and get data. This API is good enough for an integration with external applications that need real-time query capability. The API, however, does not have the power to perform batch data processing to create data aggregations and complex pipelines to generate analytical insights. This batch processing capability comes with low-level abstractions such as MapReduce or the high-level flexibility of Pig.

Java MapReduce jobs can be written to access data stored in HBase and process it, but Pig scores heavily for simplicity and terse-optimized code when compared to the Java code that one has to write to access the data in HBase.

Accessing the data stored in HBase with the operators in Pig enables the data to be manipulated in the Pig data pipeline and consumed for transformation using the batch processing. Storing the data into HBase from a Pig relation, enables HBase to provide the application's access to query it in real time.

As the data resides in HDFS in the form of Indexed Storefiles, Pig needs to be told how to serialize and deserialize data to and from the HBase format in a way that Pig can understand and process. Pig needs to understand explicitly how to translate between column families, columns in the HBase abstractions, and Pig's native data types. This pattern explains how to accomplish the tasks of ingesting and egressing data to and from HBase using the `HBaseStorage` Pig function.

 Unlike the MongoDB example, here we read the HBase files that are already stored in HDFS. We do not connect to the HBase servers and read the data from them over the network.

Use cases

The following are the use cases for Pig to ingest and egress data from HBase:

- Use the ingestion design pattern to create a data pipeline to integrate real-time data residing in HBase to perform analytics.

- Use the ingestion design pattern to access data in HBase to perform high-level data aggregates in Pig for consumption in downstream systems. Pig can act as an ETL hub to transform data in HBase to integrate it with other applications' data.

- Use the egress design pattern to store the contents of a flat file existing in HDFS into an HBase table. This pattern is also useful to store the results of a complex data integration or transformation pipeline in HBase for the purpose of real-time querying.

Pattern implementation

The following sections describe the pattern implementation of HBase ingest pattern followed by HBase egress.

The ingress implementation

Data in HBase can be ingested in the following two ways:

- The first option is to export entire tables using MapReduce EXPORT job that reads parallelly to get the contents of the table into a HDFS sequence file. A deserializer can be written in Java or Pig to access the contents of this sequence file for later manipulation. This option is slightly difficult to implement owing to the fact that we have to access the contents of HBase from the backend and then deserialize the files. Moreover, this works on one table at a time and to access multiple tables; the list of tables have to be iterated.

- The second option is to implement the HBase ingest design pattern to use the Pig's built-in load function called `HBaseStorage`. This is a straightforward option to connect to the HBase table and get the contents of the table directly into a Pig relation. The tasks of deserialization to map the HBase types to Pig types and execution of MapReduce jobs that performs parallel import are taken care of by Pig. `HBaseStorage` also comes with the additional advantage of loading data into Pig relations, using all the column families or only a subset of columns of the column families. As the columns contain key value types, they can be typecast to the Pig's map type.

The egress implementation

Pig implements the egress design pattern using the `HBaseStorage` function. This pattern is very similar to the ingest pattern implementation, except for the usage of the `STORE` clause. The `STORE` clause conveys to the Pig compiler what data to extract from the Pig relation specified and serializes it into the HBase table in the parameters.

The ingress and egress implementation options are illustrated in the following diagram:

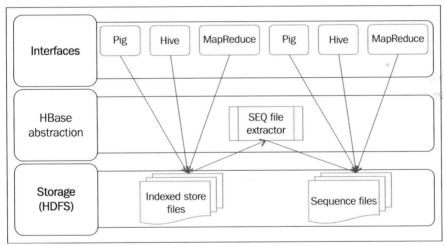

HBase Integration with Pig

Code snippets

The following code example uses a dataset that has sample synthetic retail transactions. It contains attributes such as the transaction date, customer ID, product subclass, product ID, amount, asset, and sales price. This data is already stored in HBase to illustrate this example. The HBase table hbase://retail_ transactions is accessed through the Pig Latin's HBaseStorage function.

The ingress code

The following code snippet illustrates the ingestion of the HBase data into a Pig relation:

```
/*
Load data from HBase table retail_transactions, it contains the
  column families transaction_details, customer_details and
  product_details.
The : operator is used to access columns in a column family.
First parameter to HBaseStorage is the list of columns and the
  second parameter is the list of options
The option -loadkey true specifies the rowkey should be loaded as
  the first item in the tuple, -limit 500 specifies the number of
  rows to be read from the HBase table
*/
transactions = LOAD 'hbase://retail_transactions'
  USING org.apache.pig.backend.hadoop.hbase.HBaseStorage(
  'transaction_details:transaction_date
    customer_details:customer_id customer_details:age
    customer_details:residence_area
    product_details:product_subclass product_details:product_id
    product_details:amount product_details:asset
    product_details:sales_price', '-loadKey true -limit 500')
  AS (id: bytearray, transaction_date: chararray, customer_id:
    int, age: chararray, residence_area: chararray,
    product_subclass: int, product_id: long, amount: int, asset:
    int, sales_price: int);

/*
* Some processing logic goes here which is deliberately left out
  to improve readability
*/

-- Display the contents of the relation transactions on the
  console
DUMP transactions;
```

The egress code

The following code illustrates content storage of a Pig relation into HBase table:

```
/*
Load the transactions dataset using PigStorage into the relation
  transactions
*/
transactions = LOAD
  '/user/cloudera/pdp/datasets/hbase/transactions.csv' USING
  PigStorage( ',' ) AS (
    listing_id: chararray,
    transaction_date: chararray,
    customer_id: int,
    age: chararray,
    residence_area: chararray,
    product_subclass: int,
    product_id: long,
    amount: int,
    asset: int,
    sales_price: int);


/*
* Some processing logic goes here which is deliberately left out
  to improve readability
*/


/*
Use HBaseStorage to store data from the Pig relation transactions
  into a HBase table hbase://retail_transactions.
The individual contents of transactions are mapped to three column
  families transaction_details, product_details and
  customer_details.
*/
STORE transactions INTO 'hbase://retail_transactions' USING
  org.apache.pig.backend.hadoop.hbase.HBaseStorage
  ('transaction_details:transaction_date
  customer_details:customer_id customer_details:age
  customer_details:residence_area product_details:product_subclass
  product_details:product_id product_details:amount
  product_details:asset product_details:sales_price');
```

Results

As a result of applying the HBase data ingestion pattern, the data in the HBase table represented by the column families and the corresponding columns will be loaded in a Pig relation. In this design pattern, the type of result loaded into the Pig relation varies based on the parameters passed. If you specify columns using the column family and a column identifier (CFName:CName), then the resultant type will be a tuple that consists of scalar values. If you specify the columns using a column family name along with a part of the column name followed by an asterisk (CFName:CN*), the resultant column type would be a MAP of the column descriptors as keys.

It is important to note that while retrieving a time series or event-based data stored in HBase, Pig cannot be used to get time stamp information for an HBase value.

As a result of applying the HBase data egress pattern, the data in the pig relation is stored into the HBase table, mapped to the respective column families and the corresponding columns.

Additional information

- `http://pig.apache.org/docs/r0.11.1/func.html#HBaseStorage`

The complete code and datasets for this section is in the following GitHub directories:

- `chapter2/code/`
- `chapter2/datasets/`

The ingress and egress patterns for structured data

The following section takes the example of Hive as one of the sources from where we can ingest structured data and discuss different ways to do that. Hive is selected to illustrate the structured data ingest pattern since it is the most widely used data sink to consume structured data in the enterprise. Also, by understanding this pattern, you can extend it to other structured data.

The Hive ingress and egress patterns

The Hive ingestion pattern describes how you can use Pig Latin to ingest and egress data to and from the Hive tables into the Hadoop File System to further process on your data pipeline.

We will discuss the relevance of Hive to the enterprise and understand the various ways in which the Hive data is stored internally (RCFile, the sequence file, and so on) and accessed externally (HQL and Pig/MapReduce). You will explore the use cases where the Hive data is used in conjunction with Pig. You will also understand how Pig makes the ingestion of the Hive data a lot easier with the ready-made functions provided and then comprehend the role of the Hadoop ecosystem component, HCatalog, to simplify the connection and access the mechanism of Hive tables with Pig.

The subsequent discussion of the implementation-level detail of this pattern is meant to familiarize you with the important concepts and alternatives as applicable. An example code snippet is used to enable the better understanding of the pattern from the Pig language perspective, followed by the results of using the pattern.

Background

Hive makes Hadoop development easy for programmers who are familiar with SQL and have worked on RDBMS. Hive uses HDFS for the physical storage of the data and it gives a table-level abstraction from a logical perspective. Hive implements its own SQL-like dialect, HiveQL, to access data and manipulate it. HiveQL provides operators, such as SELECT, GROUP, and JOIN, that are converted into MapReduce before being executed on the Hadoop cluster.

In the enterprises, Hive has gained widespread acceptance for use cases of data warehouses, BI-analytics, dashboards, and so on. All these use cases have the common thread of data in Hive being already cleansed, properly labeled, type casted, and neatly organized in tables so that any ad-hoc query or report can be generated effortlessly. Contrasting with this situation is the one with Pig, whose use cases have to deal with freshly minted data from varied sources, which is messy and without a name, category, or metadata associated to make sense out of it. Hence, the relevance of Pig in researching the data itself: to create a quick prototype and find sense in the seeming randomness of the schema-less data.

The storage of Hive data in HDFS is done through the serialization of Hive table's content into a physical file that can be stored in the HDFS. In the context of Hive, the HDFS is used to provide the features of high availability, fault tolerance, and the ability to run MapReduce on the Hive-specific files. Currently, Hive supports four different files for storage: plain text file, binary sequence file, ORC file, and the RCFile. Each of these file formats have their own serialization and deserialization functions associated, which converts the table-level abstraction of the data stored in Hive into a file that is stored in the HDFS.

Hive stores the information about what goes into the physical files in an external metadata store implemented on an RDBMS (Derby by default and MySQL by choice). This metadata store contains all the information of tables, schema, types, physical file mapping, and so on. Whenever a user performs a data manipulation operation, this metastore is first queried for the whereabouts of the data and then the actual data is accessed.

Motivation

Hive stores the data in a ready-to-use format for ad-hoc analytics and reporting. The data ingestion pattern is relevant to the Hive data that is ingested and integrated with the newly arrived data in the Pig data pipeline; then the combined data from Hive and Pig is aggregated, summarized, and transformed for further use in advanced analytical models.

The data egress pattern is applicable to the data already existing in a Pig data pipeline and there are ways to store it directly into a Hive table.

The external Hadoop ecosystem components, such as Pig, HBase, or MapReduce, access Hive data by understanding which storage format (text, RCFile, or sequence file) is used to store Hive data in HDFS, along with the metadata information of the tables and schemas from the metastore.

This ingress and egress design patterns describe ways to read and write data to and from Hive using Pig.

 Similar to HBase, we load Hive files that are already in HDFS. This is in contrast to MongoDB where we read the data directly from an external source and not from HDFS.

Use cases

The primary use case of the Hive ingest design pattern is to provide Pig access to the data stored in Hive. Pig uses this data for the following reasons:

- To integrate it with other unstructured sources
- To cleanse and transform the combined data
- To aggregate and summarize using a combination of other data sources in the Pig pipeline

The primary use case of the Hive egress design pattern is to provide a mechanism for the transformed data in the Pig pipeline to be stored in the Hive table. You may consider using this design pattern for the following purposes:

- To export data to Hive after integrating it with external data in the Pig data pipeline
- To export cleansed and transformed data to Hive from the Pig data pipeline
- To export aggregates to Hive or to some other downstream systems for the purpose of further processing or analytics

Pattern implementation

The following sections describes the pattern implementation of Hive ingest pattern followed by Hive egress:

The ingress implementation

The following are the two ways to load the Hive data into a Pig Latin relation:

- One way is to explicitly specify the deserializer to retrieve data from Hive. As an illustration, `HiveColumnarLoader` is a deserializer for Pig and is specific to data loaded or serialized into Hive using the RCFile format. Similarly, we can use Piggybank's `SequenceFileLoader` to load data already stored in the `SequenceFile` format from Hive. Both these examples are closely coupled with the location of the files, the format of the schemas used to store them, if compression is used or not, and so on.
- The second way is to use the HCatalog's capability to accomplish the loading of Hive data into Pig. This process has many advantages compared to the previous point. HCatalog provides an abstract way of looking at the storage of the files. It wraps the metastore and the storage information from the HDFS to provide a uniform perspective of accessing the tables. Using HCatalog, you no longer need to worry about the storage location of the file, the format of the schema, or if the compression is used or not. All you have to specify is the table name to the HCatalog loader and it does the necessary plumbing behind the scenes to diagram out the underlying storage format, location, and schema. The user is now made agnostic of the table's location, partitions, schema, compression type, and storage format. HCatalog simplifies this through a table-level abstraction and does the hard work under the covers.

The egress implementation

The egress design pattern is implemented using the HCatalog capability to store the data from a Pig relation into a Hive table. HCatalog provides an HCatStorer interface, which stores the contents of a Pig relation into a Hive table managed by HCatalog. For more information on why HCatalog interfaces are the best choice to perform load and store operations, please refer to the second point in the previous *The ingress implementation* section.

The approach followed by these design patterns is illustrated in the following diagram:

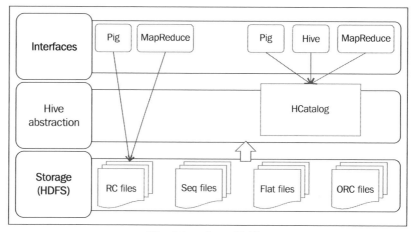

Hive integration with Pig

Code snippets

The following code example uses a sample retail transactions dataset. It contains attributes such as `Transaction ID`, `Date`, `Customer ID`, `Amount`, `Category`, `Product`, `City`, `State`, and `Spend by`. This data is already stored in Hive to illustrate this example. The Hive's native storage RCFile, which has the contents for this table, is used to illustrate direct access; `HCatalogLoader` is also illustrated in the next example.

The ingress Code

The following code illustrates ingesting data from Hive.

Importing data using RCFile

The following code illustrates the usage of `HiveColumnarLoader` that loads data from a Hive table stored in a RCFile:

```
/*
Register the Piggybank jar file to be able to use the UDFs in it
*/
REGISTER '/usr/share/pig/contrib/piggybank/java/piggybank.jar';

-- Register Hive common and exec jars
REGISTER '/usr/lib/hive/lib/hive-common-0.11.0.1.3.0.0-107.jar';
REGISTER '/usr/lib/hive/lib/hive-exec-0.11.0.1.3.0.0-107.jar';

/*
Load retail_transactions_rc  RCfile and specify the names of the
  columns of the table and their types in the constructor of
  HiveColumnarLoader.
*/
transactions = LOAD '/apps/hive/warehouse/transactions_db.db/retail_
transactions_rc'
  USING org.apache.pig.piggybank.storage.
  HiveColumnarLoader('transaction_no int,transaction_date
  string,cust_no int,amount double,category string,product
  string,city string,state string,spendby string');

/*
* Some processing logic goes here which is deliberately left out
  to improve readability
*/

/*
Display the contents of the relation transactions on the console
*/
DUMP transactions;
```

Importing data using HCatalog

The following code illustrates the loading of data from Hive using HCatalog:

```
/*
Specify the table name as the input to the HCatLoader function
  provided by HCatalog.
This function abstracts the storage location, files type, schema
  from the user and takes only the table name as input
*/
```

```
transactions = LOAD 'transactions_db.retail_transactions' USING
    org.apache.hcatalog.pig.HCatLoader();

/*
* Some processing logic goes here which is deliberately left out
  to improve readability
*/

/*
Display the contents of the relation transactions on the console
*/
DUMP transactions;
```

The egress code

The following code illustrates the egression of data to Hive using HCatStorer:

```
-- Register piggybank and hcatalog-pig-adapter jars
REGISTER '/usr/share/pig/contrib/piggybank/java/piggybank.jar';
REGISTER '/usr/lib/hcatalog/share/hcatalog/hcatalog-pig-
    adapter.jar';

/*
Load the transactions dataset into the relation transactions
*/
transactions = LOAD '/user/cloudera/pdp/datasets/hive/retail_
transactions.csv' USING
    org.apache.pig.piggybank.storage.CSVLoader() AS
    (transaction_no:int, transaction_date:chararray, cust_no:int,
    amount:double, category:chararray, product:chararray,
    city:chararray, state:chararray, spendby:chararray);

/*
* Some processing logic goes here which is deliberately left out to
improve readability
*/

/*
Specify the Hive table name transactions_db.retail_transactions as
    the input to the HCatStorer function.
The contents of the relation transactions are stored into the Hive
    table.
*/
STORE transactions INTO 'transactions_db.retail_transactions'
    using org.apache.hcatalog.pig.HCatStorer();
```

Results

After applying the ingest design pattern, the data in Hive tables is loaded in a Pig relation and is ready to be further processed. While using HCatLoader, it is important to interpret correctly how the data types of HCatalog are mapped to Pig types. All the primitive types of Pig are mapped to their HCatalog's corresponding types, except for the bytearray type that is mapped to binary in HCatalog. In the complex data types, the map of HCatalog is mapped to a map in Pig, a list of HCatalog is mapped to a bag in Pig, and struct of HCatalog is mapped to a tuple in Pig.

Applying the egress design pattern, the data in the Pig relation is stored in the Hive tables to report and perform ad-hoc analyses in Hive. All the schema conversion rules mentioned for HCatLoader in the previous paragraph are applicable to HCatStorer too. The HCatStorer class takes a string parameter that represents the key-value pair of a partitioned table. If you want to store the contents of a Pig relation in a partitioned table, this argument should be mandatorily specified.

Additional information

- `http://pig.apache.org/docs/r0.11.0/api/org/apache/pig/piggybank/storage/HiveColumnarLoader.html`
- `https://cwiki.apache.org/confluence/display/Hive/HCatalog+LoadStore`

The complete code and datasets for this section is in the following GitHub directories:

- `chapter2/code/`
- `chapter2/datasets/`

The ingress and egress patterns for semi-structured data

This section describes design patterns for semi-structured data such as XML, JSON, and the mainframe data. We have chosen XML and JSON as they are the most popular encoding formats for Internet data exchange. There is a wealth of data locked in documents, journals, and content management systems that could potentially be benefitted through analytics. The choice of the mainframe data for this use case is primarily due to the fact that this is a relatively unexplored territory in many enterprises that could gain eventual popularity as new patterns emerge.

The mainframe ingestion pattern

The mainframe ingestion pattern describes how you can use Pig Latin to ingest the data exported from mainframes into the Hadoop File System to be further processed on your data pipeline.

We will discuss the relevance of processing data stored in the mainframe to the enterprise, and get a deeper understanding of the various ways in which the mainframe stores the data internally and accesses it. We will also discuss the motivation to perform the ingest and the use cases where the mainframe data is used in conjunction with Pig. You will also understand how Pig makes the ingestion of this data a lot more intuitive (using UDFs) than doing it using MapReduce code written in Java.

The subsequent discussion of the implementation-level detail of this pattern is meant to familiarize you with the important concepts and alternatives as applicable. An example code snippet is used to enable the better understanding of the pattern from the Pig language perspective, followed by the results of using the pattern.

Background

Mainframes seem to have a long life ahead, and it is hard to imagine a world without these workhorses crunching those transactions continuously for decades. Such is the stability of these machines that even at extreme throughput of data, they perform faithfully without ever blinking for a second. No wonder these wonders of engineering have been the backbone of businesses ranging from aircrafts and automobiles to financial services and governments by selling, tracking, inserting, and updating every transaction for these entities continuously for years at a stretch.

With the experience of powering the industrial revolution in the 1960s, the mainframes have evolved with time, to become even more powerful and handle the specific high throughput transactional workloads they are designed for. Today, they use custom-built processors and other high-end hardware to implement virtualization, scale vertically, and exhibit transactional integrity, despite extreme throughput. Mainframes can clearly deliver superlative results than any other architecture at extreme throughput combined with unbelievably high-availability levels with reliability and top-notch security baked in.

Motivation

Hadoop is increasingly playing a vital role to offload much of the transactional data from mainframes and perform batch processing on it. This is in tune with improving the transaction throughput and batch processing times for the mainframes, by moving the processing from an expensive and custom-built system to the commodity hardware housing the Hadoop framework. Similarly, when the batch processing capability of a mainframe is not efficiently scalable (within a price point versus performance band), it is advantageous to offload processing to Hadoop, which does it at a better price/performance ratio. This is represented in the following diagram:

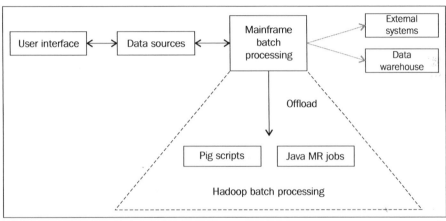

Mainframe batch processing and offloading to Hadoop

Use cases

This design pattern can be applied to address the following use cases:

- To migrate data from mainframes to Pig for integration with data from other systems and create advanced analytics
- To offload noncritical batch workloads to Pig and free up the mainframe throughput considerably
- To rewrite COBOL code in Pig to bring in the advantages of reuse, maintainability, simplicity, and compactness

Pattern implementation

By offloading, the relevant processing to Hadoop implies rewriting the code written in COBOL to MapReduce and transferring data from the mainframes.

COBOL is the *lingua franca* for the mainframes to access databases such as DB2, perform batch processing, and process online transactions. It is not suitable to implement sophisticated algorithms on, which could benefit newer business requirements such as risk modeling, predictive analytics, and so on.

To migrate the COBOL code to MapReduce, we can choose parts of functionalities implemented in the mainframe that are amenable to the constructs of a mapper and reducer. As an illustration, the legacy COBOL code to sort billions of records, merge them with other data sources and group them, and performe complex transformations can be implemented in Pig more efficiently than COBOL. Add to the Pig code the power of a Java UDF, which performs advanced analytics on the data pipeline; this combination could work wonders. Thus, migrating code to Pig Latin to perform specific processing effectively could pay rich dividends.

Migrating the mainframe data has its own set of challenges. Typically, mainframes internally store various types of data in VSAM files, flat files, and a DBMS. For Hadoop to access this data, it has to be converted into a format it can comprehend and then physically transfer it through a file transfer mechanism to the Hadoop cluster. VSAM files can be converted into flat files for Hadoop consumption using specific utilities such as IDCAMS.

Every mainframe DBMS have their specialized utilities that understand the DBMS internal file storage format and convert them to flat files. We may have to deal with the conversion of these flat files from one code page in the mainframes to another in the target machines of the Hadoop cluster. Generally, the flat files exported from the mainframes are in the denormalized CSV format. This is represented in following diagram:

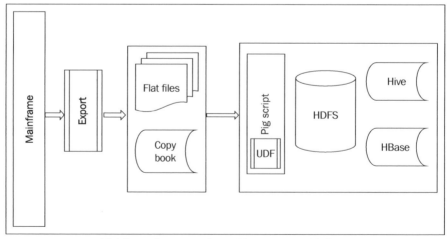

Mainframe data extraction and ingestion into Hadoop

To understand the physical layout and definition of each column in the CSV format, a mainframe-specific copybook is used. In Hadoop, this information provided by the copybook is used as a schema to parse the CSV and decode the meaning of the contents of the CSV file. Thus, the ingestion of the mainframe data requires two inputs: one is the flat file itself and the other is the copybook.

Pig has a built-in loader that can read CSV files, but the parsing has to be done on the CSV in conjunction with the contents of the copybook. Hence, a Java UDF or a custom loader has to be written to accomplish this.

Code snippets

The following code example uses a dataset that has sample vehicle insurance claims data related to vehicle repair charges claims, from a mainframe to a CSV file. The metadata and physical layout of the data elements in the VSAM file is defined in the copybook. The copybook contains fields such as `claim`, `policy`, `vehicle`, `customer`, and `garage details`. The Java code snippet in the following section parses the copybook, retrieves the metadata, and uses it to load the data in the CSV file.

The following Pig script uses a custom loader implementation to load data extracted from mainframes into a CSV file. Here, the `VSAMLoader` uses the copybook file to determine the metadata of the CSV file and loads it:

```
/*
Register custom UDF vsamloader.jar and  cb2java jar which is a
  dynamic COBOL copybook parser for Java
*/
REGISTER '/home/cloudera/pdp/jars/vsamloader.jar';
REGISTER '/home/cloudera/pdp/jars/cb2java0.3.1.jar';


/*
Load the contents of the automobile insurance claims dataset using
  custom UDF.
VSAMLoader uses the copybook file to parse the data and returns
  the schema to be used to load the data
*/
data = LOAD '/user/cloudera/pdp/datasets/vsam/automobile_
  insurance_claims_vsam.csv' USING
  com.mycustomloader.vsamloader.VSAMLoader();


/*
* Some processing logic goes here which is deliberately left out
  to improve readability
*/
```

```
-- Display the contents of the relation data on the console
DUMP data;

-- Display the schema of the relation data
DESCRIBE data;
```

The following is a Java code snippet of VSAMLoader, which is a custom
loader implementation:

```
@Override
public ResourceSchema getSchema(String arg0, Job arg1) throws
   IOException {
     .

     .
  while (it.hasNext()) {
    Map.Entry pairs = (Map.Entry) it.next();
    //Get the next key/value pairs
    String key = (String) pairs.getKey();
    String value = (String) pairs.getValue();
    /*For Group and Alphanumeric types in copybook, return
    pig compliant type chararray*/
    if (value.toString()
    .equals("class net.sf.cb2java.copybook.Group")
    || value.toString().equals("class
      net.sf.cb2java.copybook.AlphaNumeric")){
        fieldSchemaList.add(new FieldSchema(key,
          org.apache.pig.data.DataType.CHARARRAY));
      }
    /*For Decimal type in copybook, return
    pig compliant type integer*/
    else if (value.toString()
    .equals("class net.sf.cb2java.copybook.Decimal")){
      fieldSchemaList.add(new FieldSchema(key,
        org.apache.pig.data.DataType.INTEGER));
    }
    // Else return default bytearray
    else
    {
        fieldSchemaList.add(new FieldSchema(key,
        org.apache.pig.data.DataType.BYTEARRAY));
    }
    }
  return new ResourceSchema(new Schema(fieldSchemaList));
}
```

In the custom loader code of the `vsamloader` jar implementation, we use an external API to parse the copybook file and get all the values. We then implement an interface called `LoadMetaData` from Pig API and its `getSchema()` method, which will return the schema that we obtained by parsing the copybook. An `ArrayList` class of type `FieldSchema` is used, which will eventually be populated with the column names and their data types in the copybook file. This `ArrayList` is returned as the new schema, which will be used by Pig while it is loading the VSAM file.

Results

The result of applying the pattern on the data extract of the mainframe is the loading of the data in the flat file into the Pig Latin relation, ready to be further processed. As there are no ready-made functionalities available in Pig to understand the copybook format, we have extended Pig through a custom loader. Care has to be taken to properly map the schema in the custom loader as not all data types of COBOL can be readily mapped to the Java counterparts. For example, COBOL has limited support for Boolean and datetype and we have to implement specialized conversion to process it in Java to get accurate results. Please see the links in the next section for more information.

Additional information

- `http://pig.apache.org/docs/r0.11.1/udf.html#load-store-functions`
- `http://pic.dhe.ibm.com/infocenter/dmanager/v7r5/index.jsp?topic=%2Fcom.ibm.dserver.rulestudio%2FContent%2FBusiness_Rules%2F_pubskel%2FInfocenter_Primary%2Fps_DS_Rule_Designer772.html`
- `http://www.3480-3590-data-conversion.com/article-reading-cobol-layouts-1.html`

The complete code and datasets for this section is in the following GitHub directories:

- `chapter2/code/`
- `chapter2/datasets/`

XML ingest and egress patterns

This section describes how you can use Pig Latin to ingest and egress the contents of documents or logs encoded with XML to and from the Hadoop File System to be further processed on your data pipeline.

We will discuss the relevance of processing the data stored in XML to the enterprise and understand the various ways in which Pig can be used to access XML data (raw XML and binary). You will understand the pros and cons of using raw and binary XML parsing and then comprehend the motivation and the use cases where the XML data is used in conjunction with Pig. You will also understand how Pig makes the ingestion of this data a lot more intuitive and efficient (by using Avro) than doing it using the MapReduce code written in Java.

The subsequent discussion of the implementation-level detail of this pattern is meant to familiarize you with the important concepts and alternatives as applicable. An example code snippet is used to enable the better understanding of the pattern from the Pig language perspective, followed by the results of using the pattern.

Background

XML is one of the most widely used protocol for storage and transfer of data in an intuitive way, that makes comprehending the meaning of data relatively easy for humans and machines alike. XML, being a textual format rather than a binary format, has the special ability to encode data with its relevant metadata to clarify the meaning on its own. Owing to this feature, XML has become the defacto standard of data transmission for most Internet applications. The versatility of XML is evidenced in the fact that it can represent not only documents but haphazard data structures in web services. Today, we see that there are thousands of XML-based taxonomies, information exchange formats, and document formats —such as MS Office, SOAP, RSS, XHTML, and ATOM—that are being widely used. All these XML-based data storage and transmission formats contain a wealth of information from an analytics perspective.

Motivation

Using Hadoop for the ingestion and egress of XML is an inherently complex job and has some tradeoffs with flexibility. The complexity arises from the arbitrary nesting, and the space required for the metadata itself could be phenomenal. While XML gives you the flexibility to mimic the real world by encoding data with lots of metadata information by the inclusion of tags and other optional fields in the XML, this evidently results in the deep nesting of the attributes, and makes the computation even more complex and time-consuming over vast amounts of data. This implies that loading an XML document into the memory of a computer is a nontrivial, complex CPU-intensive job.

Owing to the abovementioned complexities, Hadoop offers multiple benefits to process large and complex XML data faster, using less costly operations by ingesting, transforming, and egressing XML for further consumption by downstream systems. To handle XML in Hadoop, you may have to consider the nature of processing the XML data and its context.

Motivation for ingesting raw XML

One reason to ingest and process XML in Hadoop is when you do not know the schema of the XML ahead of time and want to understand the schema as you read the files. The highlights of this approach are given as follows:

- The XML data is loaded in its raw format, its schema is discovered at the time of querying, and its transformation is performed after the discovery
- This approach is more exploratory in nature; it offers fast initial loads since the data is not cleaned up or stored in the binary format using serialization
- It supports greater flexibility so that more than one schema can be used to parse the XML for different types of analytic queries
- It is suitable for well-defined formats that could result in the XML data being parsed for every query with a slight hit on the query's performance.

Motivation for ingesting binary XML

The other reason to ingest and process XML in Hadoop is when you already know the schema of the XML and you want to perform high-performance queries on the XML. The highlights of this approach are as follows:

- The XML has to be parsed initially, serialized to disc in the binary format, split across nodes, compressed, and optimized for querying
- This approach works if there is a huge amount of cleansing and reformatting required at the load time
- It is suitable if there is a need to perform repetitive queries on the production workloads
- This approach is not very suitable if the schema is not known at the time of the load as it takes a long time to load, preprocess, and store the XML in a format that can be queried.

Motivation for egression of XML

Hadoop can be used to create and output XML files from structured data such as CSV, Hive tables, and so on, residing in HDFS. The XML files can be also be ingested directly into Hadoop so that they can be validated or transformed using Pig and written back as XML to conform to the exchange format of the downstream systems.

Use cases

The XML ingestion pattern can be used in the following use cases to address the following:

- It can be used for the ingestion of XML-based document data from content management systems such as technical documents, reference manuals, and journals. The ingestion is done prior to creating search indexes using Lucene and performing analytics on it.

- It can be adopted for the ingestion of XML logs that contain SOAP and EDXL-CAP kind of messaging texts for the request and response analysis between systems. As an example, XML-encoded messages can be picked up from the network fault management systems and analytics performed to understand or predict future failure of subsystems.

The XML egress pattern can be used in cases where it is needed to convert the structured data in HDFS (delimited flat files or hive tables) to be processed and serialized into XML, so that the upstream systems can use the XML to further process the data.

Pattern implementation

Pig provides constructs to directly load raw XML files, and supports the loading of the preprocessed XML files.

The implementation of the XML raw ingestion

The Piggybank library provides the XMLLoader function to access the contents of the XML file. The parameter of the XMLLoader function is an XML tag name that is converted internally into a single record tuple. This record contains the text enclosed within the start XML tag and the end XML tag. Using the returned tuple from the XML file, you may have to perform further parsing to decompose the record-level XML value to its constituent values; typically, a regex function, REGEX_EXTRACT, is used on a flattened projection.

The implementation of the XML binary ingestion

Converting XML into a binary format amenable for the purpose of splitting, is a two-step process.

- In the first step, in order to parse the XML document, the file can be completely read into a memory-based data structure, and a parser such as DOM can be used to randomly access all elements of the data. Alternatively, you can access the contents of the file in a serial fashion and control the parsing one step at a time. This can be done with the XML SAX parser and it is slightly slower to perform. The DOM parsing has the advantage of chaining multiple processors, but it is difficult to program, while the SAX parsing has the advantage of easy programmability and the ease of splitting. However, on the flipside, SAX is slow to perform as it is a serial access mechanism to parse the XML document.

- In the second step, to convert the parsed XML into a splittable binary format that Hadoop can process, Avro is the best choice to perform serialization that meets these criteria, and it helps to convert the XML document to a byte stream for storage in the on-disk format. Avro is specifically designed for Hadoop, making it a highly compressible and splittable binary format, which is very similar to the sequence files. Unlike the sequence files, which are accessible only through Java API, Avro files can be accessed from other languages such as C, C++, C#, Ruby, and Python. Using its unique format for interoperability, the Avro files can be transferred from being code written in one language to a different code written in another language, even from a complied language such as C to a scripting one such as Pig.

- Each Avro file wraps the underlying contents of the XML file with metadata that contains information needed to deserialize or read the contents. Avro stores both the metadata and the actual contents of the file together in a single file, making it simpler for other programs to understand the metadata first and then process the embedded data. Typically, the metadata is stored in the JSON format and the data is stored in the binary format.

- The Avro file also includes a marker that is used to split the data on the multiple nodes of the cluster. Before accessing the serialized Avro file, the XML file has to be preparsed into the Avro format, which is read into Pig Latin's relations by the usage of piggybank's `AvroStorage`.

The above implementation aspects are depicted in the following diagram:

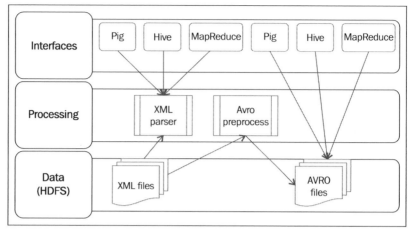

XML data ingress and egress

Code snippets

The following code example uses an XML dataset that has MedlinePlus health discussions.

The XML raw ingestion code

The XML data consists of tags for data elements such as topic title, the relevant URL, primary language, date, vocabulary, summary, membership, and other related health topics and content in other languages. The following code snippet parses the XML tags and loads the contents as a relation into the Pig Latin script:

```
-- Register piggybank jar
REGISTER '/home/cloudera/pig-
   0.11.0/contrib/piggybank/java/piggybank.jar';

/*
XMLLoader accesses the specified XML file and retrieves the record
   level value to be stored in the tuple data specified by the
   parameter to the XMLLoader.
*/
data = LOAD '/user/cloudera/pdp/datasets/xml/mplus_topics_2013-09-
   26.xml' USING org.apache.
   pig.piggybank.storage.XMLLoader('article');

/*
```

```
* Some processing logic goes here which is deliberately left out
  to improve readability
*/

/*
Print the contents of the relation data to the console
*/
DUMP data;
```

The XML binary ingestion code

The following code performs the binary ingestion of XML:

```
-- Register piggybank jar
REGISTER '/usr/share/pig/contrib/piggybank/java/piggybank.jar';


-- Register Avro and JSON jar files
REGISTER '/home/cloudera/pdp/jars/avro-1.7.4.jar';
REGISTER '/home/cloudera/pdp/jars/json-simple-1.1.1.jar';


/*
Assign the alias AvroStorage to piggybank's AvroStorage UDF
*/
DEFINE AvroStorage org.apache.pig.piggybank.
  storage.avro.AvroStorage();

/*
Load the dataset using the alias AvroStorage into the relation
  health_topics
*/
health_topics = LOAD '/user/cloudera/pdp/datasets/xml/mplus-
  topics_2013-09-26.avro' USING AvroStorage;


/*
* Some processing logic goes here which is deliberately left out
  to improve readability
*/

-- Print the contents of the relation health_topics to the console
DUMP health_topics;
```

The flow of steps involved in the conversion of the XML file to AVRO is depicted in following diagram:

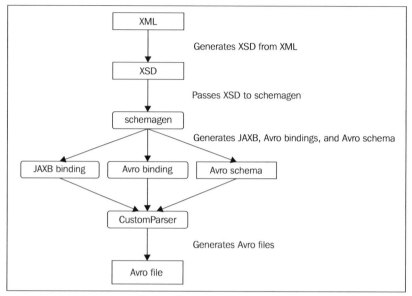

XML to Avro pre-processing

We have used a third-party tool to generate the XSD from the given XML file and schemagen to generate JAXB, Avro bindings, and Avro schema. Internally, schemagen uses the JAXB binding compiler XJC; then it generates a code model from the XSD schema file. The XJC plugin is then executed, which creates the JSON-formatted Avro schemas. The XJC plugin invokes Avro's Java schema compiler to generate new Java classes for serialization to and from Avro.

The XML egress code

The following is the Pig script to convert the contents of the CSV file into an XML format.

Pig script

A custom storage function XMLStorage is used to accomplish the conversion of the CSV file's contents into an XML format:

```
/*
Register custom UDF jar that has a custom storage function
  XMLStorage to store the data into XML file.
*/
```

```
REGISTER '/home/cloudera/pdp/jars/xmlgenerator.jar';

/*
Load the transactions dataset using PigStorage into the relation
  transactions
*/
transactions = LOAD '/user/cloudera/pdp/datasets/hbase/transactions.
csv' USING
  PigStorage( ',' ) AS (
    listing_id: chararray,
    transaction_date: chararray,
    customer_id: int,
    age: chararray,
    residence_area: chararray,
    product_subclass: int,
    product_id: long,
    amount: int,
    asset: int,
    sales_price: int);

/*
* Some processing logic goes here which is deliberately left out
  to improve readability
*/

/*
Custom UDF XMLStorage generates the XML file and stores it in the
  xml folder
*/
STORE transactions INTO '/user/cloudera/pdp/output/xml' USING
  com.xmlgenerator.XMLStorage();
```

The XML storage

The following is the code for the XML storage:

```
protected void write(Tuple tuple)
  {
    // Retrieving all fieds from the schema
    ResourceFieldSchema[] fields = schema.getFields();

    //Retrieve values from tuple
    List<Object> values = tuple.getAll();
```

```
/*creating xml element by using fields as element tag
and tuple value as element value*/
Element transactionElement =
xmlDoc.createElement(XMLStorage.elementName);
for(int counter=0;counter<fields.length;counter++)
{
  //Retrieving element value from value
  String columnValue =
  String.valueOf(values.get(counter));
  //Creating element tag from fields
  Element columnName =
  xmlDoc.createElement(fields[counter].getName().
    toString().trim());
  //Appending value to element tag
  columnName.appendChild
  (xmlDoc.createTextNode(columnValue));
  //Appending element to transaction element
  transactionElement.appendChild(columnName);
}
//Appending transaction element to root element
rootElement.appendChild(transactionElement);
}
```

The `write` method takes a tuple, which represents a row in the CSV file, as an input. This method creates an XML element for each field in the tuple. The process is repeated for all the rows in the CSV and consequently, an XML file is generated.

Results

The result of applying the pattern on the medline XML files is the loading of the data into the Pig Latin relation, which is ready to be further processed. Make sure that the XML file is formatted properly and all the elements have start and end tags, else `XMLLoader` could return an invalid value.

Applying the egress design pattern, the data in the relation transactions is written as an XML file in the specified path.

Additional information

- http://pig.apache.org/docs/r0.11.0/api/org/apache/pig/piggybank/storage/XMLLoader.html
- http://pig.apache.org/docs/r0.11.0/api/org/apache/pig/piggybank/storage/avro/AvroStorage.html

The complete code and datasets for this section is in the following GitHub directories:

- `chapter2/code/`
- `chapter2/datasets/`

JSON ingress and egress patterns

The JSON ingestion pattern describes how you can use Pig Latin to ingest and egress data represented as JSON to and from the Hadoop File System to further process it in the data pipeline.

We will discuss the relevance of processing the data stored in JSON to the enterprise and understand the various ways in which Pig can be used to access and store the JSON data (simple JSON and nested JSON). You will understand the pros and cons of using simple JSON and nested JSON parsing, comprehend the motivation, and the use cases where JSON data is used in conjunction with Pig. You will also understand how Pig makes the ingestion of this data a lot more intuitively (by using external libraries such as elephant-bird) than doing it using the MapReduce code written in Java.

The subsequent discussion of the implementation-level detail of this pattern is meant to familiarize you with the important concepts and alternatives, as applicable. An example code snippet is used to enable the better understanding of the pattern from the Pig language perspective, followed by the results of using the pattern.

Background

JSON is one more way of structuring text. JSON is a data interchange format that describes the data in a hierarchical way, so that machines and humans alike can read and perform operations on it.

JSON represents data in a much simpler way, more like the key-value pairs where the values can be very primitive, such as integers, strings, and arrays. JSON is not designed to support extremely complex and nested data types like XML does. It is less verbose and requires just a look-up function to retrieve the values, since the data is stored in key-value pairs. This makes JSON very compact and suitable to represent data more efficiently, unlike XML. In XML, data is represented in a complex nested way with rich data types, making parsing XML trees very intricate. In the real world, JSON is used to store simple data types and XML is used to model the complexity of data types, which offers features that let you be more expressive about the structure of the data.

Motivation

The rise of JSON as one of the most popular standard for data representation is largely due to the strong rise of social web companies, such as LinkedIn, Twitter, and Facebook. These enterprises along with many other firms, which have the need to exchange their internal business data (such as social conversations or any data with a smaller footprint) with the external world, are predominantly moving toward using APIs that can carry simple and efficient payload without the complexities of XML. JSON is the preferred format for these APIs owing to its simplicity and implementation as a key-value data source, enabling the ease of parsing.

Along with the rise of social media, we can see the advent of NoSQL databases that have made JSON their mainstay. Many of these databases, such as MongoDB, CouchDB, and Riak, have JSON as their primary storage format. Owing to the usage of JSON, these databases exhibit extremely high-performance characteristics along with the ability to scale horizontally. These databases are designed specifically for the needs of Internet-scale applications where the need for real-time response is paramount.

There is also an accelerated proliferation of non-social media-centric enterprises, where JSON is used currently to storelog files that have multiple headers and other key-value pairs. The log data in the JSON format represents user sessions and user activities especially well, with information on each user activity nested under the session's information. This data nesting in the JSON format provides natural advantages while performing advanced analytics. JSON is also a good choice for enterprises dealing with the sensor data, containing varied attributes collected for different measurements.

While JSON excels as a storage format of choice to perform quick retrieval and carry Internet payloads more efficiently, there are many use cases (such as log processing and sensor analysis) where data represented in JSON is not only used for lookups, but also extensively integrated with other enterprise data assets to perform analytics. This integration implies the performing of batch processing on a combination of JSON and other structured data. The ingest design patterns discussed in the following sections describe ways to accomplish the JSON ingestion into the data pipeline.

The output of a batch processing data pipeline can sometimes be summarized into ready-to-use data represented in JSON. This is applicable in use cases where the batch-processed JSON output is fed into the NoSQL databases consuming JSON, and in cases where JSON can be used as a payload for web services. The egress design pattern shows how we can use Pig to perform the conversion of data stored in the data pipeline into the JSON format.

Use cases

The following are the use cases for Pig to ingest and egress JSON data:

- Use the ingestion design pattern to integrate JSON data into Pig relation so that the combined data in the data pipeline is used for analytics.

- Use the ingestion design pattern to consume JSON APIs from Twitter and other social media sources, to perform advanced analytics such as sentiment mining.

- Use the ingestion design pattern to ingest sensor data stored in JSON for machine failure analytics.

- Use the egress design pattern to store the contents of a flat file existing in HDFS into the JSON format. This pattern is also useful to store the results of complex data integration or transformation pipeline in JSON format for downstream system access.

Pattern implementation

The following sections show the ingress and egress implementations.

The ingress implementation

JSON can be loaded into a Pig relation using the JSONLoader function, which loads the contents of the JSON file into a map. The JSONLoader function can work with or without schema information.

- In case the schema information is provided in JSONLoader, the mapping between the Pig and JSON data types is straightforward and follows the schema specified.

- In case the schema information is not provided in JSONLoader, the Pig relation's data type is set to the default bytearray, and the actual schema is inferred later in the execution cycle. To process a large JSON file and perform parallel processing on it, you may have to format the JSON file with one JSON-object format per line. This prerequisite is applicable when you need to parse a very large JSON file that exceeds the size of the HDFS-storage block, and when you have control over the format of JSON to include one JSON object per line.

- In cases where JSON files cannot be formatted to include one JSON object per line, it is not possible for MapReduce to perform a split on the JSON file, since JSON is nested and the same element is used at various levels. The JSON format is in contrast with XML, which has a start and end tag to denote the boundaries of the nested data structure. The solution for this problem is addressed in the elephant-bird library's implementation of `LZOJSONLoader`, that allows the determining of the split boundaries of the nested JSON files. The elephant-bird library is an open source library of utilities for working with JSON and other formats, courtesy of Twitter. It is available at `https://github.com/kevinweil/elephant-bird`.

The egress implementation

Use the `JsonStorage` function to store the contents of a Pig relation in the JSON format. The content of the Pig relation is stored as a single JSON line in the output. While performing schema mapping, the `JsonStorage` function maps the Pig tuples to JSON objects. Similarly, it maps the Pig map to a JSON object, while the Pig bag corresponds to the JSON array.

The general idea of how JSON is ingested and egressed using Pig is depicted in the following diagram:

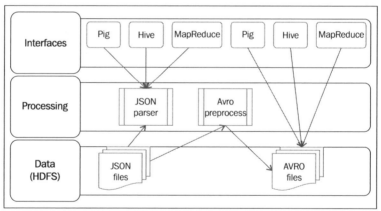

JSON Hadoop Integration

Code snippets

The following code example uses a sample dataset from the enron corpus, which has emails from 150 users with an average of 757 messages per user. The fields in the dataset are `Message ID`, `Date`, `From address`, `Subject of the email`, `Body of the email`, `To addresses`, `Addresses marked in cc`, and `Addresses marked in bcc`.

The ingress code

The following section shows the code and its explanation to ingest the data stored in the JSON format into a Pig relation.

The code for simple JSON

The code to load JSON files using `JsonLoader` is shown as follows:

```
/*
Use JSONLoader UDF, it takes in the parameter of the JSON schema
  and loads the contents of the JSON file emails.json into a map
  enron_emails
*/
enron_emails = LOAD '/user/cloudera/pdp/datasets/json/emails.json'
  USING JsonLoader('body:chararray, from:chararray, tos:chararray,
  ccs:chararray, bccs:chararray, date:chararray,
  message_id:chararray, subject:chararray');

/*
* Some processing logic goes here which is deliberately left out
  to improve readability
*/

/*
Display the contents of the relation enron_emails on the console
*/
DUMP enron_emails;
```

It is important to note that the `JsonLoader` does not use the `AS` clause to supply the schema.

The code for nested JSON

The Pig script to load nested JSON is shown as follows, and we use the elephant-bird libraries to accomplish this:

```
/*
Register elephant-bird and JSON jar files
*/
REGISTER '/home/cloudera/pdp/jars/elephant-bird-core-3.0.5.jar';
REGISTER '/home/cloudera/pdp/jars/elephant-bird-pig-3.0.5.jar';
REGISTER '/home/cloudera/pdp/jars/json-simple-1.1.1.jar';

/*
Use ElephantBird's JsonLoader for loading a nested JSON file
The parameter -nestedload denotes nested loading operation
```

```
*/
emails = LOAD '/user/cloudera/pdp/datasets/json/emails.json' USING
   com.twitter.elephantbird.pig.load.JsonLoader('-nestedLoad');

/*
* Some processing logic goes here which is deliberately left out
  to improve readability
*/

/*
Display the contents of the relation emails on the console
*/
DUMP emails;
```

The egress code

The following section shows the code and its explanation to egress data stored in a Pig relation to JSON format:

```
/*
Load the JSON file using JsonLoader to the relation enron_emails
*/
enron_emails = LOAD '/user/cloudera/pdp/datasets/json/emails.json'
   USING JsonLoader('body:chararray, from:chararray, tos:chararray,
   ccs:chararray, bccs:chararray, date:chararray,
   message_id:chararray, subject:chararray');

/*
* Some processing logic goes here which is deliberately left out
  to improve readability
*/

/*
Use JsonStorage to store the contents of the relation to a json
   file
*/
STORE enron_emails into '/user/cloudera/pdp/output/
   json/output.json' USING JsonStorage();
```

Results

Applying the ingest design pattern will result in the JSON data getting stored in a Pig relation. The `JsonLoader` stores a null in a Pig relation if the fields do not parse correctly, or if the they cannot be found. `JsonLoader` does not care about the order of the fields in the constructor; you can specify them in any order. `JsonLoader` parses them correctly as long as the field name matches. If there is a type mismatch, `JsonLoader` performs automatic typecasting based on the feasibility. It can cast an `int` to a `string`, but will not cast a `string` to an `int`. As best practice, you may consider using the `JsonLoader` function without the schema definition to understand the top-level view of all the keys in the JSON object and get a better overview of the data.

Applying the egress design pattern will result in data from a Pig relation stored in the JSON format. The `JsonStorage` function uses a buffering technique for storage in the JSON format. This buffering capability is used in the bulk loading of data and increases the performance of the storage. A fixed-size buffer in kilobytes can be specified in the `JsonStorage` constructor.

Additional information

- `http://pig.apache.org/docs/r0.11.1/func.html#jsonloadstore`
- `https://github.com/kevinweil/elephant-bird`
- `http://pig.apache.org/docs/r0.11.1/func.html#jsonloadstor`

The complete code and datasets for this section is in the following GitHub directories:

- `chapter2/code/`
- `chapter2/datasets/`

Summary

In this chapter, we started by understanding the types of data in the enterprise setting and explored the relevance of each of these data types, how they are used once they were inside the enterprise, and how Hadoop comes into the picture to process it.

In the subsequent sections, we began by looking at specific types of data more closely and applied the ingress and egress design patterns on it. We covered the most relevant data types from unstructured, structured, and semi-structured categories. We have also attempted to highlight design patterns for advanced data types such as images and mainframes to deliberate on the power of the Pig's adaptability and extensibility. In each of the design pattern showcased in this book, we began to understand the contextual relevance of the pattern from the background details, followed by the motivation and applicability of the pattern to a particular data type. The code and pattern implementation is discussed threadbare to ease the implementation aspects of the design pattern. We discussed why choosing Pig is better and talked about various options available to address specific cases within a design pattern.

In the next chapter, we will understand in greater detail the data profiling patterns that can be applied to various data formats. The goal of the next chapter is to make you adept in using Pig to *understand* the content, context, structure, and condition of data by profiling it. Pig provides a rich set of primitives to profile data and you will learn the appropriate design patterns to use in profiling enterprise-grade data. You will also learn to extend Pig's capability to cater to more advanced usages of data profiling.

3
Data Profiling Patterns

Time looking at your data is always well spent.

— Witten, et al

In the previous chapter, you studied the various patterns for ingesting and egressing different types of data into and from the Hadoop ecosystem, so that the next logical steps in the analytics process can begin. In this chapter, we will understand the most widely used design patterns related to data profiling. This chapter is all about a step-by-step approach to diagnose if your dataset has any problem, and ultimately turning the dataset into usable information.

Data profiling is a necessary first step in getting any meaningful insight into the data ingested by Hadoop, by understanding the content, context, structure, and condition of data.

The data profiling design patterns described in this chapter, collect important information on attributes of data in the Hadoop cluster, before initiating the process of cleaning the data into a more useful form. In this chapter, we will look at the following sections:

- Understanding the data profiling concepts and their implications in the context of Big Data
- Rationale for using Pig in data profiling
- Understanding the data type inference design pattern
- Understanding the basic statistical profiling design pattern
- Understanding the pattern-matching design pattern
- Understanding the string profiling design pattern
- Understanding the unstructured text profiling design pattern

Data profiling for Big Data

Bad data lurks in all of the data that is ingested by Hadoop, but its impact magnifies with the phenomenal volume and variety that constitutes Big Data. Working with missing records, malformed values, and wrong file formats amplifies the amount of wasted time. What drives us to frustration is seeing the amount of data that we can't use even though we have it, data that we have at hand and then lost, and data that was not the same as it was yesterday. In a Big Data analytics project, it is common to be handed an extremely huge dataset without a lot of information as to where it came from, how it was collected, what the fields mean, and so on. In many cases, the data has gone through many hands and multiple transformations since it was gathered, and nobody really knows what it all means anymore.

Data profiling is a measure of how good the data is and the fitness to process it in the subsequent steps. It simply indicates what is wrong with the data. Data profiling is the first short-burst analysis performed on the data to determine its suitability, understand challenges, and give a go/no-go decision early in a data-intensive endeavor. Data profiling activities provide you key insights into what the data ingested by Hadoop looks like from a qualitative perspective, and assesses the risk involved in integrating data with other sources before deriving any analytical insights. Sometimes, the profiling process is conducted at various stages in the analysis process to weed out bad data and to refine the analysis itself.

Data profiling plays a major role in improving the overall data quality, readability, and processability, by helping us understand the data from a business standpoint versus an analytical-insight standpoint. Building a data profiling framework within a Big Data information management platform such as Hadoop, ensures that the quality of data does not affect the results of reporting, analysis, forecasting, and other key business requirements that deal with decision making.

Traditionally, data profiling is done in relation to its intended use, where the purpose of using the data is defined well in advance. For Big Data projects, data may have to be used in ways not originally intended, and it has to be profiled accordingly, to address how data can be repurposed. This is due to the fact that most Big Data projects deal with exploratory analytics on ill-defined data that try to find out how the data can be used or repurposed. In order to do so, various quality measures, such as **completeness**, **consistency**, **coherence**, **correctness**, **timeliness**, and **reasonableness**, must be clearly articulated, measured, and made available to users.

In a Big Data project, metadata is collected to ascertain the data quality. This metadata includes the following:

- Data quality attributes
- Business rules
- Mappings
- Cleansing routines
- Data element profiles and measures

The measurement of data quality in a Big Data environment takes into account the following:

- Source of data
- Type of data
- The intended and unintended usage of the data
- The user group that will consume the data and the resultant analytical artifacts

Among the preceding points, the type of data plays a vital role on the data quality requirements, as outlined in the following points:

- **Profiling structured Big Data:** In a Big Data project that deals with a huge amount of structured data, an enterprise can reuse existing data quality processes that deal with relational databases, given they can scale to meet the requirements of a massive scale.

- **Profiling unstructured Big Data:** Social media related Big Data projects concern themselves with the quality issues that deal with entity extraction out of sentences expressed in non-standard language comprising of slangs and abbreviations. Analytical value from social media can be extracted by correlating it with structured transactional data, so that the relation between what is happening on the social web can be mapped to an organization's internal data, such as supply chain data or customer demographics data. To perform this kind of mapping, unstructured text has to be profiled to understand the following points:

    ◦ How to extract entities that are important for analytics
    ◦ How much of the data is misspelled
    ◦ What are the general abbreviations specific to a domain
    ◦ What criteria to use for the removal of stop words

- ○ How to perform stemming of the words
- ○ How to understand the contextual meaning of words based on preceding words

Big Data profiling dimensions

Profiling of Big Data is performed across multiple dimensions, and the choice of choosing a particular dimension, typically, depends on the analytical problem and balancing the time/quality trade-off. Some of the dimensions overlap and some are not applicable to the problem at all. The following are a few of the most important dimensions that measure the quality of Big Data:

- **Completeness:** This dimension is a measure to know if you have all the data required to answer your queries. To evaluate if your dataset is complete, start by understanding the answers that you wish to seek from the data, and determine the fields needed and the percentage of complete records required to comfortably answer these questions. The following are a few of the ways completeness can be determined:

  - ○ In cases where we have prior knowledge of the master data statistics (number of records, fields, and so on), completeness can be determined as a proportion of the ingested records to the number of master data records

  - ○ In cases where a master data statistics is not accessible, completeness is measured by the presence of **NULLS** in the following ways:

    - ○ **Attribute completeness**: It deals with the presence of NULLS in a specific attribute

    - ○ **Tuple completeness**: It deals with the number of unknown values of the attributes in a tuple

    - ○ **Value completeness**: It deals with missing complete elements or attributes in semi-structured XML data

  As one of the aspects of Big Data analysis is to ask questions that have not been asked before, checking for the completeness dimension assumes a newer meaning. In this scenario, you may consider performing an iterative *look ahead* for a generic range of questions you expect to be answered and *reason back* to figure out what sort of data is needed to answer these questions. A straightforward record-counting mechanism can be applied to check if the total expected records exist in the Hadoop cluster; but, for data size spanning petabytes, this activity can be onerous and has to be performed by applying statistical sampling. If the data is found to be incomplete, the missing records can be fixed, deleted, flagged, or ignored depending on the analytical use case.

- **Correctness:** This dimension measures the accuracy of the data. To find out if the data is accurate, you have to know what comprises inaccurate data, and this purely depends on the business context. In cases where data should be unique, duplicate data is considered inaccurate. Calculating the number of duplicate elements in data that is spread across multiple systems is a nontrivial job. The following techniques can be used to find out the measure of potential inaccuracy of data:

  ° In a dataset containing discrete values, a frequency distribution can give valuable insights into the potential inaccuracy of data; a value with relatively very low frequency could probably be incorrect.

  ° For strings, you can create string length distribution patterns and flag patterns with low frequency as potential suspects. Similarly, a string with atypical length could be flagged as incorrect.

  ° In the case of continuous attributes, you can use descriptive statistics, such as maximum and minimum to flag data as inaccurate.

  For Big Data projects, it is recommended to determine which subset of attributes are mandatory for accuracy, understand how much of the data should be accurate, and work on sampling the data to determine the accuracy

> It is important to note that in the classical *finding a needle in a haystack* kind of Big Data problem, there is a lot of analytical value hidden in inaccurate data, which can be considered as outliers. These outliers are not to be considered inaccurate, and they can be flagged and considered for further analysis in use cases such as fraud detection.

- **Coherence:** This dimension measures if the data makes sense relative to itself and determines whether records relate to each other in ways that are consistent, and follow the internal logic of the dataset. The measure of coherence of a dataset can be understood by the following methods:

  ° **Referential integrity:** This ensures that the relationships between tables remain consistent. In the Big Data context, referential integrity cannot be applied to data stored in NoSQL databases such as HBase, as there is no relational representation of the data.

  ° **Value integrity:** This ensures if the values in a table are consistent relative to themselves. Inconsistent data can be found by comparing values with a predefined set of possible values (from the master data).

Sampling considerations for profiling Big Data

Sampling of Big Data is done to understand the quality of the data, by analyzing only a subset of the population rather than reaching out to the entire population. One of the most important criteria to select a sample is its representativeness, which determines how closely the sampled subset resembles the population. Representativeness should be higher for an accurate result. Sampling size also has a considerable impact on the representative accuracy of the subset.

Sampling enormous volumes of data for profiling balances the cost-quality trade-offs, since it is very costly and complex to profile all of the population. Most of the time, the profiling activity is not devised as a mechanism to perform a full-fledged analysis on the entire data, but it is a first-pass analysis/discovery phase, to get the overall quality of data, from the Correctness, Coherence, and Completeness dimensions. The profiling activity is conducted iteratively as the data moves through the pipeline and helps in data refinement. For this reason, sampling of the data for profiling purposes has a very important role to play in Big Data.

While sampling is deemed necessary for profiling, it is recommended to tread with caution while applying sampling techniques to Big Data. Due to the implementation complexity and inapplicableness, not all data types and collection mechanisms may necessitate sampling; this is valid in cases of data that are ingested from sensors in near real time. Similarly, not all use cases may need sampling, and this is valid in cases where data is ingested for search, recommendation systems, and click stream analytics. In these cases, the data has to be looked at in its entirety, without recourse to sampling. In these cases, sampling can introduce certain biases and reduce the accuracy of the results.

The choice of appropriate sampling techniques has an impact on the overall accuracy for profiling. These techniques include non-probabilistic sampling and probabilistic sampling methods. Generally, we do not consider non-probabilistic methods to perform data profiling activities. We limit ourselves to probabilistic sampling methods, owing to the improved accuracy with less representational bias. For a better overview of the sampling techniques, please refer to the *Numerosity Reduction – Sampling Design Pattern* section in *Chapter 6, Understanding Data Reduction Patterns*.

Sampling support in Pig

Pig has native support for sampling through the usage of the SAMPLE operator. We have used the SAMPLE operator to illustrate how it works in the profiling context, using the basic statistical profiling design pattern. The SAMPLE operator helps you pick a random sample from the population using a probabilistic algorithm. The internal algorithm is quite rudimentary, and sometimes, not representative of the entire dataset that is being sampled. This algorithm internally uses the **simple random sampling technique**. The SAMPLE operator is in the process of being evolved to accommodate more esoteric sampling algorithms. More information on the path ahead can be found at https://issues.apache.org/jira/browse/PIG-1713.

Other ways to implement a robust sampling method within Pig are to extend it by using the UDF feature and by using Pig streaming.

Using Pig's extensibility feature, sampling can be implemented as a UDF, but it is complex and taxing to work with, since the biggest limitation of a UDF is that it takes only one input value and generates one output value.

You might also consider implementing sampling using streaming, which doesn't have the limitation of the UDFs. Streaming can take any number of inputs and emit any number of outputs. The language R has the needed functions to perform sampling and you can use these functions in the Pig script through Pig streaming. The limitations of this method are: it performs the sampling computation by holding most of the data in the main memory and R has to be installed on every data node of the Hadoop cluster for streaming to work.

The **Datafu** library of Pig utilities, from LinkedIn, has published a few of its own implementations for sampling. This library is now a part of Cloudera's Hadoop distribution. The following are the sampling techniques implemented by Datafu:

- **ReservoirSampling**: It generates random samples of a given size by using an in-memory reservoir
- **SampleByKey**: It generates a random sample from tuples based on a certain key. This internally uses the **Stratified Random Sampling** technique
- **WeightedSample**: It generates a random sample by assigning weights

Additional information on the Datafu sampling implementation can be found at http://linkedin.github.io/datafu/docs/current/datafu/pig/sampling/package-summary.html.

Rationale for using Pig in data profiling

Implementing the profiling code within the Hadoop environment reduces the dependency on external systems for quality checks. The high-level overview of implementation is depicted in the following diagram:

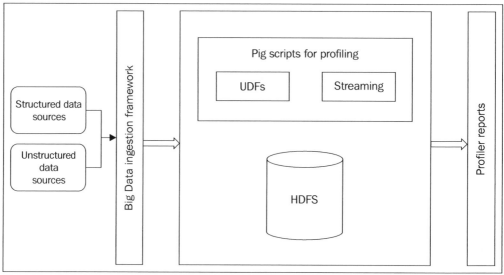

Implementing profiling in Pig

The following are the advantages of performing data profiling within the Hadoop environment using Pig:

- Implementing the design patterns in Pig reduces data movement by moving the profiling code directly to the data, resulting in performance gains and speeding up the analytics development process.

- By implementing the pattern in Pig, the data quality effort is performed alongside the data transformation in the same environment. This alleviates manual, redundant effort in performing repetitive data quality checks whenever data is ingested into Hadoop.

- Pig excels in situations where the ingested data's schema is unknown until runtime; its language features give data scientists flexibility to decipher the correct schemas at runtime and build prototype models.

- Pig's inherent ability to discover data schema and sampling gives it an edge to implement profiling code within the Hadoop environment.

- Pig has readily available functions that make writing the custom profiling code easier.

- Pig enables automating the profiling process by chaining complex profiling workflows, which comes in handy for datasets that are periodically updated.

Now that we have understood the data profiling concepts and the rationale of using Pig for profiling, we will explore few concrete design patterns in the following sections.

The data type inference pattern

This section describes the data type inference design pattern in which we use Pig scripts to capture important information about data types.

Background

Most of the ingested data in Hadoop has some associated metadata, which is a description of its characteristics. This metadata includes important information on the types of fields, their length, constraints, and uniqueness. We can also know if a field is mandatory. This metadata is also used in interpretation of the values by examining the scale, units of measurement, meaning of labels, and so on. Understanding the intended structure of a dataset helps in expounding its meaning, description, semantics, and the data quality. This analysis of data types helps us to grasp if they are syntactically consistent (different datasets having the same consistent format specification) and semantically consistent (different datasets having the same value set).

Motivation

The intent of this design pattern is to infer the data type metadata from the ingested data in Hadoop. This pattern helps you uncover the `Type` metadata that is compared to the actual data, to see if they do not agree and cause any far-reaching consequence to the analytics effort. Data types and the attributes values are scanned and compared with documented metadata, and based on this scanning, appropriate data types and data lengths are proposed.

This design pattern is used to review the structure of a dataset for which there is little or no existing metadata, or for which there are reasons to suspect the completeness or quality of existing metadata. The results of the pattern help to discover, document, and organize the "ground truth" regarding the dataset's metadata. Here, the results of data profiling are used to incrementally capture a knowledge base associated with data element structure, semantics, and its use.

Use cases

You can use this design pattern when an enormous volume of structured data has to be ingested, and there is an absence of documented knowledge about the dataset. If there is a need to use the undocumented data for further analysis or the need for deeper knowledge of the domain business terms, related data elements, their definitions, the reference datasets used, and structure of the attributes in the dataset, you can use this design pattern.

Pattern implementation

This pattern is implemented as a standalone Pig script that internally uses a Java UDF. The core concept in the implementation of this pattern is the discovery of the dominant data type in a column. Firstly, the column values are examined to understand if they belong to `int`, `long`, `double`, `string`, or `boolean` type. After the values are evaluated, each data type is grouped together to find the frequency. From this analysis, we can find out which one is the dominant (most frequent) data type.

Code snippets

To illustrate the working of this pattern, we have considered the retail transactions dataset stored on the **Hadoop Distributed File System (HDFS)**. It contains attributes, such as `Transaction ID`, `Transaction date`, `Customer ID`, `Phone Number`, `Product`, `Product subclass`, `Product ID`, `Sales Price`, and `Country Code`. For this pattern, we are interested in the values of the attribute `Customer ID`.

Pig script

The following is the Pig script illustrating the implementation of this pattern:

```
/*
Register the datatypeinferer and custom storage jar files
*/
REGISTER '/home/cloudera/pdp/jars/datatypeinfererudf.jar';
REGISTER
  '/home/cloudera/pdp/jars/customdatatypeinfererstorage.jar';

/*
Load the transactions dataset into the relation transactions
*/
```

```
transactions = LOAD
  '/user/cloudera/pdp/datasets/data_profiling/transactions.csv'
  USING  PigStorage(',') AS (transaction_id:long,
  transaction_date:chararray, cust_id:chararray, age:chararray,
  area:chararray, prod_subclass:int, prod_id:long, amt:int,
  asset:int, sales_price:int, phone_no:chararray,
  country_code:chararray);

/*
Infer the data type of the field cust_id by invoking the
DataTypeInfererUDF.
It returns a tuple with the inferred data type.
*/
data_types = FOREACH transactions GENERATE
  com.profiler.DataTypeInfererUDF(cust_id) AS inferred_data_type;

/*
Compute the count of each data type, total count, percentage.
The data type with the highest count is considered as dominant data
type
*/
grpd = GROUP data_types BY inferred_data_type;
inferred_type_count = FOREACH grpd GENERATE group AS
  inferred_type, COUNT(data_types) AS count;
grpd_inf_type_count_all = GROUP inferred_type_count ALL;
total_count = FOREACH grpd_inf_type_count_all GENERATE
  SUM(inferred_type_count.count) AS tot_sum,
  MAX(inferred_type_count.count) AS max_val;
percentage = FOREACH inferred_type_count GENERATE inferred_type AS
  type, count AS total_cnt,
  CONCAT((Chararray)ROUND(count*100.0/total_count.tot_sum),'%') AS
  percent,(count==total_count.max_val?'Dominant':'Other') AS
  inferred_dominant_other_datatype;
percentage_ord = ORDER percentage BY
  inferred_dominant_other_datatype ASC;

/*
CustomDatatypeInfererStorage UDF extends the StoreFunc. All the
abstract methods have been overridden to implement logic that writes
the contents of the relation into a file in a custom report like
format.
The results are stored on the HDFS in the directory datatype_inferer
*/
STORE percentage_ord INTO
  '/user/cloudera/pdp/output/data_profiling/datatype_inferer'
  using com.profiler.CustomDatatypeInfererStorage
  ('cust_id','chararray');
```

Java UDF

The following is the Java UDF code snippet:

```
@Override
  public String exec(Tuple tuples) throws IOException {

    String value = (String) tuples.get(0);
    String inferredType = null;
    try {
/*if tuples.get(0) is null it returns null else invokes getDataType()
method to infer the datatype
      */
      inferredType = value != null ? getDataType(value) : NULL;

    } catch (Exception e) {
      e.printStackTrace();
  }
    // returns inferred datatype of the input value
    return inferredType;
```

Results

The following is the result of applying the design pattern on the transactions data:

```
Column Name :  cust_id
Defined Datatype :  chararray
Inferred Dominant Datatype(s):  int, Count: 817740 Percentage: 100%
```

In the previous result, the input data column, cust_id, is evaluated to check if the values accurately reflect the defined data type. At the ingestion stage, the data type is defined as chararray. By using the data inference design pattern, the data type of the values in the cust_id column is inferred as an integer.

Additional information

The complete code and datasets for this section are in the following GitHub directories:

- Chapter3/code/
- Chapter3/datasets/

The basic statistical profiling pattern

This section describes the basic statistical profiling design pattern in which we use Pig scripts to apply statistical functions to capture important information about data quality.

Background

The previous design pattern depicts one way of inferring the data type. The next logical step in the data profiling process is to evaluate the quality metrics of the values. This is done by collecting and analyzing the data by applying statistical methods. These statistics provide a high-level overview of the suitability of the data for a particular analytical problem, and uncover potential problems early in the data lifecycle management.

Motivation

The basic statistical profiling design pattern helps to create data quality metadata that includes basic statistics, such as mean, median, mode, maximum, minimum, and standard deviation. These stats give you a complete snapshot of the entire data field, and tracking these statistics over time will give insights into the characteristics of new data that is being ingested by the Hadoop cluster. Basic statistics of new data could be checked before ingesting it into Hadoop, to be forewarned about the inconsistent data and help prevent adding low-quality data.

This design pattern tries to address the following profiling requirements:

- Range analysis methods scan values and determine if the data is subject to a total ordering, and also determine whether the values are constrained within a well-defined range
- The **sparseness** of the data can be evaluated to find the percentage of the elements that are not populated
- The **cardinality** of the dataset can be analyzed by finding the number of distinct values that appear within the data
- The **uniqueness** can be evaluated to figure out if each of the value assigned to the attribute is indeed exclusive
- **Overloading** of the data can be evaluated to check if the attribute is being used for multiple purposes
- Format evaluation can be done by resolving unrecognized data into defined formats

Use cases

The following are the use cases where the basic statistical profiling design pattern can be applied:

- This design pattern can be used to detect anomalies in the dataset, by empirically analyzing the values in a dataset to look for unexpected behaviors. This pattern examines the dataset's frequency distributions, the variance, percentage of data logged, and its relationships, to reveal potential flawed data values.

- One of the common use cases where this design pattern can be potentially used is when the data is ingested into the Hadoop cluster from legacy data sources that are still actively used. In legacy systems such as mainframes, the mainframe programmers, during the data creation process, design shortcuts and encodings, and overload a particular field for different purposes that are no longer used or understood. When such kinds of data are ingested into Hadoop, the basic statistical design pattern can help uncover this issue.

Pattern implementation

This design pattern is implemented in Pig as a standalone script, which internally uses a macro to pass parameters and retrieve the answers. Pig Latin has a set of `Math` functions that can be directly applied to a column of data. Data is first loaded into the Pig relation and then the relation is passed as a parameter to the `getProfile` macro. This macro iterates over the relation and applies the `Math` function to each of the columns. The `getProfile` macro is designed to be modular and can be applied across various datasets to get a good understanding of the data profile.

Code snippets

To illustrate the working of this pattern, we have considered the retail transactions dataset stored on the HDFS. It contains attributes, such as `Transaction ID`, `Transaction date`, `Customer ID`, `Phone Number`, `Product`, `Product subclass`, `Product ID`, `Sales Price`, and `Country Code`. For this pattern, we will be profiling the values of the attribute `Sales Price`.

Pig script

The following is the Pig script illustrating the implementation of this pattern:

```
/*
Register the datafu and custom storage jar files
*/
```

```
REGISTER '/home/cloudera/pdp/jars/datafu.jar';
REGISTER '/home/cloudera/pdp/jars/customprofilestorage.jar';

/*
Import macro defined in the file numerical_profiler_macro.pig
*/
IMPORT '/home/cloudera/pdp/
  data_profiling/numerical_profiler_macro.pig';

/*
Load the transactions dataset into the relation transactions
*/
transactions = LOAD
  '/user/cloudera/pdp/datasets/data_profiling/transactions.csv'
  USING  PigStorage(',') AS (transaction_id:long,
  transaction_date:datetime, cust_id:long, age:chararray,
  area:chararray, prod_subclass:int, prod_id:long, amt:int,
  asset:int, sales_price:int, phone_no:chararray,
  country_code:chararray);

/*
Use SAMPLE operator to pick a subset of the data, at most 20% of the
data is returned as a sample
*/
sample_transactions = SAMPLE transactions 0.2;

/*
Invoke the macro getProfile with the parameters sample_transactions
which contains a sample of the dataset and the column name on which
the numerical profiling has to be done.
The macro performs numerical profiling on the sales_price column and
returns various statistics like variance, standard deviation, row
count, null count, distinct count and mode
*/
result =  getProfile(sample_transactions,'sales_price');

/*
CustomProfileStorage UDF extends the StoreFunc. All the abstract
methods have been overridden to implement logic that writes the
contents of the relation into a file in a custom report like format.
The results are stored on the HDFS in the directory numeric
*/
STORE result INTO
  '/user/cloudera/pdp/output/data_profiling/numeric' USING
  com.profiler.CustomProfileStorage();
```

Macro

The following is the Pig script showing the implementation of the `getProfile` macro:

```
/*
Define alias VAR for the function datafu.pig.stats.VAR
*/
DEFINE VAR datafu.pig.stats.VAR();

/*
Define the macro, specify the input parameters and the return value
*/
DEFINE getProfile(data,columnName) returns numerical_profile{

/*
Calculate the variance, standard deviation, row count, null count and
distinct count for the column sales_price
*/
data_grpd = GROUP $data ALL;
numerical_stats = FOREACH data_grpd
{
  variance = VAR($data.$columnName);
  stdDeviation = SQRT(variance);
  rowCount = COUNT_STAR($data.$columnName);
  nullCount = COUNT($data.$columnName);
  uniq = DISTINCT $data.$columnName;
  GENERATE 'Column Name','$columnName' AS colName,
    'Row Count',rowCount,'Null Count' , (rowCount - nullCount),
    'Distinct Count',COUNT(uniq),
    'Highest Value',MAX($data.$columnName) AS
    max_numerical_count,'Lowest Value',MIN($data.$columnName) AS
    min_numerical_count, 'Total Value',SUM($data.$columnName) AS
    total_numerical_count,'Mean Value', AVG($data.$columnName) AS
    avg_numerical_count,'Variance',variance AS    variance,'Standard
    Deviation', stdDeviation AS stdDeviation,'Mode' as
    modeName,'NONE' as modevalue;
}

/*
Compute the mode of the column sales_price
*/
groupd = GROUP $data BY $columnName;
groupd_count = FOREACH groupd GENERATE 'Mode' as modeName, group
  AS mode_values, (long) COUNT($data) AS total;
groupd_count_all = GROUP groupd_count ALL;
```

```
frequency = FOREACH groupd_count_all GENERATE
  MAX(groupd_count.total) AS fq;
filterd = FILTER groupd_count BY (total== frequency.fq AND total>1
  AND mode_values IS NOT NULL);
mode   = GROUP filterd BY modeName;

/*
Join relations numerical stats and mode. Return these values
*/
$numerical_profile = JOIN numerical_stats BY modeName FULL,
  mode BY group;
};
```

Results

By using the basic statistical profiling pattern, the following results are obtained:

```
Column Name: sales_price
Row Count: 163794
Null Count: 0
Distinct Count: 1446
Highest Value: 70589
Lowest Value: 1
Total Value: 21781793
Mean Value: 132.98285040966093
Variance: 183789.18332067598
Standard Deviation: 428.7064069041609
Mode: 99
```

The previous results summarize the properties of the data, its row count, the null count, and the number of distinct values. We also learn about the key characteristics of the data with respect to central tendency and dispersion. Mean and mode are few of the measures of central tendency; variance is one method of knowing data dispersion.

Additional information

The complete code and datasets for this section are in the following GitHub directories:

- `Chapter3/code/`
- `Chapter3/datasets/`

The pattern-matching pattern

This section describes the pattern-matching design pattern in which we use Pig scripts to match numeric and text patterns, to ascertain if the data is coherently relative to itself and thus, get a measure of data quality.

Background

In the enterprise context, examining the data for coherence comes after the data has been ingested and its completeness and correctness has been ascertained. The values of a given attribute can come in different shapes and sizes. This is especially true for fields requiring human input, where the values are entered according to the whims of the user. Assuming a column representing the phone number field is coherent, it can be said that all the values represent valid phone numbers since they match the expected format, length, and data type (numeric), thus meeting the expectation of the system. Wrongly representing data in incorrect format leads to inaccurate analytics, and in the Big Data context, its sheer volume can amplify this inaccuracy.

Motivation

Profiling the data from the pattern-matching perspective, measures the consistency of data and the amount of data matching an expected pattern. This profiling process finds out if the values are consistently relative to themselves by comparing these values with a predefined set of possible values. It captures the essence of the data and tells you if a field is completely numeric or has consistent length. It also gives other format-specific information about the data. Pattern evaluation is done by resolving unrecognized data into defined formats. Abstract type recognition is done on the data to perform a semantic data-type association based on pattern analysis and usage. Identifying the percentage inaccuracy of mismatched patterns at an earlier stage of the analytics cycle ensures better cleaning of data and reduced effort.

Use cases

This design pattern can be used to profile numerical or string data that is supposed to match a particular pattern.

Pattern implementation

This design pattern is implemented in Pig as a standalone script. This script attempts to discover patterns in the data and the common types of records by analyzing the string of data stored in the attribute. It generates several patterns that match the values in the attribute, and reports the percentages of the data that follows each candidate pattern. The script primarily performs the following tasks:

- The patterns are discovered from the tuples; the count and percentage of each of them are calculated
- Examines the discovered patterns and classifies them as valid or invalid

Code snippets

To illustrate the working of this pattern, we have considered the retail transactions dataset stored in HDFS. It contains attributes such as Transaction ID, Transaction date, Customer ID, Phone Number, Product, Product subclass, Product ID, Sales Price, and Country Code. For this pattern, we are interested in the values of the attribute Phone Number.

Pig script

The following is the Pig script illustrating the implementation of this pattern:

```
/*
Import macro defined in the file pattern_matching_macro.pig
*/
IMPORT '/home/cloudera/pdp/data_profiling/pattern_matching_macro.pig';

/*
Load the dataset transactions.csv into the relation transactions
*/
transactions = LOAD
  '/user/cloudera/pdp/datasets/data_profiling/transactions.csv'
  USING  PigStorage(',') AS (transaction_id:long,
  transaction_date:datetime, cust_id:long, age:chararray,
  area:chararray, prod_subclass:int, prod_id:long, amt:int,
  asset:int, sales_price:int, phone_no:chararray,
  country_code:chararray);

/*
Invoke the macro and pass the relation transactions and the column
phone_no as parameters to it.
The pattern matching is performed on the column that is passed.
```

```
This macro returns the phone number pattern, its count and the
percentage
*/
result = getPatterns(transactions, 'phone_no');

/*
Split the relation result into the relation valid_pattern if the
phone number pattern matches any of the two regular expressions.
The patterns that do not match any of the regex are stored into the
relation invalid_patterns
*/
SPLIT result INTO valid_patterns IF (phone_number MATCHES
  '([0-9]{3}-[0-9]{3}-[0-9]{4})' or phone_number MATCHES
  '([0-9]{10})'), invalid_patterns OTHERWISE;

/*
The results are stored on the HDFS in the directories valid_patterns
and invalid_patterns
*/
STORE valid_patterns INTO '/user/cloudera/pdp/output/
  data_profiling/pattern_matching/valid_patterns';
STORE invalid_patterns INTO '/user/cloudera/pdp/output/
  data_profiling/pattern_matching/invalid_patterns';
```

Macro

The following is the Pig script showing the implementation of the getPatterns macro:

```
/*
Define the macro, specify the input parameters and the return value
*/
DEFINE getPatterns(data,phone_no) returns percentage{

/*
Iterate over each row of the phone_no column and transform each
value by replacing all digits with 9 and all alphabets with a to form
uniform patterns
*/
transactions_replaced = FOREACH $data
{
  replace_digits = REPLACE($phone_no,'\\d','9');
  replace_alphabets = REPLACE(replace_digits,'[a-zA-Z]','a');
  replace_spaces = REPLACE(replace_alphabets,'\\s','');
  GENERATE replace_spaces AS phone_number_pattern;
}
/*
Group by phone_number_pattern and calculate count of each pattern
```

```
*/
grpd_ph_no_pattern = GROUP transactions_replaced BY
  phone_number_pattern;
phone_num_count = FOREACH grpd_ph_no_pattern GENERATE group as
  phone_num, COUNT(transactions_replaced.phone_number_pattern) AS
  phone_count;

/*
Compute the total count and percentage.
Return the relation percentage with the fields phone number pattern,
count and the rounded percentage
*/
grpd_ph_no_cnt_all = GROUP phone_num_count ALL;
total_count = FOREACH grpd_ph_no_cnt_all GENERATE
  SUM(phone_num_count.phone_count) AS tot_sum;
$percentage = FOREACH phone_num_count GENERATE phone_num as
  phone_number, phone_count as phone_number_count,
  CONCAT((Chararray)ROUND(phone_count*100.0/total_count.tot_sum),
  '%') as percent;
};
```

Results

The following is the result of applying the design pattern on the transactions data. The results are stored in the folders `valid_patterns` and `invalid_patterns`.

Output in the folder `valid_patterns` is as follows:

```
9999999999   490644     60%
999-999-9999   196257     24%
```

Output in the folder `invalid_patterns` is as follows:

```
99999          8177  1%
aaaaaaaaaa   40887  5%
999-999-999a  40888  5%
aaa-aaa-aaaa  40887  5%
```

The previous results give us a snapshot of all the patterns of phone numbers that exist in the dataset, their count, and the percentage. Using this data, we can determine the percentage of inaccurate data in the dataset, and take necessary measures in the data-cleansing stage. As the relative frequency of phone numbers in the format 999-999-9999 is more, and it is a valid pattern, you can derive a rule that requires all values in this attribute to conform to this pattern. This rule can be applied in the data-cleansing phase.

Additional information

The complete code and datasets for this section are in the following GitHub directories:

- `Chapter3/code/`
- `Chapter3/datasets/`

The string profiling pattern

This section describes the string profiling design pattern in which we use Pig scripts on textual data to know important statistics.

Background

A majority of Big Data implementations deal with text data embedded in columns. To gain insight from these columns, they have to be integrated with other enterprise-structured data. This design pattern elaborates a few of the ways that help understand the quality of textual data.

Motivation

The quality of textual data can be ascertained by applying basic statistical techniques on the values of the attributes. Finding the string length is the most important dimension in selecting the appropriate data types and sizes for the target system. You can use the maximum and minimum string lengths to determine, at a glance, if the data ingested into Hadoop meets a given constraint. While dealing with data sizes in the petabyte range, limiting the character count to be just large enough optimizes storage and computation by cutting down on unnecessary storage space.

Using the string lengths, you can also determine distinct lengths of individual strings in a column and the percentage of rows in the table that each length represents.

For example, the profile of a column representing US State Codes is supposed to be two characters but if the profile gathered shows distinct values other than two characters, this indicates that the values in the column are not coherent.

Use cases

This pattern can be applied on data columns that predominantly contain text data type to find out if the text is within the constraints defined.

Pattern implementation

This design pattern is implemented in Pig as a standalone script, which internally uses a macro to retrieve the profile. Pig Latin has a set of math functions that can be directly applied to a column of data. Data is first loaded in to the Pig relation `transactions` and then the relation is passed as a parameter to the `getStringProfile` macro. This macro iterates over the relation and applies the `Math` function on each of the values. The `getStringProfile` macro is designed to be modular and can be applied across various text columns to get a good understanding of the string data profile.

Code snippets

To illustrate the working of this pattern, we have considered the retail transactions dataset stored in HDFS. It contains attributes such as `Transaction ID`, `Transaction date`, `Customer ID`, `Phone Number`, `Product`, `Product subclass`, `Product ID`, `Sales Price`, and `Country Code`. For this pattern, we are interested in the values of the attribute `Country Code`.

Pig script

The following is the Pig script illustrating the implementation of this pattern:

```
/*
Register the datafu and custom storage jar files
*/
REGISTER '/home/cloudera/pdp/jars/datafu.jar';
REGISTER '/home/cloudera/pdp/jars/customprofilestorage.jar';

/*
Import macro defined in the file string_profiler_macro.pig
*/
IMPORT
  '/home/cloudera/pdp/data_profiling/string_profiler_macro.pig';

/*
Load the transactions dataset into the relation transactions
*/
transactions = LOAD
  '/user/cloudera/pdp/datasets/data_profiling/transactions.csv'
  using PigStorage(',') as
  (transaction_id:long,transaction_date:datetime, cust_id:long,
  age:chararray, area:chararray, prod_subclass:int, prod_id:long,
  amt:int, asset:int, sales_price:int, phone_no:chararray,
  country_code:chararray);
```

```
/*
Invoke the macro getStringProfile with the parameters transactions and
the column name on which the string profiling has to be done.
The macro performs string profiling on the country_code column and
returns various statistics like row count, null count, total character
count, word count, identifies distinct country codes in the dataset
and calculates their count and percentage.
*/
result =  getStringProfile(transactions,'country_code');


/*
CustomProfileStorage UDF extends the StoreFunc. All the abstract
methods have been overridden to implement logic that writes the
contents of the relation into a file in a custom report like format.
The results are stored on the HDFS in the directory string
*/
STORE result INTO
  '/user/cloudera/pdp/output/data_profiling/string' USING
  com.profiler.CustomProfileStorage();
```

Macro

The following is the Pig script showing the implementation of the
getStringProfile macro:

```
/*
Define the macro, specify the input parameters and the return value
*/
DEFINE getStringProfile(data,columnName) returns string_profile{

/*
Calculate row count and null count on the column country_code
*/
data_grpd = GROUP $data ALL;
string_stats = FOREACH data_grpd
{
  rowCount = COUNT_STAR($data.$columnName);
  nullCount = COUNT($data.$columnName);
  GENERATE 'Column Name','$columnName' AS colName,
    'Row Count',rowCount,'Null Count' ,
    (rowCount - nullCount),
    'Distinct Values' as dist,'NONE' as distvalue;
}

/*
```

Calculate total char count, max chars, min chars, avg chars on the
column country_code
```
*/
size = FOREACH $data GENERATE SIZE($columnName) AS chars_count;
size_grpd_all = GROUP size ALL;
char_stats = FOREACH size_grpd_all GENERATE 'Total Char
  Count',SUM(size.chars_count) AS total_char_count,'Max Chars',
  MAX(size.chars_count) AS max_chars_count,'Min Chars',
  MIN(size.chars_count) AS min_chars_count,'Avg Chars',
  AVG(size.chars_count) AS avg_chars_count,'Distinct Values' as
  dist,'NONE' as distvalue;


/*
Calculate total word count, max words and min words on the column
country_code
*/
words = FOREACH $data GENERATE FLATTEN(TOKENIZE($columnName)) AS
  word;
whitespace_filtrd_words = FILTER words BY word MATCHES '\\w+';
grouped_words = GROUP whitespace_filtrd_words BY word;
word_count = FOREACH grouped_words GENERATE
  COUNT(whitespace_filtrd_words) AS count, group AS word;
word_count_grpd_all = GROUP word_count ALL;
words_stats = FOREACH word_count_grpd_all GENERATE 'Word
  Count',SUM(word_count.count) AS total_word_count,
  'Max Words',MAX(word_count.count) AS max_count,
  'Min Words',MIN(word_count.count) AS min_count,'Distinct Values'
  as dist,'NONE' as distvalue;


/*
Identify distinct country codes and their count
*/
grpd_data = GROUP $data BY $columnName;
grpd_data_count = FOREACH grpd_data GENERATE group as
  country_code, COUNT($data.$columnName) AS country_count;


/*
Calculate the total sum of all the counts
*/
grpd_data_cnt_all = GROUP grpd_data_count ALL;
total_count = FOREACH grpd_data_cnt_all GENERATE
  SUM(grpd_data_count.country_count) AS tot_sum;


/*
Calculate the percentage of the distinct country codes
*/
```

```
percentage = FOREACH grpd_data_count GENERATE country_code as
  country_code,
country_count as country_code_cnt,
  ROUND(country_count*100.0/total_count.tot_sum) as
  percent,'Distinct Values' as dist;

/*
Join string stats, char_stats, word_stats and the relation with
distinct country codes, their count and the rounded percentage. Return
these values
*/
percentage_grpd = GROUP percentage BY dist;
$string_profile = JOIN string_stats BY dist,char_stats BY dist ,
  words_stats BY dist, percentage_grpd BY group;
};
```

Results

By using the string profiling pattern, the following results are obtained:

```
Column Name: country_code
Row Count: 817740
Null Count: 0
Total Char Count: 5632733
Max Chars: 24
Min Chars: 2
Avg Chars: 6.888171056815125
Word Count: 999583
Max Words: 181817
Min Words: 90723


Distinct Values
```

country_code	Count	Percentage
US	181792	22%
U.S	90687	11%
USA	181782	22%
U.S.A	90733	11%
America	90929	11%
United States	91094	11%
United States of America	90723	11%

The previous results summarize the properties of the data, such as its row count, number of occurrences of null, and total number of characters; the `Max chars` and `Min chars` count can be used to validate the data quality by checking if the length of the values is within a range. As per the metadata, the valid value for a country code should be two characters, but the results show that the maximum character count is `24`, which implies that the data is inaccurate. The results in the `Distinct values` section show the distinct country codes in the dataset with their count and percentage. Using these results we can determine the percentage of inaccurate data in the dataset and take necessary measures in the data-cleansing stage.

Additional information

The complete code and datasets for this section are in the following GitHub directories:

- `Chapter3/code/`
- `Chapter3/datasets/`

The unstructured text profiling pattern

This section describes the unstructured text profiling design pattern in which we use Pig scripts on free-form text data to know important statistics.

Background

Text mining is done on unstructured data ingested by Hadoop to extract interesting and non-trivial meaningful patterns, from blocks of meaningless data. Text mining is an interdisciplinary field, which draws on information retrieval, data mining, machine learning, statistics, and computational linguistics, to accomplish the extraction of meaningful patterns from text. Typically, the parallel-processing power of Hadoop is used to process massive amounts of textual data, to classify documents, cluster tweets, build ontologies, extract entities, perform sentiment analysis, and so on.

This pattern discusses a way of ascertaining the quality of text data using text pre-processing techniques, such as stopword removal, stemming, and TF-IDF.

Motivation

Unstructured text is inherently inconsistent and the inconsistencies can result in inaccurate analytics. Inconsistencies in textual data arise due to the fact that there are many ways of representing an idea.

Text pre-processing enhances the quality of data to improve the accuracy of analytics and reduces the difficulty of the text mining process. The following are the steps to accomplish text pre-processing:

- One of the first steps in text pre-processing is to convert the blocks of text into tokens to remove punctuations, hyphens, brackets, and so on, and keep only the meaningful keywords, abbreviations, and acronyms for further processing. Tokenization involves a measure of a document's consistency, as there is a linear proportionality between the number of meaningless tokens eliminated and the inconsistency of data relative to itself.

- Stopword removal is the next logical step performed in text pre-processing. This step involves removal of words that do not provide any meaning or context to the document. These words are known as *stop words* and they generally contain pronouns, articles, prepositions, and so on. A stop word list is defined before actually removing them from the original text. This list can include other words that are specific to a particular domain.

- The stemming step reduces multiple forms of a word to its root form by removing or converting a word into its base word (stem). For example, agreed, agreeing, disagree, agreement, and disagreement are stemmed (depending on the specific stemming algorithm) to the word agree. This is done in order to make all the tokens in the corpus consistent.

- After the stemming process is complete, the tokens are assigned weights relative to the frequency of their occurrence by calculating the term frequency. This statistic denotes the number of times a word occurs in a document. Inverse document frequency is calculated to know the frequency of the word across all the documents. This statistic determines if a word is common or rare across all the documents. Finding the term frequency and inverse document frequency has a bearing on the quality of the text, since these statistics tell you if you can discard or use a word based on its importance relative to the document or the corpus.

Use cases

This design pattern can be used in cases that require understanding the quality of unstructured text corpora through text pre-processing techniques. This design pattern is not exhaustive and covers a few important aspects of text pre-processing and its applicability to data profiling.

Pattern implementation

This design pattern is implemented in Pig as a standalone script, which internally uses the `unstructuredtextprofiling` Java UDF to perform stemming and to generate term frequency and inverse document frequency of the words. The script performs a right outer join to remove the stop words. The list of stop words are first loaded into a relation from an external text file and then used in the outer join.

Stemming is done through the usage of the Porter Stemmer algorithm implemented in the `unstructuredtextprofiling` JAR file.

Code snippets

To demonstrate the working of this pattern, we have considered the text corpus of Wikipedia, stored in a folder accessible to the HDFS. This sample corpus consists of the wiki pages related to Computer Science and Information Technology.

Pig script

The following is the Pig script illustrating the implementation of this pattern:

```
/*
Register custom text profiler jar
*/
REGISTER '/home/cloudera/pdp/jars/unstructuredtextprofiler.jar';

/*
Load stop words into the relation stop_words_list
*/
stop_words_list = LOAD
  '/user/cloudera/pdp/datasets/data_profiling/text/stopwords.txt'
  USING PigStorage();

/*
Tokenize the stopwords to extract the words
*/
stopwords = FOREACH stop_words_list GENERATE
  FLATTEN(TOKENIZE($0));

/*
Load the dataset into the relations doc1 and doc2.
Tokenize to extract the words for each of these documents
*/
```

```
doc1 = LOAD
  '/user/cloudera/pdp/datasets/data_profiling/text/
  computer_science.txt' AS (words:chararray);
docWords1 = FOREACH doc1 GENERATE 'computer_science.txt' AS
  documentId, FLATTEN(TOKENIZE(words)) AS word;
doc2 = LOAD
  '/user/cloudera/pdp/datasets/data_profiling/text/
  information_technology.txt' AS (words:chararray);
docWords2 = FOREACH doc2 GENERATE 'information_technology.txt' AS
  documentId, FLATTEN(TOKENIZE(words)) AS word;

/*
Combine the relations using the UNION operator
*/
combined_docs = UNION docWords1, docWords2;

/*
Perform pre-processing by doing the following
Convert the data into lowercase
Remove stopwords
Perform stemming by calling custom UDF. it uses porter stemmer
algorithm to perform stemming
*/
lowercase_data = FOREACH combined_docs GENERATE documentId as
  documentId, FLATTEN(TOKENIZE(LOWER($1))) as word;
joind = JOIN stopwords BY $0 RIGHT OUTER, lowercase_data BY $1;
stop_words_removed = FILTER joind BY $0 IS NULL;
processed_data = FOREACH stop_words_removed GENERATE documentId as
  documentId, com.profiler.unstructuredtextprofiling.Stemmer($2)
  as word;

/*
Calculate word count per word/doc combination using the Group and
FOREACH statement and the result is stored in word_count
*/
grpd_processed_data = GROUP processed_data BY (word, documentId);
word_count = FOREACH grpd_processed_data GENERATE group AS
  wordDoc,
  COUNT(processed_data) AS wordCount;

/*
Calculate Total word count per document using the Group and FOREACH
statement and the result is stored in total_docs_wc
*/
```

```
grpd_wc = GROUP word_count BY wordDoc.documentId;
grpd_wc_all = GROUP grpd_wc ALL;
total_docs = FOREACH grpd_wc_all GENERATE
  FLATTEN(grpd_wc),
  COUNT(grpd_wc) AS totalDocs;
total_docs_wc = FOREACH total_docs GENERATE
  FLATTEN(word_count),
  SUM(word_count.wordCount) AS wordCountPerDoc,
  totalDocs;

/*
Calculate Total document count per word is using the Group and FOREACH
statement and the result is stored in doc_count_per_word
*/
grpd_total_docs_wc = GROUP total_docs_wc BY wordDoc.word;
doc_count_per_word = FOREACH grpd_total_docs_wc GENERATE
  FLATTEN(total_docs_wc),
  COUNT(total_docs_wc) AS docCountPerWord;

/*
Calculate tfidf by invoking custom Java UDF.
The overall relevancy of a document with respect to a term is computed
and the resultant data is stored in gen_tfidf
*/
gen_tfidf = FOREACH doc_count_per_word GENERATE $0.word AS word,
  $0.documentId AS documentId,
  com.profiler.unstructuredtextprofiling.GenerateTFIDF(wordCount,
  wordCountPerDoc,
  totalDocs,
  docCountPerWord) AS tfidf;

/*
Order by relevancy
*/
orderd_tfidf = ORDER gen_tfidf BY word ASC, tfidf DESC;

/*
The results are stored on the HDFS in the directory tfidf
*/
STORE orderd_tfidf into
  '/user/cloudera/pdp/output/data_profiling/
  unstructured_text_profiling/tfidf';
```

Java UDF for stemming

The following is the Java UDF code snippet:

```java
public String exec(Tuple input) throws IOException {
    //Few declarations go here
    Stemmer s = new Stemmer();
    //Code for exception handling goes here
    //Extract values from the input tuple
    String str = (String)input.get(0);

    /*
    Invoke the stem(str) method of the class Stemmer.
    It return the stemmed form of the word
    */
    return s.stem(str);
}
```

Java UDF for generating TF-IDF

The following is the Java UDF code snippet for computing TF-IDF:

```java
public class GenerateTFIDF extends EvalFunc<Double>{
  @Override
  /**
  *The pre-calculated wordCount, wordCountPerDoc, totalDocs and
docCountPerWord are passed as parameters to this UDF.
  */
  public Double exec(Tuple input) throws IOException {
    /*
    Retrieve the values from the input tuple
    */
    long countOfWords = (Long) input.get(0);
    long countOfWordsPerDoc = (Long) input.get(1);
    long noOfDocs = (Long) input.get(2);
    long docCountPerWord = (Long) input.get(3);
    /*
    Compute the overall relevancy of a document with respect to a
term.
    */
    double tf = (countOfWords * 1.0) / countOfWordsPerDoc;
    double idf = Math.log((noOfDocs * 1.0) /
      docCountPerWord);
    return tf * idf;
  }
}
```

Results

The following are the results after applying the design pattern on the `computer_science` and `information_technology` wiki text corpus:

```
associat  information_technology.txt  0.0015489322470613302
author  information_technology.txt  7.744661235306651E-4
automat  computer_science.txt  8.943834587870262E-4
avail  computer_science.txt  0.0
avail  information_technology.txt  0.0
babbag  computer_science.txt  8.943834587870262E-4
babbage'  computer_science.txt  0.0026831503763610786
base  information_technology.txt  0.0
base  computer_science.txt  0.0
base.  computer_science.txt  8.943834587870262E-4
basic  information_technology.txt  7.744661235306651E-4
complex.  computer_science.txt  8.943834587870262E-4
compon  information_technology.txt  0.0015489322470613302
compsci  computer_science.txt  8.943834587870262E-4
comput  computer_science.txt  0.0
comput  information_technology.txt  0.0
computation  computer_science.txt  8.943834587870262E-4
computation.  computer_science.txt  8.943834587870262E-4
distinguish  information_technology.txt  7.744661235306651E-4
distribut computer_science.txt  0.0
distribut information_technology.txt  0.0
divid  computer_science.txt  8.943834587870262E-4
division.  computer_science.txt  8.943834587870262E-4
document  information_technology.txt  7.744661235306651E-4
encompass  information_technology.txt  7.744661235306651E-4
engin  computer_science.txt  0.0035775338351481047
engine.[5]  computer_science.txt  8.943834587870262E-4
enigma  computer_science.txt  8.943834587870262E-4
enough  computer_science.txt  0.0017887669175740523
enterprise.[2]  information_technology.txt  7.744661235306651E-4
entertain  computer_science.txt  8.943834587870262E-4
```

The original text is passed through the stopword removal and stemming phases, and term frequency-inverse document frequency is then calculated. The results show the word, the document it belongs to, and the TF-IDF. Words with high TF-IDF imply a strong relationship with the document they appear in, and words with a relatively low TF-IDF are considered low quality and can be ignored.

Additional information

The complete code and datasets for this section are in the following GitHub directories:

- `Chapter3/code/`
- `Chapter3/datasets/`

Summary

In this chapter, we build upon what we've learned from *Chapter 2, Data Ingest and Egress Patterns*, where we have integrated data from multiple source systems and ingested it into Hadoop. The next step is to find clues about the data type by looking at the constituent values. The values are examined to see if they are misrepresented, if their units are misinterpreted, or if the context of units is derived incorrectly. This sleuthing mechanism is discussed in more detail in the data type inference pattern.

In the basic statistical profiling pattern, we examine if the values meet the quality expectations of the use case by collecting statistical information on the numeric values to find answers to the following questions: For a numeric field, are all the values numeric? Do all of the values of enumerable fields fall into the proper set? Do the numeric fields meet the range constraint? Are they complete?, and so on.

The pattern-matching design pattern explores a few techniques to measure the consistency of both the numerical and text columnar dataset through its data type, data length, and regex patterns. The next pattern uncovers the quality metrics of columns representing string values by using various statistical methods. This is explained in detail in the string profiling design pattern. The unstructured text profiling design pattern is an attempt to formalize the text pre-processing techniques, such as stopword removal, stemming, and TF-IDF calculation, to understand the quality of unstructured text.

In the next chapter, we will focus on data validation and cleansing patterns that can be applied to a variety of data formats. After reading this chapter, the audience will be able to choose the right pattern in order to validate the accuracy and completeness of data by using techniques, such as constraint checks and regex matching. We will also discuss data cleansing techniques, such as filters and statistical cleansing, in the next chapter.

4
Data Validation and Cleansing Patterns

In the previous chapter, you have studied the various patterns related to data profiling, through which you understood the different ways to get vital information about the attributes, content, context, structure, and condition of data residing in the Hadoop cluster. These data profiling patterns are applied in the data lifecycle before initiating the process of cleaning the data into a more useful form.

The following are the design patterns covered in this chapter:

- **Constraint validation and cleansing pattern**: This explains the validation of the data against a set of constraints to check if there are any missing values, if the values are within a range specified by a business rule or if the values conform to referential integrity and unique constraints. Depending on the business rule, either the invalid records are removed or appropriate cleansing steps are applied to the invalid data.

- **Regex validation and cleansing pattern**: This demonstrates validation of data by matching it with a specific pattern or length using regular expressions and pattern-based filtering of records to cleanse invalid data.

- **Corrupt data validation and cleansing pattern**: This sets the context to understand corruption of data ingested from various sources. This pattern details the impact of noise and outliers on data and the methods to detect and cleanse them.

- **Unstructured text data validation and cleansing pattern**: This demonstrates ways to validate and cleanse an unstructured data corpus by performing pre-processing steps, such as lowercase conversion, stopword removal, stemming, punctuation removal, extra spaces removal, identifying numbers, and identifying misspellings.

Data validation and cleansing for Big Data

Data validation and cleansing deal with the detection and removal of incorrect records from the data. The process of data validation and cleansing ensures that the inconsistencies in the data are identified well before the data is used in the analytics process. The inconsistent data is then replaced, modified, or deleted to make it more consistent.

Most of the data validation and cleansing is performed by analyzing the static constraints based on the schema. Examining the schema in conjunction with the constraints tells us about the existence of missing values, null values, ambiguity in representation, foreign key constraints, and so on.

Data validation and cleansing assume an increasingly important role in deriving value from the perspective of Big Data. While cleaning Big Data, one of the biggest trade-offs to be considered is the **time-quality** trade-off. Given that there is unlimited time, we can improve the quality of the bad data, but the challenge in devising a good data cleansing script is to cover as much data as possible within the time constraints and perform the cleansing successfully.

In a typical Big Data use case, the different types of data that are integrated can add to the complexity of the cleansing process. High-dimensional data from federated systems have their own cleansing approaches, whereas the huge volumes of longitudinal data differ in their cleansing approach. Streaming data could be time-series data that can be efficiently handled using a real-time cleansing approach rather than a batch-cleansing mechanism. Unstructured data, descriptive data, and web data have to be handled using a text pre-processing cleansing approach.

Bad data can result from various touch points in the Hadoop environment, and the following points outline the common cleansing issues mapped to these touch points:

- **Cleansing issues in Big Data arising from data gathering**: Inconsistency in data can arise due to errors in the methods of data gathering. These methods can range from manual entry to social media data (where nonstandard words are used), entering duplicate data, and measurement errors.

- **Cleansing issues in Big Data arising from improper data delivery**: This could be due to improper conversion of data after it has entered into an upstream system integrated with Hadoop. The reasons for bad data arising out of improper data delivery include inappropriate aggregation, nulls converted to default values, buffer overflows, and transmission problems.

- **Cleansing issues in Big Data arising from problems in data storage**: Inconsistent data could be the result of problems in physical and logical storage of data. Data inconsistency as a result of physical storage is a rare cause; it happens when data is stored for an extended period of time and tends to get corrupted, which is known as **bit rot**. The following issues result from storing data in logical storage structures: inadequate metadata, missing links in entity relationships, missing timestamps, and so on.

- **Cleansing issues in Big Data arising from data integration**: Integrating data from heterogeneous systems has a significant contribution to bad data, typically resulting in issues related to inconsistent fields. Varying definitions, differing field formats, incorrect time synchronization and the idiosyncrasies of legacy data, and wrong processing algorithms contribute to this.

Generally, the first step in Big Data validation and cleansing is to explore the data using various mathematical techniques to detect the existence of any inaccuracies in the data. This initial exploration is done by understanding the data type and domain of each attribute, its context, the acceptable values, and so on; after this, the actual data is validated to verify conformance to the acceptable limits. This gives an initial estimate on the characteristics of the inaccuracies and its whereabouts. In the validation phase, we can conduct this exploration activity by specifying the expected constraints to find and filter data not meeting the expected constraints, and then take required action on the data, in the cleansing step.

A sequence of data cleansing routines is run iteratively after we have explored the data and located the anomalies in it. These data cleansing routines refer to the master data and relevant business rules to perform cleansing and achieve the end result of a higher quality data. Data cleansing routines work to *clean* the data by filling in missing values, smoothing noisy data, identifying or removing outliers, and resolving inconsistencies. After the cleansing is performed, an optional control step is performed where the results are evaluated and exceptions are handled for the tuples not corrected within the cleansing process.

Choosing Pig for validation and cleansing

Implementing the validation and cleansing code in Pig within the Hadoop environment, reduces the time-quality trade-off and the requirement to move data to external systems to perform cleansing. The high-level overview of implementation is depicted in the following diagram:

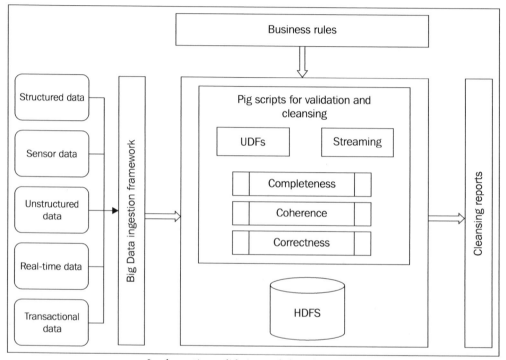

Implementing validation and cleansing in Pig

The following are the advantages of performing data cleansing within the Hadoop environment using Pig:

- Improved overall performance since validation and cleansing are done in the same environment. There is no need to transfer data to external systems for cleansing.

- Pig is highly suitable to write code for validating and cleansing scripts since the built-in functions are geared towards processing messy data and for exploratory analysis.

- Pig enables automating of the cleansing process by chaining complex workflows, which is very handy for datasets that are periodically updated.

The constraint validation and cleansing design pattern

The constraint validation and cleansing pattern deals with validating the data against a set of rules and techniques and then cleansing the invalid data.

Background

Constraints tell us about the properties that the data should comply with. They can be applied to the entire database, a table, a column, or an entire schema. These constraints are rules created at design time to prevent the data from getting corrupt and reduce the overhead of processing wrong data; they dictate what values are valid for a data.

Constraints, such as null checks and range checks, can be used to know if the data ingested in Hadoop is valid or not. Often, constraint validation and cleansing on the data in Hadoop can be performed based on the business rules that actually determine the type of constraint that has to be applied on a particular subset of data.

In cases where a given column has to belong to a particular type, a data type constraint is applied. When we want to enforce a constraint, such as numbers or dates should fall within a specified range, a range constraint is applied. These range constraints typically specify a minimum and maximum value for comparison. Mandatory constraint enforces a hard validation rule to ensure that certain important fields do not remain empty, which in essence checks for null or missing values and eliminates them using a range of methods. Set membership constraint enforces the rule that the data values should always be from a pre-determined set of values.

Invalid data could be a result of ingesting data into Hadoop from legacy systems where there are no constraints implemented in the software and ingesting data from sources such as spreadsheets where it is relatively difficult to set a constraint on what a user chooses to enter in a cell.

Motivation

The constraint validation and cleansing design pattern implements a Pig script to validate the data by examining if it is within certain, specified, and mandatory range constraints and then cleans it.

There are many ways to check if the data residing in Hadoop abides by the mandatory constraints, and one of the most useful ways is to check for null or missing values. If there are missing values in a given set of data, it is important to understand if these missing values account for the lack of data quality, since in many situations it is okay to have missing values in the data.

Finding null or missing values is relatively simple, but cleansing them by filling the missing values with the appropriate values is a complex task and typically depends on the business case.

Based on the business case, the null values can be ignored or they can be manually entered as a part of the cleansing process, but this method is the least recommended. For categorical variables, a constant global label such as "XXXXX" can be used to depict missing values, in cases where this label cannot clash with other existing values of the table or the missing values can be replaced by the most frequently occurring value (mode). Depending on the data distribution, it is recommended to use the mean value for data that is in normal distribution and the median value for data that is in skewed distribution. The usage of mean and median is applicable only to numerical data types. Using a probabilistic measure, such as Bayesian inference or a decision tree, the missing values can be calculated in a more precise manner than the other cases, but this is a time consuming method.

The range constraints limit the values that can be used in the data by specifying the upper and lower limits of valid values. The design pattern first performs the validity check of the data and finds out if the data is not within the range specified. This invalid data is cleansed as per the business rules by filtering the invalid data, or by replacing the invalid values with the maximum range value if the invalid data is higher than the range; conversely, the invalid value is replaced with the minimum range value if the invalid data is lower than the range.

Unique constraints limit the existence of a value to be unique across a table. This is applicable to primary keys where the existence of duplicate values amounts to invalid data. A table can have any number of unique constraints with the primary key defined as one of them. After the data is ingested by Hadoop, we can use this design pattern to perform validation to find if the data adheres to the unique constraints and cleanse it by removing the duplicates.

Use cases

You can use this design pattern when an enormous volume of structured data is ingested and you want to perform integrity checks on the data by validating it against the mandatory, range, and unique constraints and then cleanse it.

Pattern implementation

This design pattern is implemented in Pig as a standalone script. The script loads the data and validates it based on the constraints specified. The following is a brief description of how the pattern is being implemented:

- **Mandatory constraints**: The script checks the data for invalid and missing data, which does not abide by the mandatory constraints, and cleanses it by replacing the missing values by the median.

- **Range constraints**: The script has a range constraint defined, which states that the valid values of the column `claim_amount` should be between a lower and upper bound. The script validates the data, and finds all the values that are outside the range. In the cleansing step, these values are filtered; they can also be updated to the minimum and maximum values of the range as per a predefined business rule.

- **Unique constraints**: The script performs a check to verify if the data is distinct and then cleanses it by removing duplicate values.

Code snippets

To illustrate the working of this pattern, we have considered an automobile insurance claims dataset stored on the HDFS that contains two files. `automobile_policy_master.csv` is the master file; it contains a unique ID, vehicle details, price, and the premium paid for it. The master file is used to validate the data present in the claims file. The `automobile_insurance_claims.csv` file contains automobile insurance claims data, specifically the vehicle repair charges claims; it contains attributes, such as `CLAIM_ID`, `POLICY_MASTER_ID`, `VEHICLE_DETAILS`, and `CLAIM_DETAILS`. For this pattern, we will be performing constraint validation and cleansing on `CLAIM_AMOUNT`, `POLICY_MASTER_ID`, `AGE`, and `CITY`, as given in the following code:

```
/*
Register Datafu and custom jar files
*/
REGISTER '/home/cloudera/pdp/jars/datatypevalidationudf.jar';
REGISTER  '/home/cloudera/pdp/jars/datafu.jar';

/*
Define aliases for Quantile UDF from Datafu and custom UDF
DataTypeValidationUDF.
The parameters to Quantile constructor specify list of quantiles to
compute
The parameter to the DataTypeValidationUDF constructor specifies the
Data type that would be used for validation
*/
```

```
DEFINE Quantile datafu.pig.stats.Quantile('0.25','0.5','0.75');
DEFINE
  DataTypeValidationUDF com.validation.DataTypeValidationUDF
  ('double');

/*
Load automobile insurance claims data set into the relation claims and
policy master data set into the relation policy_master
*/
claims = LOAD
  '/user/cloudera/pdp/datasets/data_validation/
  automobile_insurance_claims.csv' USING  PigStorage(',') AS
  (claim_id:chararray, policy_master_id:chararray,
  registration_no:chararray, engine_no:chararray,
  chassis_no:chararray,
  customer_id:int,age:int,first_name:chararray,
  last_name:chararray,street:chararray,
  address:chararray,  city:chararray,  zip:long,
  gender:chararray, claim_date:chararray,
  garage_city:chararray,bill_no:long,claim_amount:chararray,
  garage_name:chararray,claim_status:chararray);
policy_master = LOAD
  '/user/cloudera/pdp/datasets/data_validation/
  automobile_policy_master.csv' USING  PigStorage(',') AS
  (policy_master_id:chararray, model:int, make:chararray,
  price:double, premium:float);

/*
Remove duplicate tuples from the relation claims to ensure that the
data meets unique constraint
*/
claims_distinct = DISTINCT claims;

/*
Invoke the custom DataTypeValidationUDF with the parameter claim_
amount.
The UDF returns the tuples where claim_amount does not match the
specified data type (double), these values are considered as invalid.
Invalid values are stored in the relation invalid_claims_amt
*/
claim_distinct_claim_amount = FOREACH claims_distinct GENERATE
  claim_amount AS claim_amount;
invalid_c_amount = FOREACH claim_distinct_claim_amount GENERATE
  DataTypeValidationUDF(claim_amount) AS claim_amount;
invalid_claims_amt = FILTER invalid_c_amount BY claim_amount IS
  NOT NULL;
```

```
/*
Filter invalid values from the relation claims_distinct and segregate
the valid and invalid claim amount
*/
valid_invalid_claims_amount_join = JOIN invalid_claims_amt BY
  claim_amount RIGHT, claims_distinct BY claim_amount;
valid_claims_amount = FILTER valid_invalid_claims_amount_join BY
  $0 IS NULL;
invalid_claims_amount = FILTER valid_invalid_claims_amount_join BY
  $0 IS NOT NULL;


/*
For each invalid_claims_amount, generate all the values and specify
the reason for considering these values as invalid
*/
invalid_datatype_claims = FOREACH invalid_claims_amount GENERATE
  $1 AS claim_id,$2 AS policy_master_id, $3 AS registration_no,
  $4 AS engine_no, $5 AS chassis_no,$6 AS customer_id,$7 AS age,
  $8 AS first_name,$9 AS last_name, $10 AS street, $11 AS address,
  $12 AS city, $13 AS zip, $14 AS gender, $15 AS claim_date,
  $16 AS garage_city,$17 AS bill_no, $18 AS claim_amount,$19 AS
  garage_name, $20 AS claim_status,'Invalid Datatype for
  claim_amount' AS reason;

valid_datatype_claims = FOREACH valid_claims_amount GENERATE $1 AS
  claim_id,$2 AS policy_master_id, $3 AS registration_no,
  $4 AS engine_no, $5 AS chassis_no,$6 AS customer_id,$7 AS age,
  $8 AS first_name,$9 AS last_name, $10 AS street, $11 AS address,
  $12 AS city, $13 AS zip, $14 AS gender, $15 AS claim_date,
  $16 AS garage_city,$17 AS bill_no, $18 AS claim_amount,
  $19 AS garage_name, $20 AS claim_status;


/*
Compute quantiles using Datafu's Quantile UDF
*/
groupd = GROUP valid_datatype_claims ALL;
quantiles = FOREACH groupd {
  sorted = ORDER valid_datatype_claims BY age;
  GENERATE Quantile(sorted.age) AS quant;
}


/*
Check for occurrence of null values for the column Age which is a
numerical field and for city which is a categorical field.
The nulls in age column are replaced with median and the nulls in city
column are replaced with a constant string XXXXX.
```

```
*/
claims_replaced_nulls = FOREACH valid_datatype_claims GENERATE $0,
   $1 ,$2 , $3 ,$4 , $5 ,(int) ($6 is null ? FLOOR
   (quantiles.quant.quantile_0_5) : $6) AS age, $7, $8 ,$9 , $10 ,
   ($11 is null ? 'XXXXX' : $11) AS city, $12, $13 , $14 , $15 ,
   $16 ,(double)$17 , $18 ,$19;


/*
Ensure Referential integrity by checking if the policy_master_id in
the claims dataset is present in the master dataset.
The values in the claims dataset that do not find a match in the
master dataset are considered as invalid values and are removed.
*/
referential_integrity_check = JOIN claims_replaced_nulls BY
   policy_master_id, policy_master BY policy_master_id;
referential_integrity_invalid_data = JOIN policy_master BY
   policy_master_id RIGHT, claims_replaced_nulls BY
   policy_master_id;
referential_check_invalid_claims = FILTER
   referential_integrity_invalid_data BY $0 IS NULL;


/*
For each referential_check_invalid_claims, generate all the values and
specify the reason for considering these values as invalid
*/
invalid_referential_claims = FOREACH
   referential_check_invalid_claims GENERATE  $5 ,$6, $7, $8 ,$9 ,
   $10 , $11, $12, $13 , $14 , $15 , $16 ,$17 , $18 ,$19,
   $20,  $21 ,(chararray) $22 , $23 ,$24,
   'Referential check Failed for policy_master_id' AS reason;


/*
Perform Range validation by checking if the values in the claim_amount
column are within a range of 7% to 65% of the price in the master
dataset.
The values that fall outside the range are considered as invalid
values and are removed.
*/
referential_integrity_valid_claims = FILTER
   referential_integrity_check BY
   ( claims_replaced_nulls::claim_amount>=
   (policy_master::price*7/100) AND
   claims_replaced_nulls::claim_amount<=
   (policy_master::price*65/100 ));
valid_claims = FOREACH referential_integrity_valid_claims GENERATE
   $0, $1 ,$2 , $3 ,$4 , $5 ,$6 , $7, $8 ,$9 , $10 , $11 , $12,
   $13 , $14 , $15 , $16 ,$17 , $18 ,$19;
```

```
invalid_range = FILTER referential_integrity_check BY
  ( claims_replaced_nulls::claim_amount<=
  (policy_master::price*7/100) OR
  claims_replaced_nulls::claim_amount>=
  (policy_master::price*65/100 ));

/*
For each invalid_range, generate all the values and specify the reason
for considering these values as invalid
*/
invalid_claims_range = FOREACH invalid_range GENERATE $0, $1 ,$2 ,
  $3 ,$4 , $5 ,$6, $7, $8 ,$9 , $10 , $11, $12, $13 , $14 , $15 ,
  $16 ,(chararray)$17 , $18 ,$19,
  'claim_amount not within range' AS reason;

/*
Combine all the relations containing invalid values.
*/
invalid_claims = UNION
  invalid_datatype_claims,invalid_referential_claims,
  invalid_claims_range;

/*
The results are stored on the HDFS in the directories valid_data and
invalid_data
The values that are not meeting the constraints are written to a
file in the folder invalid_data. This file has an additional column
specifying the reason for elimination of the record, this can be used
for further analysis.
*/
STORE valid_claims INTO
  '/user/cloudera/pdp/output/data_validation_cleansing/
  constraints_validation_cleansing/valid_data';
STORE invalid_claims INTO
  '/user/cloudera/pdp/output/data_validation_cleansing/
  constraints_validation_cleansing/invalid_data';
```

Results

The following is a snippet of the original dataset; we have eliminated a few columns to improve readability.

```
claim_id,policy_master_id,cust_id,age,city,claim_date,claim_amount
A123B39,A213,39,34,Maryland,5/13/2012,147157
A123B39,A213,39,34,Maryland,5/13/2012,147157
A123B13,A224,13,,Minnesota,2/18/2012,8751.24
```

```
A123B70,A224,70,59,,4/2/2012,8751.24
A123B672,A285AC,672,52,Las Vegas,10/19/2012,7865.73
A123B726,A251ext,726,26,Las Vegas,4/6/2013,4400
A123B21,A214,21,41,Maryland,2/28/2009,1230000000
A123B40,A214,40,35,Austin,6/30/2009,29500
A123B46,A220,46,32,Austin,12/29/2011,13986 Amount
A123B20,A213,20,42,Redmond,5/18/2013,147157 Price
A123B937,A213,937,35,Minnesota,9/27/2009,147157
```

The following is the result of applying this pattern to the dataset:

- Valid data

  ```
  A123B39,A213,39,34,Maryland,5/13/2012,147157
  A123B13,A224,13,35,Minnesota,2/18/2012,8751.24
  A123B70,A224,70,59,XXXXX,4/2/2012,8751.24
  A123B937,A213,937,35,Minnesota,9/27/2009,147157
  ```

- Invalid data

  ```
  A123B672,A285AC,672,52,Las Vegas,10/19/2012,7865.73,
    Referential check Failed for policy_master_id
  A123B726,A251ext,726,26,Las Vegas,4/6/2013,4400,
    Referential check Failed for policy_master_id
  A123B21,A214,21,41,Maryland,2/28/2009,1230000000,
    claim_amount not within range
  A123B40,A214,40,35,Austin,6/30/2009,29500,
    claim_amount not within range
  A123B46,A220,46,32,Austin,12/29/2011,13986 Amount,
    InvalidDatatype for claim_amount
  A123B20,A213,20,42,Redmond,5/18/2013,147157 Price,
    InvalidDatatype for claim_amount
  ```

The resultant data is divided into valid and invalid data. In the previous results, the duplicate record with claim_id A123B39 is removed, the null value for age is replaced by 35 (median) for the record with claim_id A123B13, and the null value for city is replaced by XXXXX for the record with claim_id A123B70. Along with these, the valid data has the list of records that match the data type, range, and referential integrity constraints on the columns claim_amount and policy_master_id. The invalid data is written to a file in the folder invalid_data. The last column of the file mentions the reason for considering the record as invalid.

Additional information

The complete code and datasets for this section are in the following GitHub directories:

- `Chapter4/code/`
- `Chapter4/datasets/`

The regex validation and cleansing design pattern

This design pattern deals with using the regex functions to validate the data. The regex functions can be used to validate the data to match a specific length or pattern and to cleanse the invalid data.

Background

This design pattern discusses ways to use a regex function to identify and clean data that has invalid field lengths. The pattern also identifies all the occurrences of values with the specified date format from within the data and removes the invalid values that do not comply with the format specified.

Motivation

Identifying string data with incorrect length is one of the quickest ways to understand if the data is accurate. Often we will need this string length parameter to judge the data without actually looking deeper into the data. This will be useful in use cases where it is mandatory to have an upper limit to the string length, such as the US state codes that generally have an upper limit of length as two.

Finding all the patterns of strings that match the date pattern is one of the most common transformations done on data. Dates are prone to be represented in multiple ways (DD/MM/YY, MM/DD/YY, YYYY/MM/DD, and so on). Transformation includes finding the occurrence of these patterns and standardizing all of these formats into a uniform date format that is mandated by the business rule.

Use cases

Regular expressions are used in cases that require full or partial pattern matches on strings. The following are a few common use cases that come up while doing **extract, transform, and load** (ETL):

- **String length and pattern validation**: Regular expressions are used to validate the data if the structure of the data is in a standard format and if the data matches a specified length. For example, it can help validate data if the field starts with an alphabet and is followed by a three-digit number.

- **Filtering fields that do not match a specific pattern**: This can be used in the cleansing phase if your business case mandates you to eliminate the data that does not match a specific pattern; for example, filtering the records where dates do not match a predefined format.

- **Splitting string into tokens**: Unstructured text can be parsed and split into tokens using regular expressions. A common example is splitting the text into words by tokenizing it with \s, which denotes splitting by space. Another use could be to split a string using a pattern to get the prefix or suffix. For example, extracting the numeric value of 100 from a string "100 dollars".

- **Extracting data that matches a pattern**: This has uses where you want to extract some text that matches a pattern out of a huge file. Logfile pre-processing is an example for this; you can form a regular expression to extract the request or response patterns from a huge log and further analysis can be performed on the extracted data.

Pattern implementation

This design pattern is implemented in Pig as a standalone script. The script loads the data and validates it against the regular expression patterns.

- **String pattern and length**: The script validates the values in the policy_master_id column to match a predefined length and pattern. The values that do not match the pattern or length are removed.

- **Date format**: The script validates values in the column claim_date to match the MM/DD/YYYY date format; the records with invalid date format are filtered.

Code snippets

To illustrate the working of this pattern, we have considered an automobile insurance claims dataset stored on the HDFS that contains two files. `automobile_policy_master.csv` is the master file; it contains a unique ID, vehicle details, price, and the premium paid for it. The master file is used to validate the data present in the claims file. The `automobile_insurance_claims.csv` file contains automobile insurance claims data, specifically the vehicle repair charges claims; it contains attributes, such as `CLAIM_ID`, `POLICY_MASTER_ID`, `VEHICLE_DETAILS`, and `CLAIM_DETAILS`. For this pattern, we will be performing regex validation and cleansing on `POLICY_MASTER_ID` and `CLAIM_DATE`, as given in the following code:

```
/*
Load automobile insurance claims dataset into the relation claims
*/
claims = LOAD
  '/user/cloudera/pdp/datasets/data_validation/
  automobile_insurance_claims.csv' USING  PigStorage(',') AS
  (claim_id:chararray, policy_master_id:chararray,
  registration_no:chararray, engine_no:chararray,
  chassis_no:chararray,
  customer_id:int,age:int,first_name:chararray,
  last_name:chararray,street:chararray,address:chararray,
  city:chararray,zip:long,gender:chararray, claim_date:chararray,
  garage_city:chararray,bill_no:long,claim_amount:chararray,
  garage_name:chararray,claim_status:chararray);


/*
Validate the values in the column policy_master_id with a regular
expression to match the pattern where the value should start with an
alphabet followed by three digits.
The values that do not match the pattern or length are considered as
invalid values and are removed.
*/
valid_policy_master_id = FILTER claims BY policy_master_id MATCHES
  '[aA-zZ][0-9]{3}';


/*
Invalid values are stored in the relation invalid_length
*/
invalid_policy_master_id = FILTER claims BY NOT
  (policy_master_id MATCHES '[aA-zZ][0-9]{3}');
invalid_length = FOREACH invalid_policy_master_id GENERATE $0,
  $1 ,$2 , $3 ,$4 , $5 ,$6 , $7, $8 ,$9 , $10 , $11, $12, $13 ,
  $14 , $15 , $16 ,$17 , $18 ,$19,
  'Invalid length or pattern for policy_master_id' AS reason;
```

```
/*
Validate the values in the column claim_date to match MM/DD/YYYY
format, also validate the values given for MM and DD to fall within 01
to 12 for month and 01 to 31 for day
The values that do not match the pattern are considered as invalid
values and are removed.
*/
valid_claims = FILTER valid_policy_master_id BY
   ( claim_date MATCHES '^(0?[1-9]|1[0-2])[\\/]
   (0?[1-9]|[12][0-9]|3[01])[\\/]\\d{4}$');


/*
Invalid values are stored in the relation invalid_date
*/
invalid_dates = FILTER valid_policy_master_id BY NOT
   ( claim_date MATCHES '^(0?[1-9]|1[0-2])[\\/]
   (0?[1-9]|[12][0-9]|3[01])[\\/]\\d{4}$');
invalid_date = FOREACH invalid_dates GENERATE $0, $1 ,$2 , $3 ,
   $4 , $5 ,$6 , $7, $8 ,$9 , $10 , $11, $12, $13 , $14 , $15 ,
   $16 ,$17 , $18 ,$19,
   'Invalid date format for claim_date' AS reason;


/*
Combine the relations that contain invalid values.
*/
invalid_claims = UNION invalid_length,invalid_date;


/*
The results are stored on the HDFS in the directories valid_data and
invalid_data
The invalid values are written to a file in the folder invalid_
data. This file has an additional column specifying the reason for
elimination of the record, this can be used for further analysis.
*/
STORE valid_claims INTO
   '/user/cloudera/pdp/output/data_validation_cleansing/
   regex_validation_cleansing/valid_data';
STORE invalid_claims INTO
   '/user/cloudera/pdp/output/data_validation_cleansing/
   regex_validation_cleansing/invalid_data';
```

Results

The following is a snippet of the original dataset; we have eliminated a few columns to improve readability.

```
claim_id,policy_master_id,cust_id,age,city,claim_date,claim_amount
A123B1,A290,1,42,Minnesota,1/5/2011,8211
A123B672,A285AC,672,52,Las Vegas,10/19/2012,7865.73
A123B726,A251ext,726,26,Las Vegas,4/6/2013,4400
A123B2,A213,2,35,Redmond,1/22/2009,147157
A123B28,A221,28,19,Austin,6/37/2012,31930.2
A123B888,A247,888,49,Las Vegas,21/20/2012,873
A123B3,A214,3,23,Maryland,7/8/2011,8400
```

The following is the result of applying this pattern to the dataset:

- Valid data

  ```
  A123B1,A290,1,42,Minnesota,1/5/2011,8211
  A123B2,A213,2,35,Redmond,1/22/2009,147157
  A123B3,A214,3,23,Maryland,7/8/2011,8400
  ```

- Invalid data

  ```
  A123B672,A285AC,672,52,Las Vegas,10/19/2012,7865.73,
      Invalid length or pattern for policy_master_id
  A123B726,A251ext,726,26,Las Vegas,4/6/2013,4400,
      Invalid length or pattern for policy_master_id
  A123B28,A221,28,19,Austin,6/37/2012,31930.2,
      Invalid date format for claim_date
  A123B888,A247,888,49,Las Vegas,21/20/2012,873,
      Invalid date format for claim_date
  ```

As shown previously, the resultant data is divided into valid and invalid data. Valid data has the list of records that match the regex pattern for validating `policy_master_id` and `claim_date`. The invalid data is written to a file in the folder `invalid_data`; the last column of the file mentions the reason for considering this record as invalid. We chose to filter invalid data; however, the cleansing technique depends on the business case where the invalid data might have to be transformed to valid data.

Additional information

The complete code and datasets for this section are in the following GitHub directories:

- `Chapter4/code/`
- `Chapter4/datasets/`

The corrupt data validation and cleansing design pattern

This design pattern discusses data corruption from the perspective of the corrupt data being treated as a noise or as an outlier. The techniques to identify and cleanse the corrupt data are discussed in detail.

Background

This design pattern explores the usage of Pig to validate and cleanse corrupt data from a dataset. It tries to set the context of data corruption from various sources of Big Data ranging from sensor to structured data. This design pattern probes the data corruption angle from two perspectives, one is noise and the other is outliers, as given in the following list:

- Noise can be defined as a random error in measurement that has caused corrupt data to be ingested along with the correct data. The amount of error is not too far away from the expected value.

- Outliers are also a kind of noise but the value of error is too far away from the expected value. Outliers can have a very high influence on the accuracy of an analysis. They are often measurements or recording errors. Some of them can represent phenomena of interest, something significant from the viewpoint of the application domain, which implies that not all outliers should be eliminated.

Data corruption can manifest as noise or outliers, the major difference between them being the degree of variation to the expected value. Noisy data varies to a lesser degree and has values closer to the original data, whereas outliers vary to a large degree and the values are way off the original data. Illustrating the example in the following set of numbers, 4 can be considered as noise and 21 as an outlier.

A = [1,2,1,4,1,2,1,1,1,2,21,1,2,2]

Corrupt data increases the amount of effort required to perform analytics and also adversely affects the accuracy of the data mining analysis. The following points illustrate a few sources of data corruption as applicable to Big Data:

- **Data corruption in sensor data**: Sensor data has become one of the biggest sources of volume amongst the wide array of Big Data sources that pervades our data universe. These sensors generally generate a huge amount of data over a very long period of time and this leads to various computational challenges arising due to the inaccuracy of data. Hadoop is extensively used in mining longitudinal sensor data for patterns and one of the biggest challenges faced in this process is the natural errors and incompleteness of the sensor data. The sensors have inadequate battery life because of which many of them probably may not be able to send accurate data over an extended period of time, thus corrupting the data.

- **Data corruption in structured data**: In the structured Big Data context, any data, be it numeric or categorical, that has been stored in Hadoop in such a manner that it cannot be read or used by any of the data processing routines written for the data can be considered corrupt.

Motivation

Corrupt data can be validated and cleansed by applying appropriate noise and outlier detection techniques. The common techniques employed for this purpose are binning, regression, and clustering, as given in the following list:

- **Binning**: This technique can be used to identify noise and outliers. This technique is also used for removal of noisy data by applying a smoothing function. Binning works by creating a set of sorted values partitioned into bins. These values are partitioned by equal frequency or equal width. In order to smoothen the data (or remove noise), the original data values that are in a given partition or a bin, are replaced by the mean or median of that partition. In the current design pattern, we will be illustrating the applicability of binning to remove noise.

- **Regression**: It is a technique that fits the data values to a function. Noise removal can be done using regression by identifying the regression function and removing all the data values that lie far away from the function's predicted value. Linear regression finds the "most appropriate" line function to fit two variables so that one variable can be used to predict the other. Multiple linear regressions, similar to linear regressions, is where more than two variables are involved and the data is fit to a poly-dimensional surface.

- **Clustering**: Outlier analysis can be performed using clustering by grouping similar values together to find the values that are outside of the cluster and may be considered as an outlier. A cluster consists of values that are similar to other values in the same cluster and at the same time, dissimilar to the values in the other clusters. A cluster of values can be treated as a group to compare with other cluster values at macro level.

One more method of finding the outliers is to compute the **interquartile range (IQR)**. In this method, three quartiles (Q1, Q2, and Q3) are first calculated from the values. The quartiles divide the values into four equal groups with each group comprising a quarter of data. The upper fence and lower fence are calculated using the three quartiles and any value above or below these two fences is considered as an outlier. The fences are a guideline to define the range outside which an outlier exists. In the current design pattern, we are using this method to find the outliers.

Use cases

You can consider using this design pattern to cleanse corrupt data by removing noise and outliers. This design pattern will be helpful to understand how to classify data into noise or outliers and then remove them.

Pattern implementation

This design pattern is implemented as a standalone Pig script using a third-party library `datafu.jar`. The script has the implementation for identifying and removing noise and outliers.

Binning techniques identify and remove noise. In binning, the values are sorted and are distributed into a number of bins. The minimum and maximum values are identified for each bin and are set as bin boundaries. Each bin value is replaced by the nearest bin boundary value. This method is called smoothing by bin boundaries. To identify outliers, we are using the standard box plot rule method; it finds outliers based on the upper and lower quartiles of the data distribution. The Q1 and Q3 of the data distribution and their interquartile distance is calculated, using *(Q1 - c * IQD, Q3 + c *IQD)*, which gives the range that that the data should fall in. Here, c is a constant with a value 1.5. The values that fall outside this range are considered outliers. The script uses the Datafu library to calculate quartiles.

Code snippets

To illustrate the working of this pattern, we have considered an automobile insurance claims dataset stored on the HDFS that contains two files. `automobile_policy_master.csv` is the master file; it contains a unique ID, vehicle details, price, and the premium paid for it. The master file is used to validate the data present in the claims file. The `automobile_insurance_claims.csv` file contains automobile insurance claims data, specifically vehicle repair charges claims; it contains attributes, such as `CLAIM_ID`, `POLICY_MASTER_ID`, `VEHICLE_DETAILS`, and `CLAIM_DETAILS`. For this pattern, we will be performing corrupt data validation and cleansing on `CLAIM_AMOUNT` and `AGE`, as given in the following code:

```
/*
Register Datafu jar file
*/
REGISTER  '/home/cloudera/pdp/jars/datafu.jar';


/*
Define alias for the UDF quantile
The parameters specify list of quantiles to compute
*/
DEFINE Quantile datafu.pig.stats.Quantile('0.25','0.50','0.75');


/*
Load automobile insurance claims data set into the relation claims
*/
claims = LOAD
  '/user/cloudera/pdp/datasets/data_validation/
  automobile_insurance_claims.csv' USING  PigStorage(',') AS
  (claim_id:chararray, policy_master_id:chararray,
  registration_no:chararray, engine_no:chararray,
  chassis_no:chararray,
  customer_id:int,age:int,first_name:chararray,
  last_name:chararray,street:chararray,address:chararray,
  city:chararray,zip:long,gender:chararray, claim_date:chararray,
  garage_city:chararray,bill_no:long,claim_amount:double,
  garage_name:chararray,claim_status:chararray);


/*
Sort the relation claims by age
*/
```

```
claims_age_sorted = ORDER claims BY age ASC;

/*
Divide the data into equal frequency bins.
Minimum and maximum values are identified for each bin and are set as
bin boundaries.
Replace each bin value with the nearest bin boundary.
*/
bin_id_claims = FOREACH claims_age_sorted GENERATE
  (customer_id - 1) * 10 / (130- 1 + 1) AS bin_id, $0 ,$1 ,$2 ,
  $3 ,$4 ,$5 ,$6 ,$7 ,$8 ,$9 ,$10 ,$11 ,$12 ,$13 ,$14 ,$15 ,
  $16 ,$17 ,$18 ,$19 ;
group_by_id = GROUP bin_id_claims BY bin_id;
claims_bin_boundaries = FOREACH group_by_id
{
  bin_lower_bound=(int) MIN(bin_id_claims.age);
  bin_upper_bound = (int)MAX(bin_id_claims.age);
  GENERATE bin_lower_bound AS bin_lower_bound, bin_upper_bound AS
  bin_upper_bound, FLATTEN(bin_id_claims);
};
smoothing_by_bin_boundaries = FOREACH claims_bin_boundaries
  GENERATE $3 AS claim_id,$4 AS policy_master_id,$5 AS
  registration_no,$6 AS engine_no,$7 AS chassis_no,
  $8 AS customer_id,( ( $9 - bin_lower_bound ) <=
  ( bin_upper_bound - $9 ) ? bin_lower_bound : bin_upper_bound )
  AS age,$10 AS first_name,$11 AS last_name,$12 AS street,
  $13 AS address,$14 AS city,$15 AS zip,$16 AS gender,
  $17 AS claim_date,$18 AS garage_city,$19 AS bill_no,
  $20 AS claim_amount,$21 AS garage_name,$22 AS claim_status;

/*
Identify outliers present in the column claim_amount by calculating
the quartiles, interquartile distance and the upper and lower fences.
The values that do not fall within this range are considered as
outliers and are filtered out.
*/
groupd = GROUP smoothing_by_bin_boundaries ALL;
quantiles = FOREACH groupd {
  sorted = ORDER smoothing_by_bin_boundaries BY claim_amount;
  GENERATE Quantile(sorted.claim_amount) AS quant;
}
valid_range = FOREACH quantiles GENERATE
  (quant.quantile_0_25 - 1.5 *
  (quant.quantile_0_75 - quant.quantile_0_25)) ,
  (quant.quantile_0_75 + 1.5 *
  (quant.quantile_0_75 - quant.quantile_0_25));
```

```
claims_filtered_outliers = FILTER smoothing_by_bin_boundaries BY
  claim_amount>= valid_range.$0 AND claim_amount<= valid_range.$1;


/*
Store the invalid values in the relation invalid_claims
*/
invalid_claims_filter = FILTER smoothing_by_bin_boundaries BY
  claim_amount<= valid_range.$0 OR claim_amount>= valid_range.$1;
invalid_claims = FOREACH invalid_claims_filter GENERATE $0 ,$1 ,
  $2 ,$3 ,$4 ,$5 ,$6 ,$7 ,$8 ,$9 ,$10 ,$11 ,$12 ,$13 ,$14 ,
  $15 ,$16 ,$17 ,$18 ,$19,
  'claim_amount identified as Outlier' as reason;


/*
The results are stored on the HDFS in the directories valid_data and
invalid_data
The invalid values are written to a file in the folder invalid_
data. This file has an additional column specifying the reason for
elimination of the record, this can be used for further analysis.
*/
STORE invalid_claims INTO
  '/user/cloudera/pdp/output/data_validation_cleansing/
  corrupt_data_validation_cleansing/invalid_data';
STORE claims_filtered_outliers INTO
  '/user/cloudera/pdp/output/data_validation_cleansing/
  corrupt_data_validation_cleansing/valid_data';
```

Results

The following is a snippet of the original dataset; we have eliminated a few columns to improve readability.

```
claim_id,policy_master_id,cust_id,age,city,claim_date,claim_amount
A123B6,A217,6,42,Las Vegas,6/25/2010,-12495
A123B11,A222,11,21,,11/5/2012,293278.7,claim_amount identified as
  Outlier
A123B2,A213,2,42,Redmond,1/22/2009,147157,claim_amount identified
  as Outlier
A123B9,A220,9,21,Maryland,9/20/2011,13986
A123B4,A215,4,42,Austin,12/16/2011,35478
```

The following is the result of applying this pattern on the dataset:

- Valid data

```
A123B6,A217,6,42,Las Vegas,6/25/2010,-12495
A123B9,A220,9,21,Maryland,9/20/2011,13986
A123B4,A215,4,42,Austin,12/16/2011,35478
```

- Invalid data

```
A123B11,A222,11,21,,11/5/2012,293278.7,
   claim_amount identified as Outlier
A123B2,A213,2,42,Redmond,1/22/2009,147157,
   claim_amount identified as Outlier
```

As shown previously, the resultant data is divided into valid and invalid data. Valid data has the list of records where the noise is smoothened for the `age` column. Outlier detection is done on the `claim_amount` column, the lower and upper fences are identified as `-34929.0` and `70935.0`; the values that do not fall in this range are identified as outliers and are written to a file in the folder `invalid_data`. The last column of this file shows the reason for considering this record as invalid. The outliers are filtered and the data is stored in the `valid_data` folder. The previous script removes the outliers; however, this decision can vary as per the business rule.

Additional information

The complete code and datasets for this section are in the following GitHub directories:

- `Chapter4/code/`
- `Chapter4/datasets/`

The unstructured text data validation and cleansing design pattern

The unstructured text validation and cleansing pattern demonstrates ways to cleanse unstructured data by applying various data pre-processing techniques.

Background

Processing huge amounts of unstructured data with Hadoop is a challenging task in terms of cleaning it and making it ready for processing. Textual data, which includes documents, mails, text files, and chat files, is inherently unorganized without a defined data model when it is ingested by Hadoop.

In order to open the unstructured data for analysis, we have to bring in a semblance of structure to it. The foundation of organizing unstructured data is to integrate it with structured data existing in the enterprise by performing a planned and controlled cleansing transformation and flow of data across the data store, for operational and/or analytical use. Integration of unstructured data is necessary to make the queries and analytics performed on the resultant data meaningful.

One of the first steps after unstructured data ingestion is to discover the metadata from the textual data and organize it in a way that facilitates further processing, thus removing a few of the irregularities and ambiguities from the data. This metadata creation itself is a multistep iterative process employing various data parsing, cleansing, and transformation techniques ranging from simple entity extraction and semantic tagging to natural language processing using artificial intelligence algorithms.

Motivation

This design pattern demonstrates one way to cleanse an unstructured data corpus by performing pre-processing steps, such as lowercase conversion, stopword removal, stemming, punctuation removal, extra spaces removal, identifying numbers, and identifying misspellings.

The motivation for this pattern is to understand the various kinds of inconsistencies in unstructured data and help identify these issues and cleanse them.

Unstructured data is prone to multiple quality issues ranging from integrity to inconsistency. The following are the common cleansing steps for unstructured text:

- Textual data can also be represented using alternative forms of spellings; for instance, a name can be written in different ways and searching for that particular name will not give a result if it is spelled differently but still refers to the same entity. This aspect can be considered as a form of misspelling. Integrating and cleansing these alternative spellings to refer to the same entity would mitigate the ambiguity. Effective conversion of unstructured text to structured format requires us to take into account all the alternative spellings.

- Misspellings also account for many irregularities that will affect the accuracy of the analytics. In order to make the data processable, we have to identify the misspelled words and replace them with the correct ones.

- Numerical value identification from within the text enables us to pick all the numbers. These extracted numbers can be included or eliminated from further processing depending on the business context. Data cleansing can also be performed by extracting numbers from text; for instance, if the text consists of a phrase "one thousand", it can be transformed into 1000 so that appropriate analytics can be performed.

- Extraction of data, which matches certain patterns using regex, can be a cleansing method. For instance, dates can be extracted from within the text by specifying a pattern. If the extracted dates are not in the standard format (DD/MM/YY), standardizing the dates could be one of the cleansing activities performed to read and index the unstructured data by date.

Use cases

You can consider using this design pattern to cleanup the unstructured data by removing misspellings, punctuations, and so on after the data has already been ingested by Hadoop.

Pattern implementation

This design pattern is implemented as a standalone Pig script, which internally uses right-outer join to remove the stop words. The list of stop words are first loaded into a relation from an external text file and then used in the outer join.

The LOWER function is used to convert all the words into lower case. Punctuations are removed by using the REPLACE function matching the specific literal. Similarly, numbers are removed by matching all the patterns of numbers in the text using REPLACE.

The code for implementing the misspelled words uses a Bloom filter, which has been recently included in Pig 0.10 version as a UDF.

The Bloom filter is a space-optimized data structure specifically used to filter a smaller dataset from a larger dataset by testing whether an element belonging to the smaller dataset is a member of the larger one or not. The Bloom filter achieves drastic space optimization by internally implementing a clever mechanism to store each element to use a constant amount of memory no matter the size of the element. Even though the Bloom filter has an enormous space advantage compared to other structures, the filtering is not completely accurate since there can be scope for false positives.

Pig has support for the Bloom filters through calls to `BuildBloom`, which builds a Bloom filter by loading and training it from the list of values loaded from the dictionary corpus stored in a Pig relation. The trained Bloom filter, stored in a distributed cache and passed on to the `Mapper` function internally, is used to perform the actual filtering operation on the input data by doing a `FILTER` operation using the `BLOOM` UDF. The resultant set filtered would be the correctly spelled words after the Bloom filter has eliminated all the misspelled words.

Code snippets

To demonstrate the working of this pattern, we have considered the text corpus of Wikipedia stored in a folder accessible to the HDFS. This sample corpus consists of the wiki pages related to Computer Science and Information Technology. A few misspelled words are deliberately introduced into the corpus to demonstrate the functionality of this pattern.

```
/*
Define alias for the UDF BuildBloom.
The first parameter to BuildBloom constructor is the hashing technique
to use, the second parameter specifies the number of distinct elements
that would be placed in the filter and the third parameter is the
acceptable rate of false positives.
*/
DEFINE BuildBloom BuildBloom('jenkins', '75000', '0.1');

/*
Load dictionary words
*/
dict_words1 = LOAD
  '/user/cloudera/pdp/datasets/data_validation/unstructured_text/
  dictionary_words1.csv' as (words:chararray);
dict_words2 = LOAD
  '/user/cloudera/pdp/datasets/data_validation/unstructured_text/
  dictionary_words2.csv' as (words:chararray);

/*
Load stop words
*/
stop_words_list = LOAD
  '/user/cloudera/pdp/datasets/data_validation/unstructured_text/
  stopwords.txt' USING PigStorage();
stopwords = FOREACH stop_words_list GENERATE
  FLATTEN(TOKENIZE($0));
```

```
/*
Load the document corpus and tokenize to extract the words
*/
doc1 = LOAD
  '/user/cloudera/pdp/datasets/data_validation/unstructured_text/
  computer_science.txt' AS (words:chararray);
docWords1 = FOREACH doc1 GENERATE FLATTEN(TOKENIZE(words)) AS
  word;
doc2 = LOAD
  '/user/cloudera/pdp/datasets/data_validation/unstructured_text/
  information_technology.txt' AS (words:chararray);
docWords2 = FOREACH doc2 GENERATE FLATTEN(TOKENIZE(words)) AS
  word;

/*
Combine the contents of the relations docWords1 and docWords2
*/
combined_docs = UNION docWords1, docWords2;

/*
Convert to lowercase, remove stopwords, punctuations, spaces, numbers.
Replace nulls with the value "dummy string"
*/
lowercase_data = FOREACH combined_docs GENERATE
  FLATTEN(TOKENIZE(LOWER($0))) as word;
joind = JOIN stopwords BY $0 RIGHT OUTER, lowercase_data BY $0;
stop_words_removed = FILTER joind BY $0 IS NULL;
punctuation_removed = FOREACH stop_words_removed
{
  replace_punct = REPLACE($1,'[\\p{Punct}]','');
  replace_space = REPLACE(replace_punct,'[\\s]','');
  replace_numbers = REPLACE(replace_space,'[\\d]','');
  GENERATE replace_numbers AS replaced_words;
}
replaced_nulls = FOREACH punctuation_removed GENERATE
  (SIZE($0) > 0 ? $0 : 'dummy string') as word;

/*
Remove duplicate words
*/
unique_words_corpus = DISTINCT replaced_nulls;

/*
```

```
Combine the two relations containing dictionary words
*/
dict_words = UNION dict_words1, dict_words2;


/*
BuildBloom builds a bloom filter that will be used in Bloom.
Bloom filter is built on the relation dict_words which contains all
the dictionary words.
The resulting file dict_words_bloom is used in bloom filter by passing
it to Bloom.
The call to bloom returns the words that are present in the
dictionary, we select the words that are not present in the dictionary
and classify them as misspelt words. The misspelt words are filtered
from the original dataset and are stored in the folder invalid_data.
*/
dict_words_grpd = GROUP dict_words all;
dict_words_bloom = FOREACH dict_words_grpd GENERATE
  BuildBloom(dict_words.words);
STORE dict_words_bloom into 'dict_words_bloom';
DEFINE bloom Bloom('dict_words_bloom');
filterd = FILTER unique_words_corpus BY NOT(bloom($0));
joind = join filterd by $0, unique_words_corpus by $0;
joind_right = join filterd by $0 RIGHT, unique_words_corpus BY $0;
valid_words_filter = FILTER joind_right BY $0 IS NULL;
valid_words = FOREACH valid_words_filter GENERATE $1;
misspellings = FOREACH joind GENERATE $0 AS misspelt_word;


/*
The results are stored on the HDFS in the directories valid_data and
invalid_data.
The misspelt words are written to a file in the folder invalid_data.
*/
STORE misspellings INTO
  '/user/cloudera/pdp/output/data_validation_cleansing/
  unstructured_data_validation_cleansing/invalid_data';
STORE valid_words INTO
  '/user/cloudera/pdp/output/data_validation_cleansing/
  unstructured_data_validation_cleansing/valid_data';
```

Results

The following are the words that are identified as misspellings and are stored in the folder `invalid_data`. We chose to filter these words from the original dataset. However, this depends on the business rule; if the business rule mandates that misspelt words have to be replaced with their correct spellings, the appropriate steps have to be taken to correct the spellings.

```
sme
lemme
puttin
speling
wntedly
mistaces
servicesa
insertingg
missspellingss
telecommunications
```

Additional information

The complete code and datasets for this section are in the following GitHub directories:

- `Chapter4/code/`
- `Chapter4/datasets/`

Summary

In this chapter, you have studied various Big Data validation and cleansing techniques that deal with the detection and cleansing of incorrect or inaccurate records from the data. These techniques ensure that the inconsistencies in the data are identified by validating the data against a set of rules before the data is used in the analytics process, and then the inconsistent data is replaced, modified, or deleted as per the business rule to make it more consistent. In this chapter, we build upon our learnings from the previous chapter on data profiling.

In the next chapter, we will focus on the **data transformation patterns** that can be applied to a variety of data formats. After reading this chapter, readers will be able to choose the right pattern to transform the data by using techniques such as aggregation, generalizations, and joins.

5
Data Transformation Patterns

In the last chapter, you learned about various patterns related to data validation and cleansing from which you understood that there are ways to detect and remove incorrect or inaccurate records from the data. By the time data validation and cleansing is complete, the inconsistencies in the data are identified even before the data is used in the next steps of the analytics life cycle; then, the inconsistent data is replaced, modified, or deleted to make it more consistent.

In this chapter, you will learn about various design patterns related to data transformation, such as structured to hierarchical, normalization, integration, aggregation, and generalization design patterns.

Data transformation processes

The process of data transformation is one of the fundamental building blocks and a vital step in the knowledge discovery process of Big Data analytics. Data transformation is an iterative process that modifies the source data into a format that enables the analytics algorithms to be applied effectively. Transformation improves the performance and accuracy of the algorithms by ensuring that the data is stored and retrieved in a format that is conducive for applying the analytics. This is done by improving the overall quality of the source data.

Data transformation for Big Data predominantly consists of the following major processes:

- **Normalization**: This transformation scales the attribute data to bring it within a specified range. Typically, an attribute value is transformed to fit the range between 0 and 1. This is done to remove certain unwanted effects of certain attributes on the analytics. The normalization transformation is different from the first, second, and third normal form used in the relational database design.

- **Aggregation**: This transformation applies summary operations on the data, for example, computing monthly and yearly summaries from the daily stock data, thus creating a data cube for performing analysis in multiple dimensions and granularities.

- **Generalization**: In this transformation, the low-level raw data is replaced by higher level abstractions using concept hierarchies. For example, low-level data such as street can be replaced by higher abstractions such as city or state depending on the analytics use case.

- **Data integration**: It is the process of joining the data from multiple input pipelines of similar or dissimilar structure into a single output pipe.

The following sections elaborate the most commonly used Pig design patterns that help in data transformation.

The structured-to-hierarchical transformation pattern

The structured-to-hierarchical transformation pattern deals with transforming the data by generating a hierarchical structure, such as XML or JSON from the structured data.

Background

The structured-to-hierarchical transformation pattern creates a new hierarchical structure, such as JSON or XML out of data that is stored in flat, row-like structures. It is a data transformation pattern that creates new records, which are represented in a different structure when compared to the original records.

Motivation

Hadoop is good at integrating data from multiple sources, but performing joins for the analytics just in time is always a complex and time-consuming operation.

In order to perform certain types of analytics efficiently (such as logfile analysis), the data is sometimes not required to be stored in a normalized form in Hadoop. Storing the data in the normalized form in multiple tables creates an additional step of joining all the data together to perform analytics on it—joins are generally performed on normalized structured data for integrating it from multiple sources that have a foreign-key relationship.

Instead, raw data is nested in a hierarchical fashion by denormalizing them. This pre-processing of data will ensure that the analysis is performed efficiently.

NoSQL databases, such as HBase, Cassandra, or MongoDB facilitate the storage of flat data in column families or JSON objects. Hadoop can be used to perform the task of integrating data from multiple sources in a batch mode and creating hierarchical data structures that could be readily inserted into these databases.

Use cases

This design pattern is predominantly applicable to integrate structured and row-based data from multiple disjointed data sources. The specific objective of this integration is to convert the data into a hierarchical structure so that the data is ready for analysis.

This pattern is also useful to convert data from a single source to a hierarchical structure, which is then used to load data into columnar and JSON databases.

Pattern implementation

Pig has out-of-the-box support for hierarchical data in the form of tuples and bags that are used to represent nested objects in a single row. The COGROUP operator groups data in one or more relations and creates a nested representation of the output tuples.

This design pattern is implemented in Pig as a standalone script. The script shows the usage of this pattern by generating a hierarchical representation of data from a structured format. The script loads a denormalized CSV file and passes it to a custom Java UDF. The Java UDF uses XMLParser to build an XML file. A custom storage function stores the result in the XML format.

Code snippets

To illustrate the working of this pattern, we have considered a manufacturing dataset stored on HDFS. The file `production_all.csv` contains denormalized data derived from `production.csv` and `manufacturing_units.csv`. We will convert the structured data from the CSV format to a hierarchical XML format.

The Pig script for the structured-to-hierarchical design pattern is as follows:

```
/*
Register the piggybank jar and generateStoreXml jar, it is a custom
storage function which generates an XML representation and stores it
*/
```

```
REGISTER '/home/cloudera/pdp/jars/generateStoreXml.jar';
REGISTER '/usr/share/pig/contrib/piggybank/java/piggybank.jar';


/*
Load the production dataset into the relation production_details
*/
production_details = LOAD
  '/user/cloudera/pdp/datasets/data_transformation/
  production_all.csv' USING  PigStorage(',') AS
  (production_date,production_hours,manufacturing_unit_id,
  manufacturing_unit_name,currency,product_id,product_name,
  quantity_produced);

/*
Call the custom store function TransformStoreXML to transform the
contents into a hierarchical representation i.e XML and to store it in
the directory structured_to_hierarchical
*/
STORE production_details INTO
  '/user/cloudera/pdp/output/data_transformation/
  structured_to_hierarchical' USING
  com.xmlgenerator.TransformStoreXML
  ('production_details','production_data');
```

The following is a snippet of the Java UDF used by the previous Pig script to perform structured-to-hierarchical transformation:

```
/**
 * data from tuple is appended to xml root element
 * @param tuple
 */
protected void write(Tuple tuple)
{
  // Retrieving all fields from the schema
  ResourceFieldSchema[] fields = schema.getFields();
  //Retrieve values from tuple
  List<Object> values = tuple.getAll();
  /*Creating xml element by using fields as element tag
and tuple value as element value*/
  Element transactionElement =
    xmlDoc.createElement(TransformStoreXML.elementName);
  for(int counter=0;counter<fields.length;counter++)
  {
    //Retrieving element value from values
```

```
        String columnValue =
          String.valueOf(values.get(counter));
        //Creating element tag from fields
        Element columnName =
          xmlDoc.createElement
          (fields[counter].getName().toString().trim());
        //Appending value to element tag

        columnName.appendChild(xmlDoc.createTextNode(columnValue));
        //Appending element to transaction element
          transactionElement.appendChild(columnName);
      }
      //Appending transaction element to root element
      rootElement.appendChild(transactionElement);
    }
```

Results

The following is a snippet of the XML file that is generated as a result of the code being executed on the input:

```
<?xml version="1.0" encoding="UTF-8" standalone="no" ?>
<production_details>
  <production_data>
    <production_date>2011-01-01T00:00:00</production_date>
    <production_hours>7</production_hours>
    <manufacturing_unit_id>1</manufacturing_unit_id>
    <manufacturing_unit_name>unit1</manufacturing_unit_name>
    <currency>USD</currency>
    <product_id>C001</product_id>
    <product_name>Refrigerator 180L</product_name>
    <quantity_produced>49</quantity_produced>
  </production_data>
  <production_data>

    .
    .
    .

  </production_data>
  .
  .
  .
</production_details>
```

Additional information

The complete code and datasets for this section are in the following GitHub directories:

- `Chapter5/code/`
- `Chapter5/datasets/`

The data normalization pattern

The data normalization design pattern discusses ways to perform normalization or standardization of data values.

Background

Normalization of data implies fitting, adjusting, or scaling the data values measured on different scales to a notionally common range. As a simplistic example, joining datasets that consist of different units for distance measurement, such as kilometers and miles, can provide varying results when they are not normalized. Hence, they are normalized to bring them back to one common unit, such as kilometers or miles, so that the effect of different units of measurement is not felt by the analytics.

Motivation

In Big Data, it is common to encounter varying values in the same data attribute while integrating multiple data sources.

Normalization performs data pre-processing and transformation by changing the original data and scaling it to bring it within a specified range (for example, in the range 0 to 1), and assigning equal weight for all attributes. Before normalization is performed on the data, any outliers are removed from it. Data normalization is required in scenarios when analytics can be affected by the choice of the unit of measurement and by values that are in the higher range.

Normalization is used in analytics such as clustering, which is a distance-based method where it prevents attributes with higher values from dominating attributes with lesser values. The techniques to perform normalization on numeric and non numeric data are as follows:

- **Normalizing numeric data**: Numeric data is normalized using methods such as min-max normalization, thus transforming the data to a value between a specified range [newMin, newMax]. The minValue and maxValue are usually identified from the dataset and the normalization is done by applying the following formula for each value:

  normalizedValue = [((value - minValue) / (maxValue - minValue))*(newMax - newMin) + newMin]

- **Normalizing non-numeric data**: Non numeric data is normalized by first converting them into numeric data and then performing the normalizing operation on it. As an example, if the values of a rating attribute can be excellent, very good, good, average, below average, poor, or worst, they can be converted into numeric values of 1 through 7; thus, normalization can be performed on these numeric values to fit in the model.

Use cases

You can consider using this design pattern as a pre-processing technique for performing analytics. This pattern can be used in analytics' use cases to avoid attributes with initially higher values from dwarfing attributes with initially lower values.

This pattern can be considered as a method to encapsulate the original data as it transforms the original data by normalizing it.

Pattern implementation

This design pattern is implemented in Pig as a standalone script. The use case identifies similar manufacturing units for a given product; it demonstrates normalization. The script loads the data and computes `total produced quantity` and `total production hours` for each manufacturing unit for the product `C001`. Each manufacturing unit is represented by `product`, `total produced quantity`, and `total production hours`. The script normalizes `total number of units produced` and `total production hours` using the min-max normalization technique to bring all the values to the same scale (range 0 to 1). The script then computes the Euclidean distance between these points. The smaller the distance, the more similar the manufacturing units are.

Code snippets

To illustrate the working of this pattern, we have considered a manufacturing dataset stored on the HDFS. The file `production.csv` contains production information of each manufacturing unit; this file contains attributes such as `production_date`, `production_hours`, `manufacturing_unit_id`, `product_id`, and `produced_quantity`. We will be calculating `total produced quantity` and `total production hours` for each manufacturing unit for the product `C001`, as shown in the following code:

```
/*
Load the production dataset into the relation production
*/
production = LOAD
  '/user/cloudera/pdp/datasets/data_transformation/
  production.csv' USING PigStorage(',') AS
  (production_date:datetime,production_hours:int,
  manufacturing_unit_id:chararray,product_id:chararray,
  produced_quantity:int);

/*
Filter the relation products to fetch the records with product id C001
*/
production_filt = FILTER production BY product_id=='C001';

/*
Calculate the total production hours and total produced quantity of
product C001 in each manufacturing unit
*/
production_grpd = GROUP production_filt BY
  (manufacturing_unit_id,product_id);
production_sum = FOREACH production_grpd GENERATE group.$0 AS
  manufacturing_unit_id, group.$1 AS product_id,(float)
  SUM(production_filt.production_hours) AS
  production_hours,(float)SUM(production_filt.produced_quantity)
  AS produced_quantity;

/*
Apply Min max normalization on total production hours and total
produced quantity for each manufacturing unit to scale the data to fit
in the range of [0-1]
*/
production_sum_grpd = GROUP production_sum ALL;
```

```
production_min_max = FOREACH production_sum_grpd GENERATE
  MIN(production_sum.production_hours)-1 AS
  min_hour,MAX(production_sum.production_hours)+1 AS max_hour,
  MIN(production_sum.produced_quantity)-1 AS min_qty,
  MAX(production_sum.produced_quantity)+1 AS max_qty;
production_norm = FOREACH production_sum
{
  norm_production_hours = (float)(((production_hours -
    production_min_max.min_hour)/(production_min_max.max_hour -
    production_min_max.min_hour))*(1-0))+1;
  norm_produced_quantity = (float)(((produced_quantity -
    production_min_max.min_qty)/(production_min_max.max_qty -
    production_min_max.min_qty))*(1-0))+1;
  GENERATE manufacturing_unit_id AS manufacturing_unit_id,
    product_id AS product_id, norm_production_hours AS
    production_hours, norm_produced_quantity AS produced_quantity;
}
prod_norm = FOREACH production_norm GENERATE manufacturing_unit_id
  AS manufacturing_unit_id,product_id AS
  product_id,production_hours AS
  production_hours,produced_quantity AS produced_quantity;


/*
Calculate the Euclidean distance to find out similar manufacturing
units w.r.t the product C001
*/
manufacturing_units_euclidean_distance  = FOREACH
  (CROSS production_norm,prod_norm) {
distance_between_points = (production_norm::production_hours -
  prod_norm::production_hours)*
  (production_norm::production_hours -
  prod_norm::production_hours) +
  (production_norm::produced_quantity -
  prod_norm::produced_quantity)*(production_norm::
  produced_quantity - prod_norm::produced_quantity);
GENERATE  production_norm::manufacturing_unit_id,
  production_norm::product_id,prod_norm::manufacturing_unit_id,
  prod_norm::product_id,SQRT(distance_between_points) as dist;
};


/*
The results are stored on the HDFS in the directory data_normalization
*/
STORE manufacturing_units_euclidean_distance INTO
  '/user/cloudera/pdp/output/data_transformation/
  data_normalization';
```

Results

The following is a snippet of the results that are generated as a result of the code being executed on the input:

```
1   C001   1   C001   0.0
1   C001   3   C001   1.413113776343348
1   C001   5   C001   0.2871426024640011
3   C001   1   C001   1.413113776343348
3   C001   3   C001   0.0
3   C001   5   C001   1.1536163027782005
5   C001   1   C001   0.2871426024640011
5   C001   3   C001   1.1536163027782005
5   C001   5   C001   0.0
```

The similarity between manufacturing units is calculated for one product (C001). As shown previously, manufacturing units 1 and 5 are similar with respect to the product C001, as the distance between them is less when compared to the distance between other units.

Additional information

The complete code and datasets for this section are in the following GitHub directories:

- Chapter5/code/
- Chapter5/datasets/

The data integration pattern

The data integration pattern deals with methods to integrate data from multiple sources and techniques to address data inconsistencies that arise out of this activity.

Background

This pattern discusses ways of integrating data from multiple sources. Data integration can sometimes lead to inconsistencies in the data, for example, different data sources may use different units of measurement. The data integration pattern deals with techniques to address data inconsistency.

Motivation

For a multitude of Big Data solutions, it is common for data to exist in various places, such as SQL tables, logfiles, and HDFS. In order to discover exciting relationships between the data that is lying at different places, they have to be ingested and integrated from different sources. On the flipside, this integration of data from multiple sources can sometimes introduce data inconsistencies too. The integration of data enables its enrichment by adding more attributes and giving it more meaning and context. It can also enable the filtering of data by removing unwanted details.

Data integration is achieved predominantly by the join operation. A join operation integrates records from more than one dataset based on a field called foreign key. The foreign key is the field in a table that is equal to the column of another table, and it is used as a means to cross-refer between tables. While this operation is fairly simple in SQL, the way MapReduce works makes it one of the most costly operations to perform on Hadoop.

The following example illustrates a simple way of understanding the different types of joins by taking an example of two datasets: A and B. The following figure represents the values in each dataset.

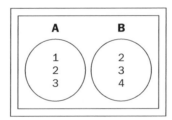

The following are different types of joins that can be performed on the datasets:

- **Inner join**: When this is performed on two datasets, all the matching records from both the datasets are returned. As shown in the following figure, it returns the matching records (**2, 3**) from both the datasets.

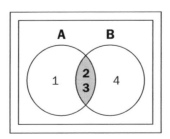

- **Left outer join**: When this is performed on two datasets, all the matching records from both the datasets are returned along with the unmatched records from the dataset on the left-hand side. As shown in the following figure, the matched records (**2, 3**) along with the unmatched record in the dataset to the left (**1**) are returned.

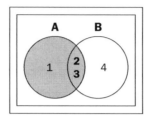

- **Right outer join**: When this is performed on two datasets, all the matching records from both the tables are returned along with the unmatched records from the dataset on the right-hand side. As shown in the following figure, the matched records (**2, 3**) along with the unmatched record in the dataset to the right (**4**) are returned.

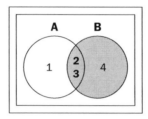

- **Full outer join**: When this is applied on two datasets, all the matching records from both the tables are returned along with the unmatched records from both tables. As shown in the following figure, the matched records (**2, 3**) along with unmatched records in both the datasets (**1, 4**) are returned.

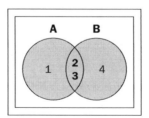

- **Cartesian join**: When the Cartesian join is performed on two datasets, each record from the first dataset and all the records of the second dataset are joined together. As shown in the following figure, the result would be (**1, 2**), (**1, 3**), (**1, 4**), (**2, 2**), (**2, 3**), (**2, 4**), (**3, 2**), (**3, 3**), and (**3, 4**).

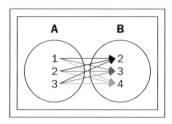

Combining data from multiple sources can result in data inconsistencies. Different data sources may use different units of measurement. For example, assume that there are two data sources, each using a different currency, say dollar versus euro. Due to this, the data integrated from these two sources is inconsistent. Another issue is that the data in each source may be represented differently, for example, true/false versus yes/ no. You have to make use of data transformation to resolve these inconsistencies.

The two broad techniques to perform the join operations in Pig are as follows:

- **Reduce-side join**: The first technique is called the reduce side join in the MapReduce terminology, and it uses the default join operator on multiple large datasets that have foreign-key relationships. This technique executes any type of join operations (inner, outer, right, left, and so on) on the datasets. Also, it works on many datasets at once. The biggest drawback of this join operation is that it puts tremendous load on the network as all of the data that is being joined is first sorted and then sent to the reducers, thereby making this operation slower to execute.

- **Replicated join:** The second technique is called the replicated join and uses the `replicated` keyword along with the `Join` operator syntax. This join technique is applicable between one very large dataset and many small datasets. Internally, this join is performed only on the mapper side and does not require the overhead sorting and shuffling of data to the reducer. The replicated join lets Pig distribute the smaller dataset (which is small enough to fit in the memory) to each node so that the dataset is joined directly to the map job, thereby eliminating the need for the reduce job. Not all types of joins are supported in the replicated join; it supports only inner and left outer joins.

Use cases

You can consider using this design pattern in the following scenarios:

- When you need to combine data from multiple sources before applying analytics on it

- To reduce the processing time by denormalizing the data; denormalization can be achieved by joining the transactions dataset with its associated master dataset(s)

- Transform data to resolve data inconsistencies that might have been introduced as a result of data integration

- Filter data using specific joins

Pattern implementation

This design pattern is implemented in Pig as a standalone script. It combines production information of all the manufacturing units, resolves data inconsistencies by transforming the data, and finds out whether each unit is performing to its optimal best.

The script first loads data of each manufacturing unit and combines them using UNION. It then denormalizes the data by applying joins on the production dataset with its master datasets to get manufacturing unit and product details. It has an implementation of the replicated join to join a huge production dataset with a smaller dataset called products. One of the units uses INR as its currency; this introduces data inconsistency. The script resolves this inconsistency by transforming the manufacturing cost attribute of the unit, which is in INR, to USD.

The script then compares the actual quantity produced with the expected quantity for each unit to find out whether each unit is performing optimally.

Code snippets

To illustrate the working of this pattern, we have considered a manufacturing dataset that is stored on the HDFS. It contains three master files; manufacturing_units.csv contains information about each manufacturing unit, products.csv contains details of the products that are manufactured, and manufacturing_units_products.csv holds detailed information of products that are manufactured in different manufacturing units. The production dataset has a separate production file for each manufacturing unit; this file contains attributes such as production_date, production_hours, manufacturing_unit_id, product_id, and produced_quantity. The following code is the Pig script illustrating the implementation of this pattern:

```
/*
Load the production datasets of five manufacturing units into the
relations
*/
production_unit_1 = LOAD
  '/user/cloudera/pdp/datasets/data_transformation/
  production_unit_1.csv' USING PigStorage(',') AS
  (production_date:datetime,production_hours:int,
  manufacturing_unit_id:chararray,product_id:chararray,
  produced_quantity:int);
production_unit_2 = LOAD
  '/user/cloudera/pdp/datasets/data_transformation/
  production_unit_2.csv' USING PigStorage(',') AS
  (production_date:datetime,production_hours:int,
  manufacturing_unit_id:chararray,product_id:chararray,
  produced_quantity:int);
production_unit_3 = LOAD
  '/user/cloudera/pdp/datasets/data_transformation/
  production_unit_3.csv' USING PigStorage(',') AS
  (production_date:datetime,production_hours:int,
  manufacturing_unit_id:chararray,product_id:chararray,
  produced_quantity:int);
production_unit_4 = LOAD
  '/user/cloudera/pdp/datasets/data_transformation/
  production_unit_4.csv' USING PigStorage(',') AS
  (production_date:datetime,production_hours:int,
  manufacturing_unit_id:chararray,product_id:chararray,
  produced_quantity:int);
production_unit_5 = LOAD
  '/user/cloudera/pdp/datasets/data_transformation/
  production_unit_5.csv' USING PigStorage(',') AS
  (production_date:datetime,production_hours:int,
  manufacturing_unit_id:chararray,product_id:chararray,
  produced_quantity:int);

/*
Combine the data in the relations using UNION operator
*/
production = UNION
  production_unit_1,production_unit_2,production_unit_3,
  production_unit_4,production_unit_5;

/*
Load manufacturing_unit and manufacturing_units_products datasets
*/
```

```
manufacturing_units_products = LOAD
  '/user/cloudera/pdp/datasets/data_transformation/
  manufacturing_units_products.csv' USING PigStorage(',') AS
  (manufacturing_unit_id:chararray,product_id:chararray,
  capacity_per_hour:int,manufacturing_cost:float);
manufacturing_units = LOAD
  '/user/cloudera/pdp/datasets/data_transformation/
  manufacturing_units.csv' USING PigStorage(',') AS
  (manufacturing_unit_id:chararray,manufacturing_unit_name:
  chararray,manufacturing_unit_city:chararray,country:chararray,
  currency:chararray);

/*
Use replicated join to join the relation production, which is huge
with a smaller relation manufacturing_units_products.
The relations manufacturing_units_products and manufacturing units are
small enough to fit into the memory
*/
replicated_join = JOIN production BY
  (manufacturing_unit_id,product_id),
  manufacturing_units_products BY
  (manufacturing_unit_id,product_id) USING 'replicated';
manufacturing_join = JOIN replicated_join BY
  production::manufacturing_unit_id, manufacturing_units BY
  manufacturing_unit_id USING 'replicated';

/*
Identify varying representation of currency and transform the values
in the attribute manufacturing_cost to USD for the units that have INR
as currency
*/
transformed_varying_values = FOREACH manufacturing_join GENERATE
  $0 AS production_date,$2 AS manufacturing_unit_id,$3 AS
  product_id,$4 AS actual_quantity_produced,
  ($1*$7) AS expected_quantity_produced,(float)((($13 == 'INR') ?
  ($8/60) : $8)*$4) AS manufacturing_cost;

/*
Calculate the expected quantity to be produced, actual quantity
produced, percentage, total manufacturing cost for each month for each
manufacturing unit and product to identify how each unit is performing
*/
transformed_varying_values_grpd = GROUP transformed_varying_values
  BY (GetMonth($0),manufacturing_unit_id,product_id);
quantity_produced = FOREACH transformed_varying_values_grpd
{
```

```
    expected_quantity_produced =
      SUM(transformed_varying_values.expected_quantity_produced);
    actual_quantity_produced =
      SUM(transformed_varying_values.actual_quantity_produced);
    percentage_quantity_produced =
      100*actual_quantity_produced/expected_quantity_produced;
    manufacturing_cost =
      SUM(transformed_varying_values.manufacturing_cost);
    GENERATE group.$0 AS production_month,group.$1 AS
      manufacturing_unit_id,group.$2 AS
      product_id,expected_quantity_produced AS
      expected_quantity_produced,actual_quantity_produced AS
      actual_quantity_produced,percentage_quantity_produced AS
      percentage_quantity_produced,ROUND(manufacturing_cost) AS
      manufacturing_cost;
}


/*
Sort the relation by the percentage of quantity produced
*/
ordered_quantity_produced = ORDER quantity_produced BY $5 DESC;

/*
The results are stored on the HDFS in the directory data_integration
*/
STORE ordered_quantity_produced INTO '/user/cloudera/pdp/output/
  data_transformation/data_integration';
```

Results

The following is a snippet of the results that are generated as a result of the code being executed on the input:

```
6    2    C003    2400    2237    93    894800
10   2    C004    1984    1814    91    816300
12   3    L002    74400   66744   89    33372
```

The first column shows the month, the second column is manufacturing unit id, and the third column represents product id. Expected quantity to be produced, actual quantity produced, percentage, and total manufacturing cost per month; all of these are calculated based on which monthly performance of each unit can be analyzed.

Additional information

The complete code and datasets for this section are in the following GitHub directories:

- `Chapter5/code/`
- `Chapter5/datasets/`

The aggregation pattern

The aggregation design pattern explores the usage of Pig to transform data by applying summarization or aggregation operations on data.

Background

Aggregation provides a summarized high-level view of the data. Aggregation combines more than one attribute into a single attribute, thus reducing the total records by treating a set of records as a single record or by paying no attention to subsections of unimportant records. Data aggregation can be performed at different levels of granularity.

Data aggregation retains the integrity of the data, though the volume of the resulting dataset is smaller than the original datasets.

Motivation

Data aggregation plays a key role in Big Data, as it is inherently difficult for huge volumes of data to provide too much of information as a whole. Instead, the data is collected on a daily basis to be aggregated into weekly data; this weekly data can be aggregated into a value for the month and so on. This enables data patterns to emerge, which can be used for analysis. A simple illustration would be to get more information about particular groups based on specific attributes, such as purchases by age, by segmenting age groups. This ability of aggregating data using specific attributes quickly provides valuable insights to conduct further analytics.

There are various techniques to aggregate data. The basic techniques employed for aggregating data include SUM, AVG, and COUNT; advanced techniques include CUBE and ROLLUP.

CUBE and ROLLUP are similar in many aspects, and they both summarize data to produce a single result set. ROLLUP calculates aggregations such as SUM, COUNT, MAX, MIN, and AVG at varying levels of hierarchy, from the subtotals up to a grand total.

CUBE enables the computation of SUM, COUNT, MAX, MIN, and AVG using all possible combinations of the values in the selected columns. Once this aggregation is computed on a set of columns, it can provide results of all possible aggregation questions on those dimensions.

Use cases

You can consider using this design pattern to produce a summarized representation of the data. We will look at a few scenarios where it is necessary to replace data with either the summary or the aggregated information. Such aggregations are done before the data is sent for analytical processing. The aggregation design pattern can be used in the following specific scenarios:

- Records containing transactional information can be aggregated based on multiple dimensions such as product or transaction date
- Individual information such as the income of each member in a family can be summarized to represent the average family income

Pattern implementation

This design pattern is implemented as a standalone Pig script. The script has the implementation to aggregate data using CUBE and ROLLUP operators that were introduced in Pig Version 0.11.0.

Aggregation is the fundamental operation that is performed on the data in the transformation phase in **Extract, Transform, and Load (ETL)**. The fastest way to aggregate data is to use ROLLUP and CUBE. In most cases, ROLLUP and CUBE provide the most meaningful aggregation of the data. This script loads production data of multiple manufacturing units. This data can be aggregated for various purposes. By applying ROLLUP on this data, we can get the following aggregations:

- The production quantity of each product in each manufacturing unit for each month
- The production quantity of each product in each manufacturing unit for all months
- The quantity of total production in each manufacturing unit
- The quantity of total production in all manufacturing units

By applying CUBE on the same dataset, we get the following aggregations in addition to the previous ones:

- The production quantity in each manufacturing unit for each month
- The production quantity of each product for each month
- The production quantity of each product
- The production quantity for each month

The additional four aggregations returned by CUBE are the result of its built-in capability to create subtotals for all possible combinations of grouping columns.

Code snippets

To illustrate the working of this pattern, we have considered a manufacturing dataset stored on the HDFS. It contains three master files: `manufacturing_units.csv` contains information about each manufacturing unit, `products.csv` contains details of the products that are manufactured, and `manufacturing_units_products.csv` holds detailed information of the products that are manufactured in different manufacturing units. The file `production.csv` contains the production information of each manufacturing unit; this file contains attributes such as `production_date`, `production_hours`, `manufacturing_unit_id`, `product_id`, and `produced_quantity`. We will be applying CUBE and ROLLUP aggregations on `manufacturing_unit_id`, `product_id`, and `production_month`, as shown in the following code:

```
/*
Load the data from production.csv, manufacturing_units_products.
csv, manufacturing_units.csv files into the relations production,
manufacturing_units_products and manufacturing_units
The files manufacturing_units_products.csv and manufacturing_units.csv
contain master data information.
*/
production = LOAD
  '/user/cloudera/pdp/datasets/data_transformation/
  production.csv' USING PigStorage(',') AS
  (production_date:datetime,production_hours:int,
  manufacturing_unit_id:chararray,product_id:chararray,
  produced_quantity:int);
manufacturing_units_products = LOAD
  '/user/cloudera/pdp/datasets/data_transformation/
  manufacturing_units_products.csv' USING PigStorage(',') AS
  (manufacturing_unit_id:chararray,product_id:chararray,
  capacity_per_hour:int,manufacturing_cost:float);
```

```
manufacturing_units = LOAD
  '/user/cloudera/pdp/datasets/data_transformation/
  manufacturing_units.csv' USING PigStorage(',') AS
  (manufacturing_unit_id:chararray,manufacturing_unit_name:
  chararray,manufacturing_unit_city:chararray,country:chararray,
  currency:chararray);

/*
The relations are joined to get details from the master data.
*/
production_join_manufacturing_units_products = JOIN production BY
  (manufacturing_unit_id,product_id), manufacturing_units_products
  BY (manufacturing_unit_id,product_id);
manufacture_join = JOIN
  production_join_manufacturing_units_products BY
  production::manufacturing_unit_id, manufacturing_units BY
  manufacturing_unit_id;

/*
The manufacturing cost attribute is converted to dollars for the units
that have currency as INR.
*/
transformed_varying_values = FOREACH manufacture_join GENERATE $2
  AS manufacturing_unit_id,$3 AS product_id,
  GetMonth($0) AS production_month,((($13 == 'INR') ? ($8/60) :
  $8)*$4) AS manufacturing_cost;

/*
Apply CUBE and ROLLUP aggregations on manufacturing_unit_id, product_
id, production_month and store the results in the relations results_
cubed and results_rolledup
*/
cubed = CUBE transformed_varying_values BY
  CUBE(manufacturing_unit_id,product_id,production_month);
rolledup = CUBE transformed_varying_values BY
  ROLLUP(manufacturing_unit_id,product_id,production_month);
result_cubed = FOREACH cubed GENERATE FLATTEN(group),
  ROUND(SUM(cube.manufacturing_cost)) AS total_manufacturing_cost;
result_rolledup = FOREACH rolledup GENERATE FLATTEN(group),
  ROUND(SUM(cube.manufacturing_cost)) AS total_manufacturing_cost;

/*
The results are stored on the HDFS in the directories cube and rollup
*/
```

```
STORE result_cubed INTO
  '/user/cloudera/pdp/output/data_transformation/data_aggregation/
  cube';
STORE result_rolledup INTO
  '/user/cloudera/pdp/output/data_transformation/data_aggregation/
  rollup';
```

Results

After applying ROLLUP on `manufacturing_unit_id`, `product_id`, and `production_month`, the following combination of results are produced:

- The production quantity of each product in each manufacturing unit for each month is as follows:

  ```
  1   C001   1    536600
  5   C002   12   593610
  ```

- The production quantity of each product in each manufacturing unit for all months is as follows:

  ```
  1   C001      7703200
  2   C003      10704000
  5   C002      7139535
  ```

- The total production quantity in each manufacturing unit is as follows:

  ```
  1        15719450
  4        15660186
  ```

- The total production quantity in all manufacturing units is as follows:

  ```
  69236355
  ```

After applying CUBE on `manufacturing_unit_id`, `product_id`, and `production_month`, the following combinations in addition to the combinations produced by ROLLUP are obtained:

- The production quantity in each manufacturing unit for each month is as follows:

  ```
  1   4    1288250
  5   12   1166010
  ```

- The production quantity of each product for each month is as follows:

  ```
  C001   8    1829330
  L002   12   101748
  L001   10   36171
  ```

- The production quantity of each product is as follows:

```
C002    15155785
C004    16830110
L002    667864
```

- The production quantity for each month is as follows:

```
2    5861625
10   5793634
11   5019340
```

As shown previously, CUBE returns four additional aggregations (production quantity in each manufacturing unit for each month, production quantity of each product for each month, production quantity of each product, and production quantity for each month) when compared to ROLLUP. This is because CUBE has the built-in capability of creating subtotals for all possible combinations of grouping columns.

Additional information

The complete code and datasets for this section are in the following GitHub directories:

- `Chapter5/code/`
- `Chapter5/datasets/`

The data generalization pattern

The data generalization pattern deals with transforming the data by creating concept hierarchies and replacing the data with these hierarchies.

Background

This design pattern explores the implementation of data generalization through a Pig script. Data generalization is the process of creating top-level summary layers called concept hierarchies that describe the underlying data concept in a general form. It is a form of descriptive approach in which the data is grouped and replaced by higher level categories or concepts by using concept hierarchies. For example, the raw values of the attribute age can be replaced with conceptual labels (such as adult, teenager, or toddler), or they can be replaced by interval labels (0 to 5, 13 to 19, and so on). These labels, in turn, can be recursively organized into higher level concepts, resulting in a concept hierarchy for the attribute.

Motivation

In the context of Big Data, a typical analytics pipeline on huge volumes of data requires the integration of multiple structured and unstructured datasets.

The data generalization process reduces the footprint of data to be analyzed in the Hadoop cluster by using generalized data that is described in a concise and summarized manner. Instead of analyzing the entire corpus of the data, the data generalization process presents general properties of the data in the form of concept hierarchies, which is helpful to get a broader, zoomed out view of an analytics trend quickly and is useful for mining at multiple levels of abstraction.

Applying data generalization may result in the loss of detail, but the resultant generalized data is more meaningful and easier to interpret in some of the analytics use cases.

Organizing data in top-level concept hierarchies enables a consistent representation of data when placed among multiple data analytics pipelines. In addition to this, analytics on a reduced dataset requires fewer input/output operations and lesser network throughput, and it is more efficient than analytics on a larger, ungeneralized dataset.

Owing to these benefits, data generalization is typically applied before analytics as a pre-processing step, rather than applying it during the mining process. There are various techniques for performing data generalization on numerical data, such as binning, histogram analysis, entropy-based discretization, chi-square analysis, cluster analysis, and discretization by intuitive partitioning. Similarly, for categorical data, generalization can be performed based on the number of distinct values of the attributes that define the hierarchy.

Use cases

You can consider using this design pattern to produce a generalized representation of the numeric and categorical structured data in analytics scenarios, where it is necessary to generalize the data for consistency using a higher level summary rather than a low-level raw data.

You can also consider using this pattern right after the data integration process as an analytics accelerator to create a reduced dataset, making it more amenable for efficient analytics.

Pattern implementation

This design pattern is implemented as a standalone Pig script. The script generates concept hierarchies for categorical data based on a number of distinct values per attribute.

The script performs the join operation on `manufacturing_unit_products`, `products`, `components`, and `product_components` relations. It then generates the concept hierarchy by selecting distinct values from the attributes `components` and `products`; the attributes are sorted in the ascending order of their distinct values. This generates a hierarchy based on the sorted order; the first attribute is at the top level of the hierarchy and the last attribute is at the bottom level of the hierarchy.

Code snippets

The master dataset `components.csv` contains component details, and the `products_components.csv` file contains component details and the count of components that are required to manufacture a product. This file contains attributes such as `product_id`, `component_id`, and `required_quantity`. The following code is the Pig script illustrating the implementation of this pattern:

```
/*
Load products_components data set into the relation products_
components
*/
products_components = LOAD
  '/user/cloudera/pdp/datasets/data_transformation/
  products_components.csv' USING PigStorage(',') AS
  (product_id:chararray,component_id:chararray,
  required_qty_per_Unit:int);


/*
Calculate the distinct count for product_id and component_id and store
the results in the relations products_unique_count and components_
unique_count
*/
products_components_grpd = GROUP products_components ALL;
products_unique_count = FOREACH products_components_grpd
{
  attribute_name = 'Products';
  distinct_prod = DISTINCT products_components.product_id;
  GENERATE attribute_name AS attribute_name, COUNT(distinct_prod)
    AS attribute_count;
}
```

```
components_unique_count = FOREACH products_components_grpd
{
  attribute_name = 'Components';
  distinct_comp = DISTINCT products_components.component_id;
  GENERATE attribute_name AS attribute_name, COUNT(distinct_comp)
    AS attribute_count;
}

/*
The relations product_unique_count and components_unique_count are
combined using the UNION operator.
This relation contains two columns attribute_name and attribute_count,
it is then sorted by attribute_count
*/
combined_products_components_count = UNION
  products_unique_count,components_unique_count;
ordered_count = ORDER combined_products_components_count BY
  attribute_count ASC;

/*
The results are stored on the HDFS in the directory data_
generalization
*/
STORE ordered_count INTO
  '/user/cloudera/pdp/output/data_transformation/
  data_generalization';
```

Results

The following is the result of applying generalization on categorical data:

```
Products    6
Components  18
```

The result shows attribute name and its unique count; the attributes are ordered by their count. The result depicts the concept hierarchy; the first attribute Products is in the top level of the hierarchy, and the last attribute Components is in the bottom level of hierarchy.

Additional information

The complete code and datasets for this section are in the following GitHub directories:

- `Chapter5/code/`
- `Chapter5/datasets/`

Summary

In this chapter, you have studied various Big Data transformation techniques that deal with transforming the structure of the data to a hierarchical representation to take advantage of Hadoop's capability to process semistructured data. We have seen the importance of performing normalization on the data before performing analysis on it. We then discussed using joins to denormalize the data joins. CUBE and ROLLUP perform multiple aggregations on the data; these aggregations provide a snapshot of the data. In data generalization, we discussed various generalization techniques for numerical and categorical data.

In the next chapter, we will focus on data reduction techniques. Data reduction aims to obtain a reduced representation of the data; it ensures data integrity, though the obtained dataset is much smaller in volume. We will discuss data reduction techniques such as dimensionality reduction, sampling techniques, binning, and clustering. After reading this chapter, you will be able to choose the right data reduction pattern.

6
Understanding Data Reduction Patterns

In the previous chapter, we learned about the various Big Data transformation techniques that dealt with transforming the structure of the data to a hierarchical representation. This was done in order to take advantage of Hadoop's capability to process semistructured data. We have seen the importance of performing normalization on the data before performing analysis on it. We then discussed using joins to denormalize the data. CUBE and ROLLUP perform multiple aggregations on the data; these aggregations provide a snapshot of the data. In the data generalization section, we discussed various generalization techniques for numerical and categorical data.

In this chapter, we will discuss design patterns that perform dimensionality reduction using the principal component analysis technique, and numerosity reduction using clustering, sampling, and histogram techniques.

Data reduction – a quick introduction

Data reduction aims to obtain a reduced representation of the data. It ensures data integrity, though the obtained dataset after the reduction is much smaller in volume than the original dataset.

Data reduction techniques are classified into the following three groups:

- **Dimensionality reduction**: This group of data reduction techniques deals with reducing the number of attributes that are considered for an analytics problem. They do this by detecting and eliminating the irrelevant attributes, relevant yet weak attributes, or redundant attributes. The principal component analysis and wavelet transforms are examples of dimensionality reduction techniques.

- **Numerosity reduction**: This group of data reduction techniques reduces the data by replacing the original dataset with a sparse representation of the data. The sparse subset of the data is computed by parametric methods such as regression, where a model is used to estimate the data so that only a subset is enough instead of the entire dataset. There are other methods such as nonparametric methods, for example, clustering, sampling, and histograms, which work without the need for a model to be built.

- **Compression**: This group of data reduction techniques uses algorithms to reduce the size of the physical storage that the data consumes. Typically, compression is performed at a higher level of granularity than at the attribute or record level. If you need to retrieve the original data from the compressed data without any loss of information, which is required while storing string or numerical data, a lossless compression scheme is used. If instead, there is a need to uncompress video and sound files that can accommodate the imperceptible loss of clarity, then lossy compression techniques are used.

The following diagram illustrates the different techniques that are used in each of the aforementioned groups:

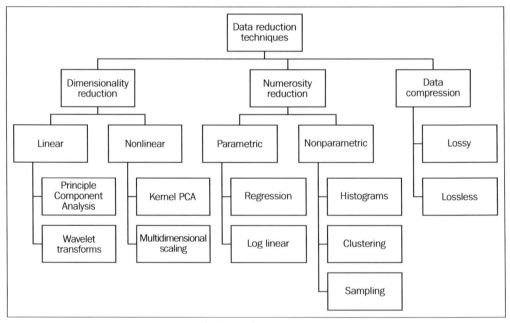

Data reduction techniques – overview

Data reduction considerations for Big Data

In Big Data problems, data reduction techniques have to be considered as part of the analytics process rather than a separate process. This will enable you to understand what type of data has to be retained or eliminated due to its irrelevance to the analytics-related questions that are asked.

In a typical Big Data analytical environment, data is often acquired and integrated from multiple sources. Even though there is the promise of a hidden reward for using the entire dataset for the analytics, which in all probability may yield richer and better insights, the cost of doing so sometimes overweighs the results. It is at this juncture that you may have to consider reducing the amount of data without drastically compromising on the effectiveness of the analytical insights, in essence, safeguarding the integrity of the data.

Performing any type of analysis on Big Data often leads to high storage and retrieval costs owing to the massive amount of data. The benefits of data reduction processes are sometimes not evident when the data is small; they begin to become obvious when the datasets start growing in size. These data reduction processes are one of the first steps that are taken to optimize data from the storage and retrieval perspective. It is important to consider the ramifications of data reduction so that the computational time spent on it does not outweigh or *erase* the time saved by data mining on a reduced dataset size. Now that we have understood data reduction concepts, we will explore a few concrete design patterns in the following sections.

Dimensionality reduction – the Principal Component Analysis design pattern

In this design pattern, we will consider one way of implementing the dimensionality reduction through the usage of **Principal Component Analysis (PCA)** and **Singular value decomposition (SVD)**, which are versatile techniques that are widely used for exploratory data analysis, creating predictive models, and for dimensionality reduction.

Background

Dimensions in a given data can be intuitively understood as a set of all attributes that are used to account for the observed properties of data. Reducing the dimensionality implies the transformation of a high dimensional data into a reduced dimension's set that is proportional to the intrinsic or latent dimensions of the data. These latent dimensions are the minimum number of attributes that are needed to describe the dataset. Thus, dimensionality reduction is a method to understand the hidden structure of data that is used to mitigate the curse of high dimensionality and other unwanted properties of high dimensional spaces.

Broadly, there are two ways to perform dimensionality reduction. One of them is the linear dimensionality reduction, examples of which are PCA and SVD. The other is the nonlinear dimensionality reduction for which kernel PCA and Multidimensional Scaling are the examples.

In this design pattern, we explore linear dimensionality reduction by implementing PCA in R and SVD in Mahout and integrating them with Pig.

Motivation

Let's first have an overview of PCA. PCA is a linear dimensionality reduction technique that works unsupervised on a given dataset by implanting the dataset into a subspace of lower dimensions, which is done by constructing a variance-based representation of the original data.

The underlying principle of PCA is to identify the hidden structure of the data by analyzing the direction where the variation of data is the most or where the data is most spread out.

Intuitively, a principal component can be considered as a line, which passes through a set of data points that vary to a greater degree. If you pass the same line through data points with no variance, it implies that the data is the same and does not carry much information. In cases where there is no variance, data points are not considered as representatives of the properties of the entire dataset, and these attributes can be omitted.

PCA involves finding pairs of eigenvalues and eigenvectors for a dataset. A given dataset is decomposed into pairs of eigenvectors and eigenvalues. An eigenvector defines the unit vector or the direction of the data perpendicular to the others. An eigenvalue is the value of how spread out the data is in that direction.

In multidimensional data, the number of eigenvalues and eigenvectors that can exist are equal to the dimensions of the data. An eigenvector with the biggest eigenvalue is the principal component.

After finding out the principal component, they are sorted in the decreasing order of eigenvalues so that the first vector shows the highest variance, the second shows the next highest, and so on. This information helps uncover the hidden patterns that were not previously suspected and thereby allows interpretations that would not result ordinarily.

As the data is now sorted in the decreasing order of significance, the data size can be reduced by eliminating the attributes with a weak component, or low significance where the variance of data is less. Using the highly valued principal components, the original dataset can be constructed with a good approximation.

As an example, consider a sample election survey conducted on a hundred million people who have been asked 150 questions about their opinions on issues related to elections. Analyzing a hundred million answers over 150 attributes is a tedious task. We have a high dimensional space of 150 dimensions, resulting in 150 eigenvalues/ vectors from this space. We order the eigenvalues in descending order of significance (for example, 230, 160, 130, 97, 62, 8, 6, 4, 2,1… up to 150 dimensions). As we can decipher from these values, there can be 150 dimensions, but only the top five dimensions possess the data that is varying considerably. Using this, we were able to reduce a high dimensional space of 150 and could consider the top five eigenvalues for the next step in the analytics process.

Next, let's look into SVD. SVD is closely related to PCA, and sometimes both terms are used as SVD, which is a more general method of implementing PCA. SVD is a form of matrix analysis that produces a low-dimensional representation of a high-dimensional matrix. It achieves data reduction by removing linearly dependent data. Just like PCA, SVD also uses eigenvalues to reduce the dimensionality by combining information from several correlated vectors to form basis vectors that are orthogonal and explains most of the variance in the data.

For example, if you have two attributes, one is sale of ice creams and the other is temperature, then their correlation is so high that the second attribute, temperature, does not contribute any extra information useful for a classification task. The eigenvalues derived from SVD determines which attributes are most informative and which ones you can do without.

Mahout's **Stochastic SVD (SSVD)** is based on computing mathematical SVD in a distributed fashion. SSVD runs in the PCA mode if the `pca` argument is set to true; the algorithm computes the column-wise mean over the input and then uses it to compute the PCA space.

Use cases

You can consider using this pattern to perform data reduction, data exploration, and as an input to clustering and multiple regression.

The design pattern can be applied on ordered and unordered attributes with sparse and skewed data. It can also be used on images. This design pattern cannot be applied on complex nonlinear data.

Pattern implementation

The following steps describe the implementation of PCA using R:

- The script applies the PCA technique to reduce dimensions. PCA involves finding pairs of eigenvalues and eigenvectors for a dataset. An eigenvector with the biggest eigenvalue is the principal component. The components are sorted in the decreasing order of eigenvalues.

- The script loads the data and uses streaming to call the R script. The R script performs PCA on the data and returns the principal components. Only the first few principal components that can explain most of the variation can be selected so that the dimensionality of the data is reduced.

Limitations of PCA implementation

While streaming allows you to call the executable of your choice, it has performance implications, and the solution is not scalable in situations where your input dataset is huge. To overcome this, we have shown a better way of performing dimensionality reduction by using Mahout; it contains a set of highly scalable machine learning libraries.

The following steps describe the implementation of SSVD on Mahout:

- Read the input dataset in the CSV format and prepare a set of data points in the form of key/value pairs; the key should be unique and the value should comprise of *n* vector tuples.

- Write the previous data into a sequence file. The key can be of a type adapted into `WritableComparable`, `Long`, or `String`, and the value should be of the `VectorWritable` type.

- Decide on the number of dimensions in the reduced space.

- Execute SSVD on Mahout with the `rank` arguments (this specifies the number of dimensions), setting `pca`, `us`, and `v` to true. When the `pca` argument is set to true, the algorithm runs in the PCA mode by computing the column-wise mean over the input and then uses it to compute the PCA space. The `USigma` folder contains the output with reduced dimensions.

Generally, dimensionality reduction is applied on very high dimensional datasets; however, in our example, we have demonstrated this on a dataset with fewer dimensions for a better explainability.

Code snippets

To illustrate the working of this pattern, we have considered the retail transactions dataset that is stored on the **Hadoop File System (HDFS)**. It contains 20 attributes, such as `Transaction ID`, `Transaction date`, `Customer ID`, `Product subclass`, `Phone No`, `Product ID`, `age`, `quantity`, `asset`, `Transaction Amount`, `Service Rating`, `Product Rating`, and `Current Stock`. For this pattern, we will be using PCA to reduce the dimensions. The following code snippet is the Pig script that illustrates the implementation of this pattern via Pig streaming:

```
/*
Assign an alias pcar to the streaming command
Use ship to send streaming binary files (R script in this use
  case) from the client node to the compute node
*/
DEFINE pcar '/home/cloudera/pdp/data_reduction/compute_pca.R'
  ship('/home/cloudera/pdp/data_reduction/compute_pca.R');


/*
Load the data set into the relation transactions
*/
transactions = LOAD '/user/cloudera/pdp/datasets/
  data_reduction/transactions_multi_dims.csv' USING
  PigStorage(',') AS (transaction_id:long,
  transaction_date:chararray, customer_id:chararray,
  prod_subclass:chararray, phone_no:chararray,
  country_code:chararray, area:chararray, product_id:chararray,
  age:int, amt:int, asset:int, transaction_amount:double,
  service_rating:int, product_rating:int, curr_stock:int,
  payment_mode:int, reward_points:int, distance_to_store:int,
  prod_bin_age:int, cust_height:int);
/*
```

```
Extract the columns on which PCA has to be performed.
STREAM is used to send the data to the external script.
The result is stored in the relation princ_components
*/
selected_cols = FOREACH transactions GENERATE age AS age, amt AS
    amount, asset AS asset, transaction_amount
    AS transaction_amount, service_rating AS service_rating,
    product_rating AS product_rating, curr_stock AS current_stock,
    payment_mode AS payment_mode, reward_points AS reward_points,
    distance_to_store AS distance_to_store, prod_bin_age AS
    prod_bin_age, cust_height AS cust_height;
princ_components = STREAM selected_cols THROUGH pcar;


/*
The results are stored on the HDFS in the directory pca
*/
STORE princ_components INTO
    '/user/cloudera/pdp/output/data_reduction/pca';
```

Following is the R code illustrating the implementation of this pattern:

```
#! /usr/bin/env Rscript
options(warn=-1)

#Establish connection to stdin for reading the data
con <- file("stdin","r")

#Read the data as a data frame
data <- read.table(con, header=FALSE, col.names=c("age", "amt",
    "asset", "transaction_amount", "service_rating",
    "product_rating", "current_stock", "payment_mode",
    "reward_points", "distance_to_store", "prod_bin_age",
    "cust_height"))
attach(data)

#Calculate covariance and correlation to understand the variation
    between the independent variables
covariance=cov(data, method=c("pearson"))
correlation=cor(data, method=c("pearson"))

#Calculate the principal components
pcdat=princomp(data)
summary(pcdat)
pcadata=prcomp(data, scale = TRUE)
pcadata
```

The ensuing code snippets illustrate the implementation of this pattern using Mahout's SSVD. The following is a snippet of a shell script with the commands for executing CSV to the sequence converter:

```
#All the mahout jars have to be included in HADOOP_CLASSPATH
  before execution of this script.
#Execute csvtosequenceconverter jar to convert the CSV file to
  sequence file.
hadoop jar csvtosequenceconverter.jar
  com.datareduction.CsvToSequenceConverter
  /user/cloudera/pdp/datasets/data_reduction/
  transactions_multi_dims_ssvd.csv
  /user/cloudera/pdp/output/data_reduction/ssvd/transactions.seq
```

The following is the code snippet of the Pig script with commands for executing SSVD on Mahout:

```
/*
Register piggybank jar file
*/
REGISTER '/home/cloudera/pig-
  0.11.0/contrib/piggybank/java/piggybank.jar';

/*
*Ideally the following data pre-processing steps have to be
  generally performed on the actual data, we have deliberately
  omitted the implementation as these steps were covered in the
  respective chapters

*Data Ingestion to ingest data from the required sources

*Data Profiling by applying statistical techniques to profile data
  and find data quality issues

*Data Validation to validate the correctness of the data and
  cleanse it accordingly

*Data Transformation to apply transformations on the data.
*/

/*
Use sh command to execute shell commands.
Convert the files in a directory to sequence files
-i specifies the input path of the sequence file on HDFS
-o specifies the output directory on HDFS
```

```
-k specifies the rank, i.e the number of dimensions in the reduced
   space
-us set to true computes the product USigma
-V set to true computes V matrix
-pca set to true runs SSVD in pca mode
*/

sh /home/cloudera/mahout-distribution-0.8/bin/mahout ssvd -i
   /user/cloudera/pdp/output/data_reduction/ssvd/transactions.seq -
   o /user/cloudera/pdp/output/data_reduction
   /ssvd/reduced_dimensions -k 7 -us true -V true -U false -pca
   true -ow -t 1

/*
Use seqdumper to dump the output in text format.
-i specifies the HDFS path of the input file
*/
sh /home/cloudera/mahout-distribution-0.8/bin/mahout seqdumper -i
   /user/cloudera/pdp/output/data_reduction/
   ssvd/reduced_dimensions/V/v-m-00000
```

Results

The following is a snippet of the result of executing the R script through Pig streaming. Only the important components in the results are shown to improve readability.

```
Importance of components:
                          Comp.1        Comp.2        Comp.3
Standard deviation    1415.7219657 548.8220571 463.15903326
Proportion of Variance   0.7895595   0.1186566   0.08450632
Cumulative Proportion    0.7895595   0.9082161   0.99272241
```

The following diagram shows a graphical representation of the results:

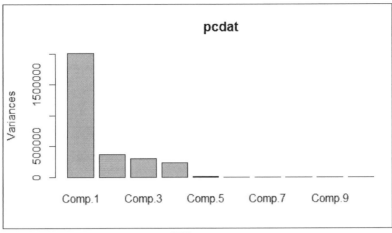

PCA output

From the cumulative results, we can explain most of the variation with the first three components. Hence, we can drop the other components and still explain most of the data, thereby achieving data reduction.

The following is a code snippet of the result attained after applying SSVD on Mahout:

```
Key: 0: Value: {0:6.78114976729216E-5,1:-2.1865954292525495E-4,2:-
    3.857078959222571E-5,3:9.172780131217343E-4,4:-
    0.0011674781643860148,5:-
    0.5403803571549012,6:0.38822546035077155}
Key: 1: Value: {0:4.514870142377153E-6,1:-1.2753047299542729E-
    5,2:0.002010945408634006,3:2.6983823401328314E-5,4:-
    9.598021198119562E-5,5:-0.015661212194480658,6:-
    0.00577713052974214}
Key: 2: Value: {0:0.0013835831436886054,1:3.643672803676861E-
    4,2:0.9999962672043754,3:-8.597640675661196E-4,4:-
    7.575051881399296E-4,5:2.058878196540628E-
    4,6:1.5620427291943194E-5}
.

.

Key: 11: Value: {0:5.861358116239576E-4,1:-
    0.001589570485260711,2:-2.451436184622473E-
    4,3:0.007553283166922416,4:-0.011038688645296836,
    5:0.822710349440101,6:0.060441819443160294}
```

The contents of the v folder show the contribution of the original variables to every principal component. The result is a 12 x 7 matrix as we have 12 dimensions in our original dataset, which were reduced to 7, as specified in the rank argument to SSVD.

The USigma folder contains the output with reduced dimensions.

Additional information

The complete code and datasets for this section are in the following GitHub directories:

- Chapter6/code/
- Chapter6/datasets/

Information on Mahout's implementation of SSVD can be found at the following links:

- https://cwiki.apache.org/confluence/display/MAHOUT/Stochastic+Singular+Value+Decomposition
- https://cwiki.apache.org/confluence/download/attachments/27832158/SSVD-CLI.pdf?version=18&modificationDate=1381347063000&api=v2
- http://en.wikibooks.org/wiki/Data_Mining_Algorithms_In_R/Dimensionality_Reduction/Singular_Value_Decomposition

Numerosity reduction – the histogram design pattern

The *Numerosity reduction – histogram design pattern* explores the implementation of the histograms technique for data reduction.

Background

Histograms belong to the numerosity reduction category of data reduction. They are nonparametric methods of data reduction in which it is assumed that the data does not fit into a predefined model or function.

Motivation

Histograms work by dividing the entire data into buckets or groups and storing the central tendency for each of the buckets. Internally, this resembles binning. Histograms can be constructed optimally using dynamic programming. Histograms differ from bar charts in that they represent continuous data categories rather than discrete categories. This implies that in a histogram, there are no gaps among columns that represent various categories.

Histograms help in reducing the categories of data by grouping a large number of continuous attributes. Representing a large number of attributes may result in a complex histogram with so many columns that it becomes difficult to interpret the information. Hence, the data is grouped into ranges that denote a continuous range of values for an attribute. The data can be grouped in the following ways:

- **Equal-width grouping technique**: In this grouping technique, each range is of uniform width.

- **Equal-frequency (or equi-depth) grouping technique**: In an equal-frequency grouping technique, the ranges are created in a way that either the frequency of each range is constant or each range contains the same number of contiguous data elements.

- **V-Optimal grouping technique**: In this grouping technique, we consider all the possible histograms for a given number of ranges and choose the one with the minimal variance.

- **MaxDiff grouping technique**: This histogram grouping technique considers grouping values into a range based on the difference between each pair of adjacent values. The range boundary is defined between each pair of adjacent points with the largest differences. The following diagram depicts sorted data that is grouped into three ranges identified by the maximum differences between 9-14 and 18-27.

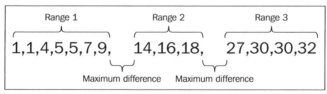

Maximum difference – illustration

In the previously mentioned grouping techniques, the V-Optimal and MaxDiff techniques are more accurate and effective for approximating both sparse and dense data, as well as highly skewed and uniform data. These histograms can also work on multiple attributes by using multidimensional histograms that can capture dependencies between attributes.

Use cases

You can consider using this design pattern in the following conditions:

- When the data does not fit into a parametric model such as regression or log-linear models
- When the data is continuous and not discrete
- When the data has ordered or unordered numeric attributes
- When the data is skewed or sparse

Pattern implementation

The script loads the data and divides it into buckets using equal-width grouping. The data for the `Transaction Amount` field is grouped into buckets. It counts the number of transactions in each bucket and returns the bucket range and the count as the output.

This pattern produces a reduced representation of the dataset where the transaction amount is divided into the specified number of buckets and the count of transactions that fall in that range. This data is plotted as a histogram.

Code snippets

To illustrate the working of this pattern, we have considered the retail transactions dataset stored on the HDFS. It contains attributes such as `Transaction ID`, `Transaction date`, `Customer ID`, `age`, `Phone Number`, `Product`, `Product subclass`, `Product ID`, `Transaction Amount`, and `Country Code`. For this pattern, we will be generating buckets on the attribute `Transaction Amount`. The following code snippet is the Pig script illustrating the implementation of this pattern:

```
/*
Register the custom UDF
*/
REGISTER '/home/cloudera/pdp/jars/databucketgenerator.jar';

/*
```

```
Define the alias generateBuckets for the custom UDF, the number of
  buckets(20) is passed as a parameter
*/
DEFINE generateBuckets com.datareduction.GenerateBuckets('20');


/*
Load the dataset into the relation transactions
*/
transactions = LOAD '/user/cloudera/pdp/datasets/
  data_reduction/transactions.csv' USING  PigStorage(',') AS
  (transaction_id:long,transaction_date:chararray,
  cust_id:chararray, age:chararray, area:chararray,
  prod_subclass:int, prod_id:long, quantity:int, asset:int,
  transaction_amt:double, phone_no:chararray,
  country_code:chararray);


/*
Maximum value of transactions amount and the actual transaction
  amount are passed to generateBuckets UDF
The UDF calculates the bucket size by dividing maximum transaction
  amount by the number of buckets.
It finds out the range to which each value belongs to and returns
  the value along with the bucket range
*/
transaction_amt_grpd = GROUP transactions ALL;
transaction_amt_min_max = FOREACH transaction_amt_grpd GENERATE
  MAX(transactions.transaction_amt) AS
  max_transaction_amt,FLATTEN(transactions.transaction_amt) AS
  transaction_amt;
transaction_amt_buckets = FOREACH transaction_amt_min_max GENERATE
  generateBuckets(max_transaction_amt,transaction_amt) ;


/*
Calculate the count of values in each range
*/
transaction_amt_buckets_grpd = GROUP transaction_amt_buckets BY
  range;
transaction_amt_buckets_count = FOREACH
  transaction_amt_buckets_grpd GENERATE group,
  COUNT(transaction_amt_buckets);


/*
The results are stored on HDFS in the directory histogram.
*/
STORE transaction_amt_buckets_count INTO
  '/user/cloudera/pdp/output/data_reduction/histogram';
```

The following code snippet is the Java UDF code that illustrates the implementation of this pattern:

```
@Override
  public String exec(Tuple input) throws IOException {
    if (input == null || input.size() ==0)
      return null;
    try{
      //Extract the maximum transaction amount
      max = Double.parseDouble(input.get(0).toString());
      //Extract the value
      double rangeval = Double.parseDouble
        (input.get(1).toString());
      /*Calculate the bucket size by dividing maximum
        transaction amount by the number of buckets.
      */
      setBucketSize();

      /*Set the bucket range by using the bucketSize and
        noOfBuckets
      */
      setBucketRange();

      /*
      It finds out the range to which each value belongs
      to and returns the value along with the bucket range
      */
      return getBucketRange(rangeval);
    } catch(Exception e){
      System.err.println("Failed to process input; error - " +
        e.getMessage());
      return null;
    }
  }
```

Results

The following is a snippet of the result of applying this pattern on the dataset; the first column is the bucket range of the `Transaction Amount` attribute and the second column is the count of transactions:

1-110	45795
110-220	50083
220-330	60440
330-440	40001
440-550	52802

The following is the histogram generated by plotting this data using gnuplot. It shows a graphical representation of the transaction amount buckets and the number of transactions in each bucket.

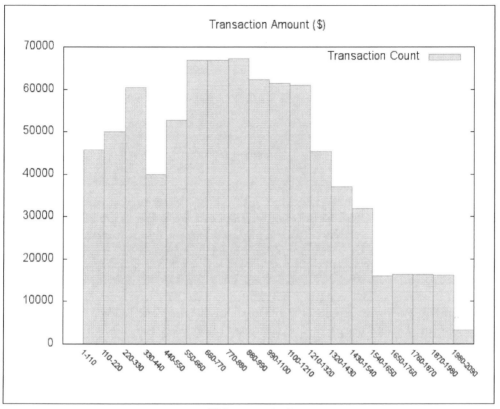

Histogram output

Additional information

The complete code and datasets for this section are in the following GitHub directories:

- Chapter6/code/
- Chapter6/datasets/

Numerosity reduction – sampling design pattern

This design pattern explores the implementation of sampling techniques for data reduction.

Background

Sampling belongs to the numerosity reduction category of data reduction. It can be used as a data reduction technique, as it represents a very large amount of data by a much smaller subset.

Motivation

Sampling is essentially a method of data reduction to determine the approximate subset of a population that has the characteristics of the entire population. Sampling is a general approach to choose a subset of data to accurately represent a population. Sampling is performed by various methods that differ in the way in which they define what goes into the subset and the way candidates are located for that subset.

In the Big Data scenario, the cost of performing analytics, such as classification and optimization, over the complete population is high; sampling helps to reduce the cost by reducing the footprint of the data used to perform the actual analytics and then extrapolating the results on the population. There would be marginal loss of accuracy, but it far outweighs the benefits of reduced time versus storage trade-offs.

When it comes to Big Data, wherever techniques of statistical sampling are applied, it is important to be cognizant of the population about which one aims to perform the analytics. Even if the data that has been collected is very big, the samples may relate only to a small part of the population, and they may not represent the whole. While picking the sample, representativeness plays a vital role, as it determines how close the sampled data is to the population.

Sampling can be performed using probabilistic and nonprobabilistic methods. The following diagram captures the broad landscape of the techniques involved in sampling:

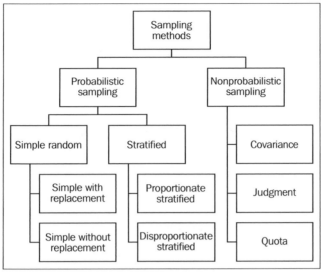

Sampling methods

Probabilistic sampling methods use random sampling, and every element in the population has a known nonzero (greater than zero) chance of getting selected into the sampled subset. Probabilistic sampling methods use weighted sampling and result in unbiased samples of the population. The following are a few probabilistic sampling methods:

- **Simple random sampling**: This is the most basic type of sampling in which every element of the population has an equal chance of being selected into the subset. The samples are objectively selected at random. The simple random sampling can be done by replacing the selected item in the population so that it can be selected again (sampling with replacement) or by not replacing the selected item in the population (sampling without replacement). Random sampling doesn't always result in a representative sample and is a costly operation to perform on a very large dataset. The representativeness of random sampling can be improved by presampling the population using stratification or clustering.

- The following diagram illustrates the difference between the **Simple Random Sampling Without Replacement (SRSWOR)** and **Simple Random Sampling With Replacement (SRSWR)**.

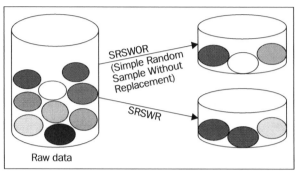

SRSWOR versus SRSWR

- **Stratified sampling**: This sampling technique is used when we already know that the population contains a number of unique categories that are used to organize the population into subpopulations (strata); individual samples can then be picked out of them. The chosen sample is forced to contain elements from each of the subpopulations. This sampling method concentrates on relevant subpopulations and ignores the irrelevant ones. The representativeness of the sample is increased by eliminating the selection by absolute randomness, as evidenced in the simple random sampling and by selecting items from the independent strata. The stratified sampling method is a more efficient sampling technique in cases where the unique categories of the strata are identified in advance. There is an overall time-cost trade-off associated with stratified sampling, as it could be tedious to initially identify the unique categories for a population that is relatively homogeneous.

- **NonProbabilistic sampling**: This sampling method selects the subset of the population without giving an equal chance of selection to some elements of the population. In this sampling, the probability of the selection of the elements cannot be accurately determined. The selection of the elements is done purely based on a few assumptions on the population of interest. Nonprobabilistic sampling score poorly to accurately represent the population, and hence the resultant analytics cannot be extrapolated from the sample to the population. Nonprobabilistic sampling methods include the covariance sampling, the judgment sampling, and the quota sampling methods.

Use cases

You can consider using the numerosity reduction sampling design pattern in the following scenarios:

- When the data is continuous or discrete

- When each element of the data has an equal chance of getting selected without affecting the representativeness of the sampling

- When the data has ordered or unordered attributes

Pattern implementation

This design pattern is implemented in Pig as a standalone script. It uses the datafu library, which has the implementation of SRSWR as a pair of UDFs, SimpleRandomSampleWithReplacementElect and SimpleRandomSampleWithReplacementVote; they implement a scalable algorithm for SRSWR. The algorithm consists of two phases: vote and elect. Candidates for each position are voted during the vote stage. One candidate per position is elected during the election stage. The output is a bag of sampled data.

The script selects a sample of 100,000 records from the transactions dataset using the SRSWR technique.

Code snippets

To illustrate the working of this pattern, we have considered the retail transactions dataset stored on the HDFS. It contains attributes such as Transaction ID, Transaction date, Customer ID, age, Phone Number, Product, Product subclass, Product ID, Transaction Amount, and Country Code. For this pattern, we will be performing SRSWR on the transactions dataset. The following code snippet is the Pig script that illustrates the implementation of this pattern:

```
/*
Register datafu and commons math jar files
*/
REGISTER '/home/cloudera/pdp/jars/datafu-1.2.0.jar';
REGISTER '/home/cloudera/pdp/jars/commons-math3-3.2.jar';
```

```
/*
Define aliases for the classes
  SimpleRandomSampleWithReplacementVote and
  SimpleRandomSampleWithReplacementElect
*/
DEFINE SRSWR_VOTE
  datafu.pig.sampling.SimpleRandomSampleWithReplacementVote();
DEFINE SRSWR_ELECT
  datafu.pig.sampling.SimpleRandomSampleWithReplacementElect();

/*
Load the dataset into the relation transactions
*/
transactions= LOAD '/user/cloudera/pdp/datasets
  /data_reduction/transactions.csv' USING  PigStorage(',') AS
  (transaction_id:long,transaction_date:chararray,
  cust_id:chararray, age:int, area:chararray, prod_subclass:int,
  prod_id:long, quantity:int, asset:int, transaction_amt:double,
  phone_no:chararray, country_code:chararray);

/*
The input to Vote UDF is the bag of items, the desired sample size
  (100000 in our use case) and the actual population size.
  This UDF votes candidates for each position
*/
summary = FOREACH (GROUP transactions ALL) GENERATE
  COUNT(transactions) AS count;
candidates = FOREACH transactions GENERATE
  FLATTEN(SRSWR_VOTE(TOBAG(TOTUPLE(*)), 100000, summary.count));

/*
The Elect UDF elects one candidate for each position and returns a
  bag of sampled items stored in the relation sampled
*/
sampled = FOREACH (GROUP candidates BY position PARALLEL 10)
  GENERATE FLATTEN(SRSWR_ELECT(candidates));

/*
The results are stored on the HDFS in the directory sampling
*/
STORE sampled into '/user/cloudera/pdp/output
  /data_reduction/sampling';
```

Results

The following is a snippet of the results obtained after applying sampling on the transactions data. We have eliminated a few columns to improve readability.

```
580493 … 1621624 … … … … 1 115 576 900-435-5791 U.S.A
193016 … 1808643 … … … … 1 119 735 9020138550 U.S.A
800748 … 199995 … … … … 1 28 1577 904-066-467q USA
```

The result is a file that contains 100,000 records, taken as a sample from the original dataset.

Additional information

The complete code and datasets for this section are in the following GitHub directories:

- `Chapter6/code/`
- `Chapter6/datasets/`

Numerosity reduction – clustering design pattern

This design pattern explores the implementation of the clustering technique for data reduction.

Background

Clustering belongs to the numerosity reduction category of data reduction. Clustering is a nonparametric model and works without the prior knowledge of a class label using unsupervised learning.

Motivation

Clustering is a general approach to solve the problem of grouping data. It can be achieved by various algorithms that differ in the way they define what goes into a group and how to find the candidates for that group. There are more than 100 different implementations of clustering algorithms that solve a variety of problems for different objectives. There is no single size that fits all the clustering algorithms for a given problem; the appropriate one has to be chosen by careful experimentation. A clustering algorithm that works on a specific data model doesn't always work on a different model. Clustering is widely used in machine learning, image analysis, pattern recognition, and information retrieval.

The objective of clustering is to partition the dataset and effectively reduce its size based on a set of heuristics. Clustering is, in a way, similar to binning, since it mimics the grouping aspect of binning; however, the difference lies in the precise way the grouping is performed in clustering.

The partitions are performed in a way that the data in one cluster is similar to another in the same cluster, but is dissimilar to other data in other clusters. Here, similarity is defined as a measure of how close the data is to each other.

K Means is one of the most widely used methods for clustering. Partitions of observations into k clusters is done by K Means of the cluster analysis; here, each observation belongs to the cluster with the nearest mean. It is an iterative process and stabilizes only if the cluster centroid does not move any further.

The quality measure of how well the clustering was performed can be ascertained by measuring the diameter or the average distance of each cluster object from the cluster centroid.

We can intuitively understand the need for clustering to reduce the numerosity of data by the example of an apparel company planning to release a new model of t-shirt into the market. If the company doesn't use a data reduction technique, it ends up manufacturing t-shirts of varying sizes to cater to different people. In order to prevent this, they reduce the data by first noting down the height and weight of people, plotting them on a graph, and dividing them into three major clusters: small, medium, and large.

The K Means method uses the dataset of height and weight (n observations) and divides them into k (that is, three) clusters. For each of the cluster (small, medium, and large), the data points inside the cluster are closer to the cluster category (that is, mean of small's height and weight). K Means has provided us with the best three sizes that will fit everyone and has thus effectively reduced the complexity of the data; instead of working on the actual data, clustering enables us to work on the replacement of the actual data by clusters themselves.

We have considered using the K Means implementation of Mahout; more information on this can be obtained from `https://mahout.apache.org/users/clustering/k-means-clustering.html`.

From a Big Data perspective, as there is a need to process a very large amount of data, there would be a time-quality trade-off to be taken into consideration for choosing a clustering algorithm. New research is underway to develop preclustering methods, which can process Big Data efficiently. However, the results of a preclustering method are an approximate prepartitioning of the original dataset, which will eventually be clustered again by traditional methods such as K Means.

Use cases

You can consider using this design pattern in the following cases:

- When the data is continuous or discrete and the class labels of the data are not known in advance
- When there is a need to preprocess the data by clustering for, eventually, performing the classification on a very large amount of data
- When the data has numeric, ordered, or unordered attributes
- When the data is categorical
- When the data is not skewed, sparsed, or smeared

Pattern implementation

The design pattern is implemented in Pig and Mahout. The dataset is loaded into Pig. The age attribute on which K Means clustering is to be performed is transformed into vectors and is stored into a Mahout-readable format. It applies Mahout's K Means clustering on the age attribute of the transactions dataset. K Means clustering partitions the observations into *k* clusters in which each observation belongs to the cluster with the nearest mean; the process is iterative and stabilizes only if the cluster centroid does not move any further.

This pattern produces a reduced representation of the dataset where the age attribute is partitioned into a predefined number of clusters. This information can be used to identify the age groups of the customers visiting the store.

Code snippets

To illustrate the working of this pattern, we have considered the retail transactions dataset stored on the HDFS. It contains attributes such as Transaction ID, Transaction date, Customer ID, age, Phone Number, Product, Product subclass, Product ID, Transaction Amount, and Country Code. For this pattern, we will be performing K Means clustering on the age attribute. The following code snippet is the Pig script that illustrates the implementation of this pattern:

```
/*
Register the required jar files
*/
REGISTER '/home/cloudera/pdp/jars/elephant-bird-pig-4.3.jar';
REGISTER '/home/cloudera/pdp/jars/elephant-bird-core-4.3.jar';
REGISTER '/home/cloudera/pdp/jars/elephant-bird-mahout-4.3.jar';
REGISTER '/home/cloudera/pdp/jars/elephant-bird-hadoop-compat-
    4.3.jar';
REGISTER '/home/cloudera/mahout-distribution-0.7/lib/json-simple-
    1.1.jar';
REGISTER '/home/cloudera/mahout-distribution-0.7/lib/guava-
    r09.jar';
REGISTER '/home/cloudera/mahout-distribution-0.7/mahout-examples-
    0.7-job.jar';
REGISTER '/home/cloudera/pig-
    0.11.0/contrib/piggybank/java/piggybank.jar';

/*
Use declare to create aliases.
declare is a preprocessor statement and is processed before running
the script
*/
%declare SEQFILE_LOADER
    'com.twitter.elephantbird.pig.load.SequenceFileLoader';
%declare SEQFILE_STORAGE
    'com.twitter.elephantbird.pig.store.SequenceFileStorage';
%declare VECTOR_CONVERTER
    'com.twitter.elephantbird.pig.mahout.VectorWritableConverter';
%declare TEXT_CONVERTER
    'com.twitter.elephantbird.pig.util.TextConverter';

/*
Load the dataset into the relation transactions
*/
transactions = LOAD
    '/user/cloudera/pdp/datasets/data_reduction/transactions.csv'
    USING  PigStorage(',') AS (id:long,transaction_date:chararray,
    cust_id:int, age:int, area:chararray, prod_subclass:int,
    prod_id:long, quantity:int, asset:int, transaction_amt:double,
    phone_no:chararray, country_code:chararray);

/*
Extract the columns on which clustering has to be performed
*/
```

```
age = FOREACH transactions GENERATE id AS tid, 1 AS index, age AS
  cust_age;

/*
Generate tuples from the parameters
*/
grpd = GROUP age BY tid;
vector_input = FOREACH grpd generate group,
  org.apache.pig.piggybank.evaluation.util.ToTuple(age.(index,
  cust_age));
/*
Use elephant bird functions to store the data into sequence file
(mahout readable format)
cardinality represents the dimension of the vector.
*/
STORE vector_input INTO
  '/user/cloudera/pdp/output/data_reduction/kmeans_preproc' USING
  $SEQFILE_STORAGE (
 '-c $TEXT_CONVERTER', '-c $VECTOR_CONVERTER -- -cardinality 100'
);
```

The following is a snippet of a shell script with the commands for executing K Means clustering on Mahout:

```
#All the mahout jars have to be included in classpath before
  execution of this script.
#Create the output directory on HDFS
  before executing VectorConverter
hadoop fs -mkdir
  /user/cloudera/pdp/output/data_reduction/kmeans_preproc_nv

#Execute vectorconverter jar to convert the input to named vectors
hadoop jar /home/cloudera/pdp/data_reduction/vectorconverter.jar
  com.datareduction.VectorConverter
  /user/cloudera/pdp/output/data_reduction/kmeans_preproc/
  /user/cloudera/pdp/output/data_reduction/kmeans_preproc_nv/

#The below Mahout command shows the usage of kmeans. The algorithm
  takes the input vectors from the path specified in the -i
  argument, it chooses the initial clusters at random, -k argument
  specifies the number of clusters as 3, -x specified the maximum
  number of iterations as 15. -dm specifies the distance measure
  to use i.e euclidean distance and a convergence threshold
  specified in -cd as 0.1
```

```
/home/cloudera/mahout-distribution-0.7/bin/mahout kmeans -i
    /user/cloudera/pdp/output/data_reduction/kmeans_preproc_nv/ -c
    kmeans-initial-clusters -k 3 -o /user/cloudera/pdp/output/
    data_reduction/kmeans_clusters -x 15 -ow -cl -dm org.apache
    .mahout.common.distance.EuclideanDistanceMeasure -cd 0.01

# Execute cluster dump command to print information about the
    cluster
/home/cloudera/mahout-distribution-0.7/bin/mahout clusterdump --
    input /user/cloudera/pdp/output/data_reduction
    /kmeans_clusters/clusters-4-final --pointsDir
    /user/cloudera/pdp/output/data_reduction
    /kmeans_clusters/clusteredPoints --output age_kmeans_clusters
```

Results

The following is a snippet of the result of applying this pattern on the transactions dataset:

```
VL-817732{n=309263 c=[1:45.552] r=[1:4.175] }
    Weight : [props - optional]:  Point:
1.0: 1 = [1:48.000]
    1.0: 2 = [1:42.000]
    1.0: 3 = [1:42.000]
    1.0: 4 = [1:41.000]
VL-817735{n=418519 c=[1:32.653] r=[1:4.850] }
    Weight : [props - optional]:  Point:
    1.0: 5 = [1:24.000]
    1.0: 7 = [1:38.000]
    1.0: 12 = [1:34.000]
    1.0: 14 = [1:23.000]
VL-817738{n=89958 c=[1:65.198] r=[1:5.972] }
    Weight : [props - optional]:  Point:
    1.0: 6 = [1:66.000]
    1.0: 8 = [1:58.000]
    1.0: 16 = [1:62.000]
    1.0: 24 = [1:74.000]
```

VL-XXXXX is the cluster identifier for a converged cluster, c is the centroid and is a vector, n is the number of points in the cluster, and r is the radius and is a vector. The data is divided into three clusters as specified in the K Means command. When this data is visualized, we can infer that values between 41 and 55 are grouped under cluster 1, 20 and 39 under cluster 2, and 56 and 74 are grouped under cluster 3.

Additional information

The complete code and datasets for this section are in the following GitHub directories:

- `Chapter6/code/`
- `Chapter6/datasets/`

Summary

In this chapter, you have studied various data reduction techniques that aim to obtain a reduced representation of the data. We have explored design patterns that perform the dimensionality reduction using the PCA technique and the numerosity reduction using the clustering, sampling, and histogram techniques.

In the next chapter, you will explore the advanced patterns that use Pig to mimic social-media data and understand the context better using text classification and other relevant techniques. We will also understand how the Pig language would evolve in the future.

7
Advanced Patterns and Future Work

In the previous chapter, you have studied various Big Data reduction techniques that aim to reduce the amount of data being analyzed or processed. We have explored design patterns that perform dimensionality reduction using the Principal Component Analysis technique and numerosity reduction using clustering, sampling, and histogram techniques.

In this chapter, we will start by discussing design patterns that primarily deal with text data and will explore a wide array of analytics pipelines that can be built using Pig as the key ingestion and processing engine.

We will be delving into the following patterns:

- Clustering textual data
- Topic discovery
- Natural language processing
- Classification

We will also speculate about what the future holds for Pig design patterns. These future trends analyze the kind of trends that are being followed now in the mainstream to modify Pig for specific use cases. These include where these trends will originate, what trends in data will affect current design patterns, and so on.

The clustering pattern

The clustering design pattern explores text clustering by calculating set similarities and clustering the results using Pig and Python.

Background

In the previous chapter, we examined how clustering can be used as a data reduction technique. We explored a clustering technique that deals with numeric data.

Clustering text automatically groups related documents into clusters that are similar to each other and separates documents that are different into different clusters. The primary reason clustering is performed is that if a corpus of documents is clustered, we divide the search space so that the search can be performed on the cluster containing the relevant documents. Clustering is one of the most important ways of improving search effectiveness and efficiency. Whether a group of documents is similar or different is not always clear and normally varies with the actual problem. For example, when clustering research articles, any two articles are considered similar if they share comparable thematic topics. When clustering websites, we are interested in clustering the pages according to the type of information they hold. For instance, to cluster university websites, we may want to separate professors' home pages from students' home pages and pages for courses from pages for research projects.

Text clustering works in situations where we need to organize multiple text documents into neatly tagged categories to make information retrieval easier. It can also be used for automated summarization of text corpus so that we can get a summary insight into the overall content of the corpus.

Text data has many unique properties, which require the design of specialized algorithms for classification. The following are a few distinctive characteristics of text representation:

- The text representation is generally very high dimensional, but the underlying data is sparse. In other words, the dictionary from which the documents are drawn may contain a million words, but a given document may contain only a few hundred words.

- These words are typically correlated with each other, implying that the principal components (or important concepts) are fewer than the words.

- The number of words in each document varies widely, requiring the word vectors to be normalized in terms of their relative frequency of presence in the document and over the entire collection. This is typically achieved by calculating the **term frequency–inverse document frequency (TF-IDF)**.

- These problems have a greater impact when we need to cluster shorter sentences or tweets.

Clustering plays a key role in retrieving vital insights from social media conversations, which are predominantly unstructured and huge in volume. As social media content is generated and delivered by one customer to other customers, the velocity of content generation is also a factor to be considered when choosing a clustering mechanism. Social media is not confined to just the content created by the microblogging platform Twitter and the social networking platform Facebook alone; there are various other sources of content that are routinely created in wikis, forums, blogs, and other media sharing platforms. These platforms predominantly create text content, with the exception of Flickr and YouTube, which create image and video data. Clustering various types of social media content provides an inherent understanding of the similarity in the relationship between documents, images, videos, network links, and other contextual information.

In this design pattern, we limit ourselves to clustering text data gleaned from social media so that we can interpret from the data if there are groups of similar people in our own social network. This similarity could be owing to the same job titles, companies, or location.

Motivation

There is a wide variety of algorithms commonly used for text clustering. We have Hierarchical Agglomerative Clustering and distance-based clustering techniques, which use a similarity function to measure the closeness between any two text objects. Many clustering algorithms predominantly differ in the way the similarity measure is calculated. The following diagram depicts the most common clustering techniques for text data:

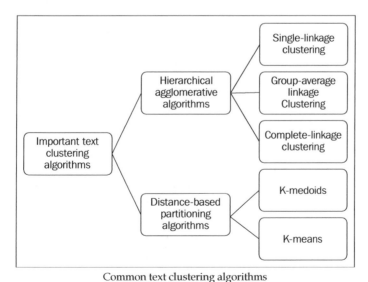

Common text clustering algorithms

The following is a brief description of the most common text clustering techniques:

- **Hierarchical Agglomerative Clustering (HAC)**: This technique is useful for supporting a variety of problems that arise while searching because it creates a tree hierarchy that can be leveraged for the search process and improves the search effectiveness and efficiency.

  The general concept of HAC algorithms is to combine documents into clusters based on their similarity to other documents. Hierarchical clustering algorithms successively combine groups based on the best pairwise similarity between these groups of documents. The similarity is computed between different sets of points in documents using the popular distance measures such as Euclidean, Manhattan, and Levenshtein. This corresponds to single-linkage, group-average linkage, and complete linkage clustering respectively. These algorithms are quite accurate, but they suffer from lack of efficiency.

- **Distance-based partitioning algorithms**: These algorithms are generally used to create a cluster of objects where hierarchy does not play an important role. There are two widely used distance-based clustering algorithms: K-medoids and K-means. These algorithms are far less accurate than the HAC algorithms, but are a lot more efficient.

  - **K-medoids clustering algorithm**: This technique uses a set of k data points from the original data as central points (or medoids) around which the clusters are developed. The central aim of the algorithm is to figure out an ideal set of documents from the original set of documents around which the clusters are built. Each document is assigned to the document nearest to it in the collection. This creates an iterative set of clusters from the document set, which are successively improved by a random process. The key disadvantages of K-medoids clustering algorithms are that they are slow as they require a large number of iterations in order to achieve convergence and that they do not work well for sparse text data sets.

  - **K-means clustering algorithm**: This technique is quite similar to K-medoids as it also uses a set of k data points around which the clusters are built. However, unlike the K-medoids, this initial set of representative points is not obtained from the original data. The initial set of representative points is obtained from methods such as the hierarchical agglomerative clustering and partial supervision techniques. The K-means algorithm is faster than the K-medoids algorithm as it reaches the convergence in far fewer iterations. The disadvantages of using the K-means method are that it is quite dependent on the accuracy of the initial set of seeds and that the centroids for a given cluster of documents may contain a large number of words.

Pig is used to ingest the source data and apply several standard transformations to the term vector representation.

1. Remove the stop words. These are words that are nondescriptive for the topic of a document (such as a, an, is, and the).

2. Stem the words using Porter stemmer so that words with different endings are mapped into a single word.

3. Measure the effect of containing rare terms in the document on the overall clustering ability and then decide to discard words that appear with less than a specified threshold frequency.

The following is a quick overview of some of the string similarity measures used to compute the closeness of strings for clustering purposes:

- **Edit distance or Levenshtein distance**: This calculates the dissimilarity of strings by counting the minimum number of replacements required to transform one string to another

- **Jaccard similarity**: This is calculated by dividing the number of items in common between the two sets by the total number of distinct items in the two sets

- **Measuring Agreement on Set-valued Items (MASI)**: This distance returns a shorter distance than the Jaccard similarity when there is partial overlapping between the sets

Use cases

The clustering design pattern can be used for the following purposes:

- Clustering data after retrieval to present more organized results to the user

- Creating hierarchical taxonomies of documents based on their similarity for browsing purposes

Pattern implementation

The use case depicted in this pattern clusters Outlook contacts with similar job titles. Conceptually, this pattern identifies which of your contacts are similar based on an arbitrary criterion such as job title. For example, this pattern can be extended to answer which of your connections have worked in companies you want to work for or where most of your connections reside geographically.

The Pig script loads the data and performs transformations on it by replacing abbreviations with their full forms and passes distinct job titles to the Python script via streaming. Passing distinct job titles ensures that the amount of data sent to the Python script is reduced.

The bulk of the clustering code is implemented in Python, which has ready-made support for clustering. The Python script is invoked via streaming in the Reduce phase. The job titles passed by Pig are read by the Python script from `stdin` and MASI distance is calculated. Clustering is done on the job title based on the distance and threshold and then the clustered job titles are written to `stdout`.

The Pig script reads the values written by Python to `stdout` and performs the name and job title association by fetching the job titles from the data available in the Pig relation.

We have explored several methods to calculate string similarity in order to cluster the job titles and zeroed in on the MASI distance for implementation in this pattern. This distance measure is deemed appropriate for our current use cases where there are overlaps in the job titles.

Code snippets

To illustrate the working of this pattern, we have exported contact names and their job titles from Outlook into a CSV file and de-identified the names. This file is stored on the HDFS.

 All the external Python modules that are not in the default Python path should be added to the `PYTHONPATH` environment variable before execution of the script.

The following code snippet is the Pig script illustrating the implementation of this pattern:

```
/*
Assign alias cluster_contacts to the streaming command
Use SHIP to send the streaming binary files (Python script) from
  the client node to the compute node
*/
DEFINE cluster_contacts 'cluster_contacts.py' SHIP
  ('cluster_contacts.py');

/*
Register the piggybank jar file
*/
```

```
REGISTER '/home/cloudera/pig-
  0.11.0/contrib/piggybank/java/piggybank.jar';

/*
Load the outlook_contacts.csv dataset into the relation
  outlook_contacts
*/
outlook_contacts = LOAD '/user/cloudera/pdp/datasets/
  advanced_patterns/outlook_contacts.csv' USING PigStorage(',') AS
  (name: chararray, job_title: chararray);

/*
Transform the job titles by replacing few abbreviations with their
  full forms
*/
transformed_job_titles = FOREACH outlook_contacts {
job_title_sr = REPLACE(job_title,'Sr', 'Senior');

.

.

job_title_vp = REPLACE(job_title_cfo,'VP', 'Vice President');

GENERATE name AS name,job_title_vp AS job_title;
}

/*
Trim spaces for the field job_title
*/
jt_trimmed = FOREACH transformed_job_titles GENERATE
  TRIM(job_title) AS job_title,name;

/*
Group outlook_contacts by job_title
Extract unique job titles and store into the relation jt_flattened
STREAM is used to send the data to the external script
The Python script executes as a reduce job as STREAM is called
  after GROUP BY
The result is stored in the relation clustered_jt
*/
jt_trimmed_grpd = GROUP jt_trimmed BY job_title;
jt_flattened = FOREACH jt_trimmed_grpd GENERATE flatten(group);
clustered_jt = STREAM jt_flattened THROUGH cluster_contacts;
```

```
/*
Clustered job titles from relation clustered_jt are typecasted to
  chararray and are assigned to relation clustered_jt_cast.
clustered_jt_cast relation contains job title clusters.
*/
clustered_jt_cast = FOREACH clustered_jt GENERATE (chararray)$0 AS
  cluster;


/*
The job titles are tokenized by using comma and are assigned to
  the relation clustered_jt_tokens along with the cluster name.
*/
clustered_jt_tokens  = FOREACH clustered_jt_cast GENERATE
  TOKENIZE(cluster,','), cluster;


/*
Each job title in job cluster is converted into a new tuple and is
  assigned to relation clustered_jt_flattened along with the
  cluster name.
*/
clustered_jt_flattened = FOREACH clustered_jt_tokens  GENERATE
  FLATTEN($0) AS cluster_job, cluster;


/*
Trim spaces in the job titles.
*/
clustered_jt_trimmed  = FOREACH clustered_jt_flattened GENERATE
  TRIM(cluster_job) AS cluster_job, cluster;


/*
Join jt_trimmed relation by job_title with the relation
  clustered_jt_trimmed by cluster_job. Project the contact name
  and cluster name.
*/
jt_clustered_joind = JOIN jt_trimmed BY
  job_title,clustered_jt_trimmed  BY cluster_job;
name_clustered_jt = FOREACH jt_clustered_joind GENERATE
  jt_trimmed::name AS name, clustered_jt_trimmed::cluster AS
  cluster;


/*
Remove duplicate tuples from relation name_clustered_jt.
*/
uniq_name_clustered_jt  = DISTINCT name_clustered_jt;
```

```
/*
Group the relation uniq_name_clustered_jt by field cluster and
  project the cluster name(consisting of a set of job titles) and
  the contact name
*/
name_clustered_jt_grpd =  GROUP uniq_name_clustered_jt  BY
  cluster;
similar_jt_clusters= FOREACH name_clustered_jt_grpd GENERATE group
  AS clustername, uniq_name_clustered_jt.name AS name;

/*
The results are stored on the HDFS in the directory clustering
*/
STORE similar_jt_clusters into
  '/user/cloudera/pdp/output/advanced_patterns/clustering';
```

The following is the Python code snippet illustrating the implementation of
this pattern:

```
#! /usr/bin/env python

# Import required modules
import sys
import csv
from nltk.metrics.distance import masi_distance

# Set the distance function to use and the distance threshold
    value
DISTANCE_THRESHOLD = 0.5
DISTANCE = masi_distance

def cluster_contacts_by_title():

# Read data from stdin and store in a list called contacts
    contacts = [line.strip() for line in sys.stdin]
    for c in contacts[:]:
        if len(c)==0 :
            contacts.remove(c)


# create list of titles to be clustered (from contacts list)
    all_titles = []
    for i in range(len(contacts)):
```

```
        title = [contacts[i]]
        all_titles.extend(title)

    all_titles = list(set(all_titles))



    # calculate masi_distance between two titles and cluster them
    based on the distance threshold, store them in dictionary
    variable called clusters
    clusters = {}
    for title1 in all_titles:
        clusters[title1] = []
        for title2 in all_titles:
            if title2 in clusters[title1] or
                clusters.has_key(title2) and title1 \
                in clusters[title2]:
                continue
            distance = DISTANCE(set(title1.split()),
                set(title2.split()))
            if distance < DISTANCE_THRESHOLD:
                clusters[title1].append(title2)



    # Flatten out clusters
    clusters = [clusters[title] for title in clusters if
        len(clusters[title]) > 1]

    # Write the cluster names to stdout
    for i in range(len(clusters)):
        print ", ".join(clusters[i])
```

Results

The following is a snippet of the results after executing the code in this pattern on the dataset. We have shown only a few of the clusters to improve readability. The comma separated list on the left shows the clustered job titles, while the names associated with the job titles are displayed on the right.

```
IT Analyst, IT Financial Analyst    {(Name268),(Name869)}
Delivery Head, Delivery Unit Head    {(Name631),(Name662)}
Data Scientist, Lead Data Scientist    {(Name50),(Name823),(Name960),
    (Name314),(Name124),(Name163),(Name777),(Name58),(Name695)}
Lead Analyst, Lead Business Analyst    {(Name667),(Name495),
    (Name536),(Name952)}
```

```
Pega Practice Head, M2M Practice Head        { (Name618), (Name322) }
Technical Lead, Lead Technical Writer        { (Name52), (Name101),
     (Name120), (Name969), (Name683) }
Vice President, Vice President Sales          { (Name894), (Name673),
     (Name72) }
Business Analyst, Lead Business Analyst        { (Name536), (Name847) }
Director - Presales, Director - Staffing       { (Name104), (Name793) }
Product Manager, Senior. Product Manager       { (Name161), (Name956) }
Technology Lead, Technology Lead Service        { (Name791), (Name257) }
```

In the following diagram, we have graphically represented a few of the clusters to improve readability:

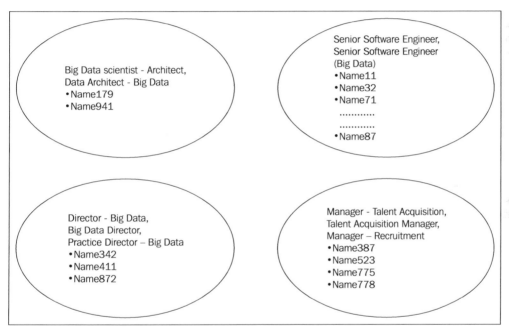

Clustering output

As shown in the preceding diagram, the first cluster consists of two contacts with the job titles **Big Data scientist – Architect** and **Data Architect – Big Data**. These two titles are similar and hence the contacts are grouped into a single cluster.

Additional information

The complete code and datasets for this section can be found in the following GitHub directories:

- `Chapter7/code/`
- `Chapter7/datasets/`

The topic discovery pattern

The topic discovery design pattern explores one way of classifying a corpus of text by the technique called **Latent Dirichlet Allocation (LDA)** using Pig and Mahout.

Background

The discovery of the hidden topic in a corpus of text is one of the latest developments in the field of natural language processing. The data posted on social media sites generally covers a wide array of subjects. However, in order to extract relevant information from these sites, we have to classify the text corpus based on the relevance of the topics hidden in the text. This will enable automated summarization of a large amount of text and find what it is really about. Prior knowledge of the topics that are thus discovered is used to classify new documents.

Motivation

The key difficulty topic models solve is that of classifying a text corpus and identifying its topic in the absence of any prior knowledge of its contents. Prior knowledge implies that the document has not been labeled before as belonging to a particular topic. Topic models use statistical methods to discover topics hidden in the text corpus.

Latent Dirichlet Allocation (LDA) is an implementation of the topic models that works by initially identifying topics from a set of words contained in a document and then grouping the documents into combinations of topics.

LDA uses a TF-vector space model to identify the meaning of the word based on its context rather than frequency. Using LDA, the word's intent is resolved by removing ambiguities. LDA uses contextual clues to connect words with the same meaning and differentiate between usages of words with multiple meanings.

We can form an intuitive understanding of topic models by considering a case where it is easy for humans to comprehend that the words "penicillin" and "antibiotics" will appear more often in documents about medicine and the words "code" and "debugger" will appear more often in documents about software. Topic models try to glean the topic from the corpus based on the word distributions and document distributions of the topics.

Let us consider the following statements:

- I ate oats and carrots for breakfast
- I love eating oranges and carrots
- Puppies and kittens are cute
- My brother brought a puppy home
- The cute rabbit is chewing a piece of carrot

LDA automatically discovers the topics these sentences contain. As an example, if we perform LDA on these sentences and perform a query for the discovered topics, the output might be as follows:

```
Topic A: 30% oats, 15% carrots, 10% breakfast, 10% chewing, … (this topic could be interpreted to be about food)
Topic B: 20% Puppies, 20% kittens, 20% cute, 15% rabbit, ... (this topic could be interpreted to be about cute animals)
Sentences 1 and 2: 100% Topic A
Sentences 3 and 4: 100% Topic B
Sentence 5: 60% Topic A, 40% Topic B
```

Pig is the glue that connects the raw data and LDA algorithm by pre-processing the data and converting it into a format amenable to the application of the LDA algorithm. It comes in handy to quickly ingest the right data from various sources, cleanse it, and transform it into the necessary format. Pig manufactures the dataset from the raw data and sends it to the LDA implementation script.

Use cases

You can consider using this design pattern on an unstructured text corpus to explore the latent intent and summarization. This pattern can also be considered in cases where we are not aware of the contents of the text corpus and cannot classify it based on a supervised classification algorithm so that we can understand even the latent topics.

Pattern implementation

To implement this pattern, we have considered a set of articles on Big Data and medicine, and we intend to find the topics inherent in the documents. This design pattern is implemented in Pig and Mahout. It illustrates one way of implementing the integration of Pig with Mahout to ease the problem of vectorizing the data and converting it into a Mahout-readable format, allowing quick prototyping. We have deliberately omitted the steps for pre-processing and vector conversion as we have already seen an example illustrating these steps in *Chapter 6, Understanding Data Reduction Patterns*.

The `sh` command in Pig is used to invoke Mahout commands that perform the pre-processing, create sparse vectors, and apply **Collapsed Variational Bayes (CVB)**, which is Mahout's implementation of LDA for topic modeling. The resultant list of words, along with their probabilities, is returned for each topic.

Code snippets

To illustrate the working of this pattern, we have considered a dataset with a couple of articles on Big Data and medicine. The files are stored on HDFS. For this pattern, we will be applying topic modeling on the text corpus to identify the topics.

The following code snippet is the Pig code illustrating the implementation of this pattern:

```
/*
Register piggybank jar file
*/
REGISTER '/home/cloudera/pig-
   0.11.0/contrib/piggybank/java/piggybank.jar';

/*
*Ideally the following data pre-processing steps have to be
   generally performed on the actual data, we have deliberately
   omitted the implementation as these steps were covered in the
   respective chapters

*Data Ingestion to ingest data from the required sources

*Data Profiling by applying statistical techniques to profile data
   and find data quality issues

*Data Validation to validate the correctness of the data and
   cleanse it accordingly
```

```
*Data Transformation to apply transformations on the data.

*Data Reduction to obtain a reduced representation of the data.
*/


/*
We have deliberately omitted the steps for vector conversion as we
  have an example illustrating these in the chapter Understanding
  Data Reduction Patterns.
*/

/*
Use sh command to execute shell commands.
Convert the files in a directory to sequence files
-i specifies the input directory on HDFS
-o specifies the output directory on HDFS
*/
sh /home/cloudera/mahout-distribution-0.8/bin/mahout seqdirectory
  -i /user/cloudera/pdp/datasets/advanced_patterns/lda -o
  /user/cloudera/pdp/output/advanced_patterns/lda/sequence_files

/*
Create sparse vectors
-i specifies the input directory on HDFS
-o specifies the output directory on HDFS
-nv to get the named vectors
*/
sh /home/cloudera/mahout-distribution-0.8/bin/mahout seq2sparse -i
  /user/cloudera/pdp/output/advanced_patterns/lda/sequence_files -
  o /user/cloudera/pdp/output/advanced_patterns/lda/sparse_vectors
  -nv -wt tf

/*
Use rowid to convert the sparse vectors by changing the text key
  to integer
-i specifies the input directory on HDFS
-o specifies the output directory on HDFS
*/
sh /home/cloudera/mahout-distribution-0.8/bin/mahout rowid -i
  /user/cloudera/pdp/output/advanced_patterns/lda/
  sparse_vectors/tf-vectors/ -o /user/cloudera/pdp/output/
  advanced_patterns/lda/matrix
```

```
/*
Use Collapsed Variational Bayes for topic modelling
-i specifies the input directory on HDFS
-o specifies the output directory on HDFS
-k specifies the number of topics
-x specifies the maximum number of iterations
-dict specifies the path to term dictionary
-dt specifies the path to document topic distribution
-mt specifies temporary directory of the model, this is useful
  when restarting the jobs
*/
sh /home/cloudera/mahout-distribution-0.8/bin/mahout cvb -i
  /user/cloudera/pdp/output/advanced_patterns/lda/matrix/matrix -o
  /user/cloudera/pdp/output/advanced_patterns/lda/lda-out -k 2 -x
  5 -dict /user/cloudera/pdp/output/advanced_patterns/lda/sparse_
  vectors/dictionary.file-* -dt /user/cloudera/pdp/output/advanced_
  patterns /lda/lda-topics -mt /user/cloudera/pdp/output/advanced_
  patterns/  lda/lda-model


/*
Display top ten words along with their probabilities for each
  topic
-i specifies the input directory on HDFS
-d specifies the path to the dictionary file
-dt specifies the type of the dictionary (sequence / text)
-sort sorts the Key/Value pairs in descending order
*/
sh /home/cloudera/mahout-distribution-0.8/bin/mahout vectordump -i
  /user/cloudera/pdp/output/advanced_patterns/lda/lda-out -d
  /user/cloudera/pdp/output/advanced_patterns/lda/sparse_vectors
  /dictionary.file-* -dt sequencefile -vs 10 -sort
  /user/cloudera/pdp/output/advanced_patterns/lda/lda-out
```

Results

The following is a snippet of the results after executing the code in this pattern on the dataset:

```
Topic 1:
   {examination:0.11428571430112491,medical:0.09999999999299336,
   follow:0.057142857068596745,may:0.057142857068595974,
   patient:0.05714285706859565,order:0.05714285706858435,
   tests:0.042857142760463936,physical:0.04285714276045852,
   signs:0.04285714276044089,other:0.028571428452333902}
```

```
Topic 2:
   {data:0.14754098319799064,parallel:0.0983606554177082,
   processing:0.08196721282428095,mapreduce:0.08196721282428092,
   big:0.06557377023085392,framework:0.06557377023085392,
   architecture:0.06557377023085391,use:0.032786885044002005,
   end:0.032786885044002005,type:0.032786885044002005}
```

The preceding result indicates discovery of two topics (Topic 1 and Topic 2) in the document and the list of the top ten words along with their probabilities for each topic. These topics are related to Big Data and medicine.

Additional information

The complete code and dataset for this section can be found in the following GitHub directories:

- Chapter7/code/
- Chapter7/datasets/

More information on Mahout's implementation of LDA can be found at https://mahout.apache.org/users/clustering/latent-dirichlet-allocation.html.

The natural language processing pattern

This design pattern explores the implementation of natural language processing on unstructured text data using Pig.

Background

Information retrieval from unstructured data, such as blogs and articles, revolves around extracting meaningful information from huge chunks of un-annotated text. The core goal of information retrieval is to extract structured information from unstructured text. This structured information is indexed to optimize the search. For example, consider the following sentence:

"Graham Bell invented the telephone in 1876"

The preceding sentence is used to extract the following structured information:

```
Inventorof (Telephone, Graham Bell)
InventedIn(Telephone, 1876)
```

There are a number of ways in which information retrieval can be performed on a corpus of text. We have studied in *The unstructured text profiling pattern* section of *Chapter 3*, *Data Profiling Patterns*, how a bag of words model based on TF-IDF helps to decompose a document into word frequencies and makes information retrieval possible by accessing the document in which a word is frequent. One of the glaring shortcomings of this model, based on TF-IDF, is that it does not require deep semantic understanding of data. Instead, these models are concerned with the syntax of the words that were separated by whitespace to break the document into a bag of words and use frequency and simple similarity metrics to determine which words were likely to be important in the data. Even though these techniques are used for a wide variety of applications, they fail in cases where we have to retrieve information dealing with the context of the data.

As an illustration, biomedical researchers often examine a large number of medical publications to glean discoveries related to genes, proteins, or other biomedical entities. To enable this effort, a simple search using keyword matching (such as TF-IDF) may not be adequate, because many biomedical entities have synonyms and ambiguous names; this makes it hard to accurately retrieve relevant documents. It is a critical task in biomedical literature mining to identify biomedical entities from text based on semantics or context and to link them to their corresponding entries in existing knowledge bases. In this design pattern, we will explore extraction of named entities from an unstructured corpus using Pig and Python.

Motivation

The two fundamental tasks of context-sensitive decomposition of data using natural language processing are named entity recognition and relation extraction.

Named entity recognition is a technique for identifying names of entities, such as "Obama", "president", and "Washington", from unstructured text and classifying them into predefined types, such as people, job, and locations. Named entity recognition generally cannot be performed using string matching since the entities of a given type can be unlimited and also since the type of the named entity can be context dependent. In the previous example, the entity "Washington" can belong to the entity types, Location or Person; to correctly determine the correct entity type, its context has to be considered. Named entity recognition is the foundational task for information extraction. The extraction of other information structures, such as relationships and events, depends on accuracy of named entity recognition as a pre-processing step.

Typically, named entity recognition is implemented using statistical sequence labeling algorithms, such as maximum entropy models, hidden Markov models, and conditional random fields.

The following are the high-level steps involved in performing named entity recognition:

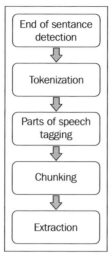

Named entity recognition

The following is a brief description of the steps involved in an NLP pipeline:

- **End of sentence detection**: This is the first step toward processing the corpus. It is performed on the entire corpus of text to split it into a collection of meaningful sentences. This step overcomes the ambiguities involved in the end-of-sentence detection where a period or other punctuation mark denotes the end of sentences and other abbreviations.

- **Tokenization**: This operates on single sentences and converts them into tokens.

- **Parts-of-speech tagging**: This assigns information about parts of speech (such as nouns, verbs, and adjectives) to each token. The parts of speech listed as a result in this step will be grouped together (for example, all the nouns may be grouped). This grouping will eventually help reasoning about the types of entities they belong to (for example, people, places, and organizations).

- **Chunking**: This performs a series of tasks such as finding noun groups and verb groups, and completes partitioning of sentences into groups of different types.

- **Extraction**: This analyzes each chunk and tags it as an entity type, such as people, places, and organizations.

The previously mentioned steps to extract entities enable us to use these entities as the basis of analysis as opposed to document-centric analysis involving keyword searches and frequency analysis. One simple way to do this analysis would be to extract all the nouns and noun phrases from the document, and index them as entities appearing in the documents.

In this design pattern, Pig is used to ingest the source data and preprocess it before the NLP algorithm is applied and the parts of speech or entities are identified.

Use cases

This design pattern can be used to address the needs of the following problem areas:

- Extracting the financial or biomedical information from news or other text corpus

- Extracting entities to automatically summarize text and creating new text by combining information from multiple documents

- Detection of certain sequences in text, which are needed prior to text clustering or indexing

Pattern implementation

To implement this pattern, we have considered a text data set containing some text on the invention of the telephone. The objective of the code is to extract named entities from the document.

This design pattern is implemented by integrating Pig and Python. Python has extensive support for processing natural language through its NLTK toolkit. The Pig script loads a text file and passes this relation to a Python script via streaming. Python's NLTK library has built-in functions to tokenize sentences and words. Its pos_tag function tags parts of speech for each token; the chunking operation finds the noun and verb groups and tags them with entity types such as people, organizations, and places. The Python script uses these functions of the NLTK library and returns the named entities to the Pig script.

Code snippets

To illustrate the working of this pattern, we have considered a text dataset extracted from the Wikipedia article on the invention of the telephone. The file is stored on HDFS. For this pattern, we will be using Pig and Python to extract named entities.

All the external Python modules not in the default Python path should be added to the `PYTHONPATH` environment variable before the execution of the script.

The following code snippet is the Pig code illustrating the implementation of this pattern:

```
/*
Assign alias ner to the streaming command
Use SHIP to send the streaming binary files (Python script) from
  the client node to the compute node
*/
DEFINE ner 'named_entities.py' SHIP ('named_entities.py');

/*
Load the dataset into the relation data
*/
data = LOAD '/user/cloudera/pdp/datasets/advanced_patterns/input.txt';

/*
STREAM is used to send the data to the external script
The result is stored in the relation extracted_named_entities
*/
extracted_named_entities = STREAM data THROUGH ner;

/*
The results are stored on the HDFS in the directory nlp
*/
STORE extracted_named_entities INTO
  '/user/cloudera/pdp/output/advanced_patterns/nlp';
```

The following code snippet is the Python code illustrating the implementation of this pattern:

```
#! /usr/bin/env python

# Import required modules

import sys
import string
import nltk


# Read data from stdin and store it as sentences
for line in sys.stdin:
```

```
if len(line) == 0: continue
sentences = nltk.tokenize.sent_tokenize(line)

# Extract words from sentences
words = [nltk.tokenize.word_tokenize(s) for s in sentences]

# Extract Part of Speech from words
pos_words = [nltk.pos_tag(t) for t in words]

# Chunk the extracted Part of Speech tags
named_entities = nltk.batch_ne_chunk(pos_words)

# Write the chunks to stdout
print named_entities[0]
```

Results

The following is a snippet of the results after executing the code in this pattern on the dataset. The tag NNP indicates a noun that is part of a noun phrase, VBD indicates a verb that's in simple past tense, and JJ indicates an adjective. For more information on the tags, refer to the Penn Treebank Project, which provides a full summary. The following is a snippet of part of speech tags that are returned:

```
(S
  (PERSON Alexander/NNP)
  (PERSON Graham/NNP Bell/NNP)
  was/VBD
  awarded/VBN
  a/DT
  patent/NN
  for/IN
  the/DT
  electric/JJ
  telephone/NN
  by/IN
  (ORGANIZATION USPTO/NNP)
  in/IN
  March/NNP
  1876/CD
  ./.)
```

We have redrawn the results for better readability, as shown in the following diagram:

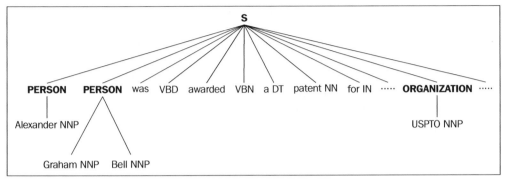

The named entity recognition output

The parts of speech tagging is done for each word. Alexander Graham Bell is identified as a person and part of speech tagging is done as an NNP (noun that is part of a noun phrase), which indicates a proper noun. USPTO is identified as an organization and is tagged as a proper noun.

Additional information

The complete code and dataset for this section can be found in the following GitHub directories:

- `Chapter7/code/`
- `Chapter7/datasets/`

Additional parts of speech tagging information is at `http://www.ling.upenn.edu/courses/Fall_2003/ling001/penn_treebank_pos.html`.

The classification pattern

This design pattern explores the implementation of classification using Pig and Mahout.

Background

Classification is one of the core concepts of predictive analytics; it is a technique in which data is labeled into categories or groups according to its characteristics. Classification is a simplified way to make decisions based on the data and its attributes. For example, in a survey questionnaire, we choose an appropriate answer or select a particular check box for a given question. Here, we are making a decision from a finite group of choices (check boxes or answers) provided to us. Sometimes, the number of choices can be as small as two (yes/no). In these cases, classification uses specific information on the input data to choose a single output from a group of predetermined responses.

Consider the case of a human being making a decision to buy a pizza. The input data for this decision making includes the price, toppings, type of crust, and so on, for multiple pizzas, and the group of predetermined choices includes *to buy* and *don't buy*. Classification helps the person involved to efficiently make the decision by looking at the input information and choosing to *buy* a pizza if it suits his taste and is within his specific price limit.

Using machine learning for classification, we can train the machine-learning algorithm to mimic human thought and perform automated decisions based on the input data characteristics. These algorithms work best when they have to decide a single output from a short list of categorical values based on the specific input characteristics.

The well-known example of predictive analysis using classification is spam detection where the machine learning algorithm uses the details of past e-mails that were labeled as spam and combines this with the attributes of e-mail messages to *decide* whether new messages are *spam* or *not spam*. Similarly, in the case of credit card fraud detection, the past history of fraudulent transactions and the attributes of the current transaction are used to decide whether the transaction is fraudulent or not.

All the classification algorithms learn how to decide based on the examples (past data). The accuracy of the decision making depends on the accuracy of the examples fed into the classification algorithm and also the quality of the input data.

Motivation

Classification is a three-step process: **training, testing**, and **production**. The training and testing are preproduction steps, which specifically use historical data to build and refine the model. This data has already been labeled with the decision (say *spam* or *not spam*). The historical data is divided into two buckets, one for building the training model and the other for testing. The training data is approximately 80 to 90 percent of the historical data and the rest is testing data. The decisions in the testing bucket are deliberately removed.

- **Training**: The input for the training step consists of example data labeled with known decisions. Based on the known decisions and the input data characteristics, the trained model performs classification in the testing step. The training model is the most important artifact in the classification engine, and it is tuned to predict as accurately as possible by supplying it with appropriately labeled example data.

- **Testing**: The input for the testing step is the trained model from the previous step plus the new examples that were withheld from the training step that have the decisions deliberately removed. As a result of the testing step, the model chooses a decision and these decisions are evaluated for accuracy. This evaluation is done by comparing known results with the results from the model. This step has a bearing on the performance on the model, which is revised accordingly. Once the model performs as expected, it is deployed into production, where more unlabelled examples are given to it.

- **Production**: The input to the production step is a set of new example data whose decision is unknown. The model deployed in production uses the inference formed out of the training and testing phase to perform the actual classification. The output of this phase is generally in line with the precision of the results obtained in the testing phase unless there is a drastic change in the input values or poor data quality. Occasionally, the samples of the production data are taken to be used as new training data so that the classification model is updated and deployed back into production.

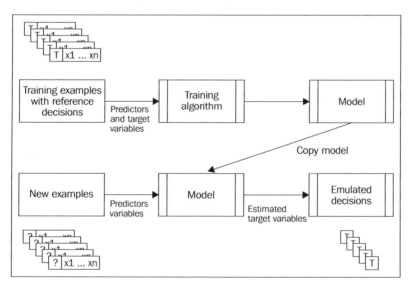

The classification process

The performance of the classification exercise can be understood by the confusion matrix. The confusion matrix contains the values of the decisions made by the model (predicted class) and the actual decisions (actual class). It generally has two rows and two columns that report the number of true positives, false negatives, false positives, and true negatives. The columns of the confusion matrix represent the predicted class, and the rows represent the actual class.

For example, if the model needs to classify e-mails as SPAM and NOT_A_SPAM and the document is actually SPAM but the model classified it as NOT_A_SPAM, then the confusion matrix is as follows:

		Predicted class	
Actual class		SPAM	NOT_A_SPAM
	SPAM	0	1
	NOT_A_SPAM	0	0

The confusion matrix

In the preceding confusion matrix illustration, the diagonal contains the counts of e-mails that the model has correctly classified and the off-diagonal contains the wrongly classified instances. The perfect classifier will have all entries classified correctly and hence will have all the counts along the diagonal.

Classification can be performed using a variety of algorithms. Each of these algorithms differs broadly based on the type of input data it can handle (such as skewed data and uniform data), the amount of data, explainability of the results, the number of attributes (with high dimensional space), the number of classifiers (such as binary yes/no or multiclassifier), speed of training and classification, parallelizablility, and so on.

The following diagram shows a snapshot of the most important classification algorithms. These algorithms have different trade-offs in terms of effectiveness, efficiency, and applicability for a given problem set.

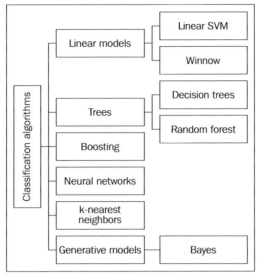

A few classification algorithms

Pig is an extremely useful language to implement the classification pipeline in production. It comes in handy to quickly explore the data, assign the right schema, ingest the right data from various sources, cleanse it, integrate the data, and transform it into the necessary format. Pig manufactures the dataset from the raw data so that classification is performed on this ready-made set.

Use cases

This design pattern can be used to address the needs of the following problem areas, but is not limited to them:

- Spam filtering
- Fraud detection
- Sentiment analysis

Pattern implementation

This design pattern is implemented in Pig and Mahout. It illustrates one way of implementing integration of Pig with Mahout to ease the problem of vectorizing the data and converting it into a Mahout-readable format, allowing quick prototyping. We have deliberately omitted the steps for pre-processing and vector conversion as we have already seen an example illustrating these steps in *Chapter 6, Understanding Data Reduction Patterns*.

Typically, the data profiling, validation and cleansing, and transformation and reduction steps can be applied using the Pig script before sending it to Mahout. In our use case, we made the assumption that the data has already been profiled, cleansed, and transformed.

The data is divided into training and test data in the ratio of 80:20. The training data is used to train the model, and the test data is used to test the model's accuracy of prediction. The decision tree model is built on the training data and is applied to the test data. The resultant matrix shows the comparison between the predicted and actual results.

Code snippets

To illustrate the working of this pattern, we have considered the German credit dataset in the UCI format. There are 20 attributes (7 numerical and 13 categorical) with 1000 instances. The file is stored on the HDFS. For this pattern, we will be using Pig and Mahout to train the model to classify people as good or bad customers based on a set of attributes; the prediction will then be tested on test data.

The following is the Pig script illustrating the implementation of this pattern:

```
/*
Register piggybank jar file
*/
REGISTER '/home/cloudera/pig-
   0.11.0/contrib/piggybank/java/piggybank.jar';

/*
*The following data pre-processing steps have to be performed
   here, we have deliberately omitted the implementation as these
   steps were covered in the respective chapters
*Data Ingestion to ingest data from the required sources
*Data Profiling by applying statistical techniques to profile data
   and find data quality issues
*Data Validation to validate the correctness of the data and
   cleanse it accordingly
*Data Transformation to apply transformations on the data.
*Data Reduction to obtain a reduced representation of the data.
*/

/*
We have deliberately omitted the steps for vector conversion as we
   have an example illustrating these in the chapter Understanding
   Data Reduction Patterns.
```

```
*/

/*
Use sh command to execute shell commands.
Generate file descriptor for the training dataset
The string C N 2 C N 2 C N 2 C N C N 2 C N C N 2 C L provides the
  description of the data.
C specifies that the first attribute is Categorical, it is
  followed by N specifying the next attribute to be Numeric. This
  is followed by 2 C which means that the next two attributes are
  Categorical.
L represents the Label
*/
sh hadoop jar /home/cloudera/mahout-distribution-
  0.8/core/target/mahout-core-0.8-job.jar
  org.apache.mahout.classifier.df.tools.Describe -p
  /user/cloudera/pdp/datasets/advanced_patterns/german-train.data
  -f /user/cloudera/pdp/datasets/advanced_patterns/german-
  train.info -d C N 2 C N 2 C N 2 C N C N 2 C N C N 2 C L


/*
Build Random Forests
-t specifies the number of decision trees to build
-p specifies usage of partial implementation
-sl specifies the number of random attributes to select for each
  node
-o specifies the output directory
-d specifies the path to the training dataset
-ds specifies the data descriptor
-Dmapred.max.split.size indicates the maximum size of each
  partition
*/
sh hadoop jar /home/cloudera/mahout-distribution-
  0.8/examples/target/mahout-examples-0.8-job.jar
  org.apache.mahout.classifier.df.mapreduce.BuildForest -
  Dmapred.max.split.size=1874231 -d /user/cloudera/pdp/datasets/
  advanced_patterns/german-train.data -ds /user/cloudera/pdp/
  datasets/advanced_patterns/german-train.info -sl 5 -p -t 100 -o
  /user/cloudera/pdp/output/advanced_patterns/classification


/*
Predict the label in the test dataset
-i specifies the file path of the test dataset
-ds specifies the dataset descriptor, we use the one generated
  for training data as the data description is the same for both
  training and test data
```

```
-m specifies the file path of the decision tree built on the
   training data
-a specifies that confusion matrix has to be calculated
-mr specifies usage of Hadoop to distribute the classification
-o specifies the output directory
*/
sh hadoop jar /home/cloudera/mahout-distribution-
   0.8/examples/target/mahout-examples-0.8-job.jar
   org.apache.mahout.classifier.df.mapreduce.TestForest -i
   /user/cloudera/pdp/datasets/advanced_patterns/german-test.data -
   ds /user/cloudera/pdp/datasets/advanced_patterns/german-
   train.info -m /user/cloudera/pdp/output/advanced_patterns
   /classification -a -mr -o /user/cloudera/pdp/output/
   advanced_patterns/classification_pred
```

Results

The following snapshot shows the results after executing the code in this pattern on the dataset:

```
=========================================================
Summary
---------------------------------------------------------
Correctly Classified Instances          :      154      77%
Incorrectly Classified Instances        :       46      23%
Total Classified Instances              :      200


=========================================================
Confusion Matrix
---------------------------------------------------------
a       b       <--Classified as
22      38      |  60        a    = 2
8       132     |  140       b    = 1
```

The decision tree output

The preceding matrix shows the comparison between the predicted and actual results. We can see that the model predicted 154 instances correctly, while it classified 46 instances incorrectly. The confusion matrix shows that out of 60 instances, 22 were correctly classified as bad customers and 38 were wrongly classified as good. Similarly, out of 140 instances, 132 were correctly classified as good customers and 8 were wrongly classified as bad.

Additional information

The complete code and dataset for this section can be found in the following GitHub directories:

- `Chapter7/code/`
- `Chapter7/datasets/`

Information on using Mahout for classification is present at `https://mahout.apache.org/users/stuff/partial-implementation.html`.

Future trends

When I began writing this book, the usage of Pig was moving quickly. Knowledge about new usage patterns, new features, and new systems that are integrated with Pig is being pushed into the public domain by a variety of industries and by academia at regular intervals. These developments will have a direct effect on the Pig design patterns explored in this book. The adoption of newer techniques will also drive the user community's documentation of Pig design patterns by sharing new patterns and by maturing the already existing patterns.

Emergence of data-driven patterns

In this book, we have extensively dealt with using Pig design patterns in the traditional enterprise settings. The future holds great promise owing to the growth of the Internet of Things phenomenon. In the future, the Internet of Things will enable every human artifact, every physical object of the world, and even every person to be plausibly networked. All of these things will be capable of being connected, read, and monitored, and data-driven intelligence will be delivered continuously.

In the traditional setting, the data journeys along familiar routes. Exclusive data and information is lodged in regular databases and analyzed in reports; it then rises up the management chain.

These familiar routes of data and information flow will change according to the newer paradigm of the Internet of Things in which data from the external world (from sensors and actuators of devices) is poised to be an important information source to drive real analytics from the truly connected world.

Emerging Pig design patterns might potentially address the impending data deluge emanating from the Internet of Things. These patterns might deal with integrating high-velocity streaming data at regular intervals and perform streaming analysis using Pig. The proposed work related to implementing Pig on Storm and Pig on Tez could be a good starting point.

The emergence of solution-driven patterns

As design patterns continue to get wider acceptance for many business problems, users tend to see the merits of grouping these patterns into manageable modular chunks of reusable pattern libraries. In this book, the emphasis was to group patterns based on the familiar route the data takes from ingestion to egression; there might be a novel grouping mechanism in which the patterns are grouped based on the functional usage. From this perspective, newer design patterns could potentially emerge to fill the gaps, which this book has not addressed.

Patterns addressing programmability constraints

Pig is designed to be a data-driven procedural language, which can perform small-scale analysis and is not suitable for implementing complex mathematical algorithms. Its mainstay is to be in front of the data pipeline trying to understand, ingest, and integrate data so that data can be analyzed by the likes of R, Weka, Python, OpenNLP, and Mahout libraries.

There is an immediate and compelling need to make the integration of these external libraries seamless with Pig, owing to the inherent complexities involved. Typically, while integrating Pig with R or any other analytics library, we encounter difficulties. These include not finding all the commonly used algorithms implemented in the library, problems registering the library functions, issues with data type incompatibilities, lack of built-in functions, and many others.

Newer design patterns could potentially emerge, resulting in a framework with closer integration between these external libraries and Pig. The extensibility features of Pig, such as streaming and UDFs, could come in handy to implement these frameworks. These design patterns take advantage of both the statistical analysis capability of the libraries and the parallel data processing capability of Pig.

Summary

In this chapter, we explored advanced patterns that specifically deal with using Pig to analyze unstructured text data using various patterns.

We started by understanding the context and the motivation behind clustering text data; we then examined in brief several techniques followed by a use case that elaborates through Pig code. Similarly, we understood the relevance of topic models to understanding the latent context of textual documents using an example of text containing Big Data and medicine. We have explored how Pig integrates with the Python's NLTK library to perform natural language processing in order to decompose a text corpus into sentences and recognize named entities; these entities are eventually used in indexing and information retrieval. In the last pattern, we considered a credit dataset to illustrate the process of classification or predictive analytics using Mahout integrated with Pig.

The *Future trends* section scratched the surface to identify future design patterns in conjunction with the evolution of Pig as a mainstream programming language to process Big Data. This section also brings into perspective the progressive nature of design patterns that enables you to identify and develop new design patterns you haven't seen before and share it with the world.

I hope that this book has provided you a springboard for readily using the design patterns mentioned in this book. This bridges the gap between theoretical understanding and practical implementation of creating complex data pipelines, and apply it in various stages of data management life cycle and analytics. Through this book, we covered the journey of Big Data from the time it enters the enterprise to its eventual use in analytics; and throughout this journey, Pig design patterns performed the role of a catalyst to guide us through the successive steps of data management life cycle and analytics.

Index

C

S

T

U

Thank you for buying
Pig Design Patterns

About Packt Publishing

Packt, pronounced 'packed', published its first book "*Mastering phpMyAdmin for Effective MySQL Management*" in April 2004 and subsequently continued to specialize in publishing highly focused books on specific technologies and solutions.

Our books and publications share the experiences of your fellow IT professionals in adapting and customizing today's systems, applications, and frameworks. Our solution based books give you the knowledge and power to customize the software and technologies you're using to get the job done. Packt books are more specific and less general than the IT books you have seen in the past. Our unique business model allows us to bring you more focused information, giving you more of what you need to know, and less of what you don't.

Packt is a modern, yet unique publishing company, which focuses on producing quality, cutting-edge books for communities of developers, administrators, and newbies alike. For more information, please visit our website: www.packtpub.com.

About Packt Open Source

In 2010, Packt launched two new brands, Packt Open Source and Packt Enterprise, in order to continue its focus on specialization. This book is part of the Packt Open Source brand, home to books published on software built around Open Source licences, and offering information to anybody from advanced developers to budding web designers. The Open Source brand also runs Packt's Open Source Royalty Scheme, by which Packt gives a royalty to each Open Source project about whose software a book is sold.

Writing for Packt

We welcome all inquiries from people who are interested in authoring. Book proposals should be sent to author@packtpub.com. If your book idea is still at an early stage and you would like to discuss it first before writing a formal book proposal, contact us; one of our commissioning editors will get in touch with you.

We're not just looking for published authors; if you have strong technical skills but no writing experience, our experienced editors can help you develop a writing career, or simply get some additional reward for your expertise.

Big Data Analytics with R and Hadoop

ISBN: 978-1-78216-328-2   Paperback: 238 pages

Set up an integrated infrastructure of R and Hadoop to turn your data analytics into Big Data analytics

1. Write Hadoop MapReduce within R.

2. Learn data analytics with R and the Hadoop platform.

3. Handle HDFS data within R.

4. Understand Hadoop streaming with R.

Securing Hadoop

ISBN: 978-1-78328-525-9   Paperback: 116 pages

Implement robust end-to-end security for your Hadoop ecosystem

1. Master the key concepts behind Hadoop security as well as how to secure a Hadoop-based Big Data ecosystem.

2. Understand and deploy authentication, authorization, and data encryption in a Hadoop-based Big Data platform.

3. Administer the auditing and security event monitoring system.

Please check **www.PacktPub.com** for information on our titles

Hadoop MapReduce Cookbook

ISBN: 978-1-84951-728-7   Paperback: 300 pages

Recipes for analyzing large and complex datasets with Hadoop MapReduce

1. Learn to process large and complex datasets, starting simply, then diving in deep.

2. Solve complex big data problems, such as classifications, finding relationships, online marketing, and recommendations.

3. More than 50 Hadoop MapReduce recipes, presented in a simple and straightforward manner, with step-by-step instructions and real-world examples.

Instant MapReduce Patterns – Hadoop Essentials How-to

ISBN: 978-1-78216-770-9   Paperback: 60 pages

Practical recipes to write your own MapReduce solution patterns for Hadoop programs

1. Learn something new in an Instant! A short, fast, focused guide delivering immediate results.

2. Learn how to install, configure, and run Hadoop jobs.

3. Seven recipes, each describing a particular style of the MapReduce program to give you a good understanding of how to program with MapReduce.

Please check **www.PacktPub.com** for information on our titles

Made in the USA
San Bernardino, CA
25 March 2016